A HISTORY OF SICILY

A HISTORY OF
SICILY

M. I. Finley,
Denis Mack Smith *and*
Christopher Duggan

ELISABETH SIFTON BOOKS

VIKING

ELISABETH SIFTON BOOKS · VIKING
Viking Penguin Inc.
40 West 23rd Street,
New York, New York 10010, U.S.A.

First American Edition
Published in 1987

ISBN 0–670–81725–2

Library of Congress Catalog Card Number 86–40426
(CIP data available)

Set in Linotron 202 Aldus
Printed in Great Britain
by Redwood Burn Ltd, Trowbridge, Wiltshire

Contents

Illustrations & Maps

Acknowledgements for the illustrations are made with thanks to the following:

Tim Benton, plates 14 and 15; D. M. Boswell, 1, 17 and 23; the Trustees of the British Museum, 16; John Freeman & Co., 5 and 6; the Mansell Collection, 4 and 7; Publifoto, Palermo, 25; Ezio Quiresi, Cremona, 11; Scala, Florence, 8 and 10; Anton Schroll & Co., Vienna, publishers of *Sicily* by H. M. Schwarz, in which plates 2, 3, 9, 12, 13, 18, 19, and 20 appeared; Società Fotografica Italiana, 21. This photograph appeared in *Messina: Prima e Dopo Il Disastro*, published by Giuseppe Principato, Messina, in 1914; Paul Watkins, 22 and 24.

Preface

This is an abridged and somewhat revised version of *A History of Sicily* by Moses Finley and Denis Mack Smith which first came out in three volumes in 1968.* The text has been reduced by about two-thirds. I have tried to correct a few anachronisms and errors, but given that my own expertise is limited largely to the present century, I have made no systematic attempt at revision. The aim throughout has been to provide a concise and hopefully readable account of Sicilian history. There will obviously be gaps, and in the eyes of some, imbalances. The weight given to the last two centuries might seem excessive. In justification I would say that much of the island's uniqueness lies in its singular, and not altogether savoury, response to the challenge of liberalism.

My own contribution, aside from abridgement, has been threefold. In the first place I have added a new final chapter covering the period from the concession of regional autonomy down to the present day. This has necessarily been brief, and also highly subjective; but that is in the nature of contemporary history. I have given particular emphasis to the twin evils of clientelism and the mafia, which strike me as the two most pressing problems facing the island. Sicily is currently in a state of high flux, and it is too early to say what the results of the big anti-mafia drive of the last few years will be. I have taken a pessimistic line, largely because my own researches into the 1920s have given me a strong sense of *déjà vu*. Many might find this perverse, and see in the revelations of Tommaso Buscetta, or indeed the plans for a bridge across the Straits of Messina, new grounds for hope. I trust they are right.

My second contribution has been in the interpretation of the mafia. Recent studies have tended to underline the fact that there is no firm evidence for a criminal organization; and my own work on the 1920s strongly supports this line. Some kind of transformation may have occurred since the war; but the evidence for this is not convincing. Indeed, both the pathology and the official diagnosis of the evil appear much the same as a century ago. To my mind, ideas about the mafia are largely subjective and

* *Ancient Sicily: To the Arab Conquest*, by M. I. Finley (revised edition 1979); *Medieval Sicily: 800–1713* and *Modern Sicily: After 1713*, by Denis Mack Smith (London, Chatto & Windus; New York, Viking Press).

stem from confusion, political calculation, and prejudice. In keeping with this view, I have altered and added to those sections in the second and third volumes that deal with the problem; and I naturally take full responsibility.

My third contribution has been stylistic. The process of abridgement has led, particularly in the first part, to a certain amount of rewriting. Though I have tried to retain the fluency of the original, the search for compression may on occasions have led to awkwardness. I should point out finally that the bibliography has been revised. It is in no sense intended to be comprehensive. Though a number of foreign works of scholarship are included, the principal aim has been to provide indications to the general reader who wishes to explore specific aspects of Sicilian history.

I am indebted to a number of people for their help. Dr Jeremy Johns of Newcastle University gave me invaluable advice on the Arab and Norman periods, as well as the bibliography. Dr Piero Corrao of Palermo University kindly read the sections relating to the fourteenth and fifteenth centuries, and made a number of very useful suggestions. Dr Timothy Davies, Peter Fraser, Professor Ben Isaac, and above all Dr Roger Wilson, kindly gave up their time to discuss specific points. I am very grateful to Humaira Ahmed for transcribing the manuscript, and to Gaia Servadio and various officials at the Bank of Sicily and the Regional Assembly for providing me with useful material. Finally I would like to thank Moses Finley and Denis Mack Smith. Their generosity, not to mention courage, in letting a young research student loose on their texts has been remarkable; and their general kindness altogether exceptional.

Christopher Duggan
February 1986

CHAPTER 1

The coming of the Greeks

Sicily is an island. Few islands have played a greater, or even comparable, role in history over long spans of time, and no other which is so small. Easily accessible by sea on all sides, it has a variegated and fertile terrain, and above all an unparalleled location. At the north-east, the Straits of Messina separating it from Italy narrow to a mere three kilometres at one point; in the west, the shortest distance from Africa is about 160 kilometres. The island has therefore been both a gateway and a crossroads, on the one hand dividing the eastern and western Mediterranean, on the other linking Europe and Africa as a stepping-stone.

This halfway position, in both location and scale, fixed the *leitmotifs* of Sicilian history. Sicily could not long live undisturbed, except in those periods when she was securely in the possession of a strong external power. The list of migrants and invaders in the course of ancient, medieval and modern history is considerable: unnamed prehistoric peoples, then Sicans, Phoenicians, Elymians, Sicels, Greeks, Carthaginians, Romans and others from Italy, mercenaries and slaves from the whole Mediterranean basin, Jews, Vandals, Saracens, Normans, Spaniards and a sprinkling of others. A few, like the Vandals, merely swept through and left no trace behind. Most stayed, however, for long periods or for all time, contributing in different ways to a continuous process of biological and cultural fusion.

Save for relatively brief periods of independence in the Middle Ages, foreign domination was the rule. That meant rule to the material advantage of the foreign power at the expense of the Sicilians, through rents, taxes and plain looting. This parasitical interest inevitably did great harm to the countryside and to the people. Yet, and this should be stressed, not everyone suffered. The traditional way of ruling Sicily has been through the agency of local magnates, both 'natives' and newcomers, who shared in the profits in return for their services in exercising administrative and police powers.

Looking at Sicily today, it is often hard to imagine what attracted so many different peoples. But the fact is that for most of its history the island was a region of exceptional fertility. This was a consequence both of its geology – a limestone base with heavy coatings of lava – and its climate. Wheat, olives, wine and fruits abounded; so too did forests, particularly in the moun-tainous regions stretching from Mount Etna west and south to Agrigento.

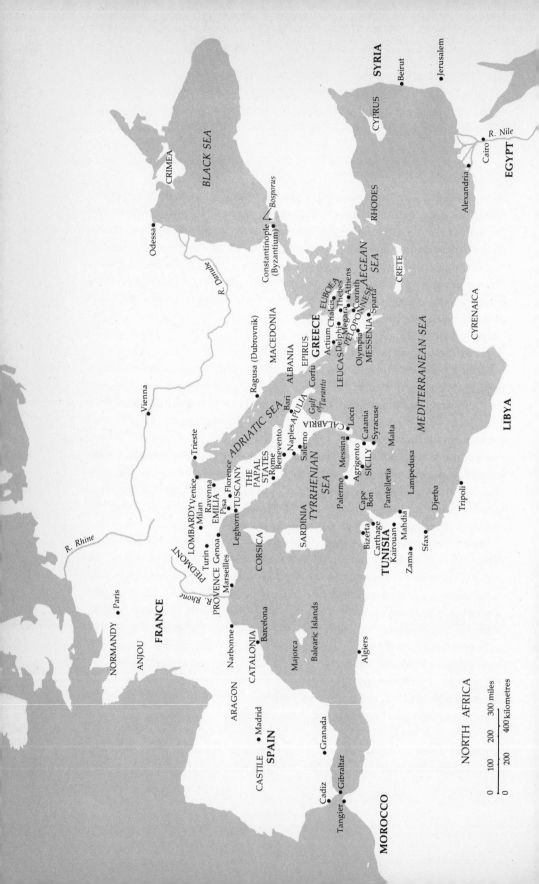

The drastic deafforestation of the island in recent centuries has not only changed its face but also its very ecology. Rainfall has dropped, springs have dried up, and not one river is any longer navigable. Human selfishness and misrule have made Sicily a pale shadow of its former self.

THE BEGINNINGS

According to the geologists, Sicily has always been an island, and the earliest migrants came by boat, sometime before 20,000 BC. Their stone tools and art – particularly the cave engravings of Levanzo and Monte Pellegrino – link them with the cultures of central and western Europe. Little seems to have changed for thousands of years, and then suddenly a revolutionary break occurred, probably some time soon after 5000 BC. This was part of a more general transformation in the central Mediterranean, that resulted in the emergence of peasant communities, still dependent on stone tools, but having at their disposal the new arts of agriculture, the domestication of animals, and pottery.

Though copper appeared in Sicily around 3000 BC, the age of metal only really began more than a thousand years later, with bronze. Prior to that another influence had made itself felt which was linked to migrations originating in the Iberian peninsula. The people involved were skilled in copper and goldwork, and they can be identified by a characteristic kind of pottery known as 'bell beakers'. Their impact on Sicily is hard to gauge; but apart from these utensils, they seem to have produced little that was new. The great migratory movements of this period may, however, have been responsible for the introduction of Indo-European dialects into Western Europe. As far as Sicily is concerned, this probably meant three languages: Sican in the west of this island, Elymian in the north-west, and Sicel in the east.

The history of the Bronze Age is bedevilled by later Greek legends. One that is particularly intriguing concerns Daedalus, the master craftsman and inventor, who escaped from Crete on waxen wings and managed to reach western Sicily. Here he was honoured by King Kokalos of the Sicans, for whom he built many marvels of engineering. But the Cretan king, so the story goes, decided to reclaim Daedalus for himself, and to this end landed with a force on the south-western coast of Sicily. Things did not go according to plan: he was tricked by Kokalos, who invited him to a feast and had him drowned while bathing. The Cretan force buried their king in a great mausoleum and then, finding all retreat cut off, settled permanently in Sicily.

Though scholars have made repeated attempts to discover in this legend a

MAP 1   The Mediterranean and Western Europe

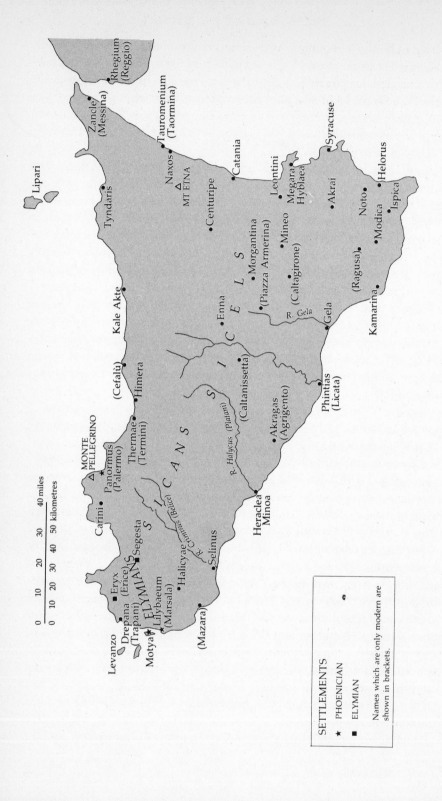

Rhegium
(Reggio)

Zancle
(Messina)

Tauromenium
(Taormina)

Lipari

Naxos
MT ETNA △

Catania

Syracuse

Helorus

Tyndaris

Centuripe

Leontini
Megara
Hyblaea
Akrai

Noto
Ispica
Modica

Mineo
(Caltagirone)

Morgantina
(Piazza Armerina)

(Ragusa)

Kale Akte

S   I   C   E   L   S

Enna

R. Gela

Gela

Kamarina

(Cefalù)

Himera

S
I
C
A
N
S

Caltanissetta
(Caltanissetta)

R. Halycus (Platani)

Akragas
(Agrigento)

Phintias
(Licata)

MONTE
△ PELEGRINO

Thermae
(Termini)

Panormus
(Palermo)

S   I   C   A   N   S

Crimisus (Belice)

R. Halycus (Platani)

Heraclea
Minoa

Carini

Segesta
Halicyae

Selinus

40 miles
30
20
10
0

50 kilometres
40
30
20
10
0

Eryx
(Erice)

ELYMIANS

Drepana
(Trapani)

Lilybaeum
(Marsala)

Levanzo

Motya

(Mazara)

SETTLEMENTS
★ PHOENICIAN
■ ELYMIAN

Names which are only modern are
shown in brackets.

kernel of truth – a reminiscence of some unsuccessful attempt by Cnossus, in its great period, to establish a settlement in Sicily – the difficulty arises that the tale is incompatible with the archaeological record. The Bronze Age objects so far found in Sicily are either imports from mainland Greece and the Aegean islands, or else local ware based on prototypes from these areas. Very few identifiably Cretan ('Minoan') artefacts are known. It is therefore hard to see why the tale of Daedalus should be given any more credence than that of Heracles, who is said to have swum the Straits of Messina and wandered about in Sicily – in all the wrong places. The capacity of the ancients for invention should not be underestimated.

How much this long period of prehistory contributed to historical Sicily is not easy to judge. There was an obvious physical contribution in that a great deal of land was cleared and brought under cultivation. The Greek settlers also found wives and a labour force among the natives. Otherwise, though, the influence of the pre-Greek populations was hardly very significant. Even in religion the main impact seems to have been topographical, with the Greeks following their predecessors in cults of dark subterranean powers associated with such natural phenomena as mountain grottoes and hot springs. But this is perhaps not surprising in an island dominated by the highest volcano in Europe, Mount Etna, which is never completely dormant.

GREEK COLONIZATION

The Greek settlement of Sicily was an impressive, yet also rather mysterious affair. The word 'colonization' is conventionally used by historians to describe the process, but it is actually misleading insofar as it suggests the establishment of subject communities overseas. The westward emigration from Greece was certainly an organized movement, equipped, armed and planned by various 'mother-cities'; but from the start the effect, and so far as we can tell the intention, was not so much to colonize as to encourage and sometimes compel men to move out permanently to new and independent communities of their own.

The Greek traditions about the opening up of Sicily and the west are very unsatisfactory. We know that Greeks were sailing in the Aegean Sea with some regularity at an early date, and that an occasional ship also entered the western Mediterranean. But Sicily lacks metals, and there is no reason why purely commercial ventures should have been calling here with any frequency. The colonization of the island seems to have had other motives behind it, and in particular the desire to make a new life on the land. Not even Syracuse was an exception here, despite its magnificent harbours.

MAP 2 Ancient Sicily

In the second half of the eighth century BC there were three foundations in the plain of Catania and its northern extension east of Mount Etna: Naxos, Leontini, and Catania itself. Syracuse, Zancle and Megara Hyblaea were settled at about the same time; and this first colonizing wave in Sicily was traditionally completed with the foundation of Gela. All of these settlements were no doubt small to start with, and numbered their households only in the hundreds. Each had an acknowledged 'mother-city', which provided the leader of the expedition and did the planning. The official founders of the four most northern colonies were Chalcidians from Euboea; Syracuse was a Corinthian settlement; and Gela owed its existence to a combined Rhodian-Cretan group.

Intensive archaeological study in the present century has shown that the successful colonies expanded rapidly. Evidence suggests that in some places the first Greek migrants and the Sicels lived side by side, and that the latter were only pushed out gradually; and until Syracuse became the dominant power in eastern Sicily at the beginning of the fifth century, the Chalcidian colonies clearly had prosperous dealings with the natives of the interior. Interaction resulted in extensive Hellenization, but this did not immediately destroy the self-consciousness of the Sicels or their desire to remain free from overlordship by the original Greek settlements. Otherwise the claim of Ducetius to be leading a Sicel revolt in the middle of the fifth century BC would be unintelligible.

At Syracuse the pattern of relations was different from that of the Chalcidian sites, for here the colonists subjugated the Sicels of their district from the very start. A similar practice was adopted by the Geloans. They settled in the coastal plain after finding it virtually unpopulated, and then proceeded to drive the Sicels out of the ring of hills to the north and occupy various sites as strong-points. No satisfactory explanation has been found for this difference of approach, but because the northern colonists were Ionian speaking and the others Dorian, some historians have suggested a basic temperamental difference as the root cause. The foundation of Himera in about 650, however, shows the irrelevance of the supposed racial factor, as Chalcideans from Zancle in this instance co-operated with Dorians from Syracuse.

The establishment of Himera, and later of Selinus and Akragas, brought the Greeks into the Sican and Elymian districts. Along with Thermae (modern Termini Imerese) and Mazara, these settlements marked their furthest westward movement. The Sicans were apparently thinner on the ground than the Sicels, and seem to have been more resistant to Hellenization; so too do the Elymians. This meant that the development in the interior west of Enna was not comparable either in scale or rapidity to the

Hellenization of the eastern regions. Though many Sican sites were transformed and fortified in the sixth century, and took on a clearly Greek aspect, they seem to have been garrison-points rather than true cities; and even in Roman times they remained insignificant in contrast with the eastern part of the interior.

The puzzling exception to this pattern of non-absorption was Segesta, which lay in Elymian territory. Though the native language remained in use here, the Greek script was adopted. Furthermore, the shell of a Doric temple was built in the late fifth century, and it still stands as one of the greatest of surviving Greek temple-remains. Most significant of all, perhaps, the Segestans became so Greek, or at least so un-barbarian, that a formal agreement could eventually be made with Selinus accepting intermarriage among their respective citizens as legitimate. This practice was by no means universal even among purely Greek cities.

Nothing has been said so far about the Phoenicians, the favourite scapegoat (as perennial aggressors) ever since antiquity. The day was to come when Carthage – a Phoenician settlement in Tunisia – would engage with the Greeks of Sicily in prolonged and violent conflict. But archaeology has now proved that it is unwarranted to read anything back from the later struggles. The Phoenician foundations in the island were concentrated in the north-west, and they were neither numerous nor expansive; and if this paucity is not enough to demonstrate Phoenician disinterest in competing with Greeks, further proof comes from the presence of Greek products in two Phoenician settlements, Motya and Palermo. The first faint hint of conflict can be dated to about 580, and then the responsibility must be assigned to Greeks not Phoenicians.

ARCHAIC SOCIETY AND POLITICS

For the 250 years that followed the initial foundations, the surviving literary tradition about Sicily is hopelessly thin. Though archaeology is of no great help either, some things can be ascertained. We know that the colonists brought with them their dialects and script, their technology, their favourite gods and myths, their cult and burial practices, their calendar, and their political and social terminology; their language remained fundamentally 'pure' Greek. As far as religion is concerned, some shifts in emphasis occurred. Demeter and her daughter Persephone were particularly popular, an indication perhaps of the fertility of the region at this time. Sicily even challenged the claim of Eleusis (near Athens) to be the place where Demeter first gave man the gift of corn, and Enna was pointed out as the site where Hades seized Persephone and brought her to his house.

Sicily was no mere outpost, for it felt itself to be, and was in almost all respects, fully Greek. A visitor from Athens or Corinth would have found himself in familiar surroundings. Each city had its unmistakably Greek central square or Agora, its public buildings, and cemeteries outside the town proper. The temples were Doric in style and were conceived on a grand scale. The oldest, which is now a pitiful ruin, was erected in Syracuse near the causeway end of the island of Ortygia. It was built of sandstone and dedicated to Apollo, and has been dated on stylistic grounds to about 575 BC. If correct, that would place it quite early in the history of this type of Greek architecture.

The initiative first taken at Syracuse was followed up in other cities in the course of the next century and a half. The result was a series of splendid monumental buildings. Though these were obviously Greek in style, a perceptive visitor would have noticed such distinctive features as the rarity of sculpted reliefs on friezes and pediments, or the carving of the lion rain-spouts at Akragas and Himera. As for sculpture, it appears that no Sicilian city developed a distinctive school of its own, apart from Selinus in the sixth century. But neither did many cities on the Greek mainland; and Sicilians were moreover handicapped by the unavailability of native marble.

The continuous traffic between Sicily and the old Greek world made it easy for Sicilian Greeks to keep in step with the mother-country. The first colonists attracted further settlers; and among the newcomers were skilled craftsmen, political exiles (including Sappho in about 600 BC), larger groups who went west for the same reasons as the first migrants, and in the end poets, architects and philosophers who came at the summons of patrons. There was also continuous commercial activity and what one might call ceremonial traffic or even pilgrimages, though without most of the usual overtones. Greeks from Sicily shared in the pan-Hellenic sentiment that was gathering around certain shrines; and we know that Sicilian Greeks consulted the oracle of Delphi and entered the festival competitions at Olympia.

Regular travel for ceremonial purposes was perhaps most common between the individual Sicilian settlement and its mother-city. The absence of political controls, or even of political ties in any proper sense, had the positive effect of keeping the way clear for other kinds of relations. It was the accepted convention, for example, to turn to the mother-city whenever a personality was required for an important occasion. In the same spirit, the new settlements were expected to send embassies regularly to the main religious festivals of the mother-city, with appropriate gifts to the patron god or goddess.

One of the more puzzling aspects in this area of interrelationships is trade. This is partly because our knowledge of Sicilian commerce for the whole archaic period rests almost entirely on the single commodity of painted pottery. During the first century of colonization, virtually all the pottery imported into Sicily was Corinthian, and Corinthian predominance continued until replaced by Athenian in the sixth century. But this happened everywhere, and to talk in terms of 'commercial rivalry', or even 'commercial imperialism', as some people have done, is dangerous. As for the carrying trade, we know little except that the Sicilian Greeks were not themselves active participants. Only Syracuse ever had a navy worth mentioning and that not before the fifth century. Internal commerce, it seems, was restricted to traffic between Greek communities and natives of the interior, rather than between the Greek cities themselves.

Euboea, Corinth, Rhodes and other Aegean islands, all appear to have exported goods to Sicily. This raises the question of what Sicily paid with. Wheat, olives, wine, timber, fruit, nuts and vegetables, and the product of pasturage and the chase were all abundant, and presumably the answer lies there. (The wealth of Akragas in the fifth century BC, according to the historians Timaeus and Diodorus, was due to its olive and wine exports to Carthage.) Only when large-scale internecine warfare developed, would enslaved captives have become an additional article of exchange. Exploitation of the sulphur resources, the only other possibility, is not confirmed before Roman times.

Though the wealth and luxury of Akragas were certainly exaggerated by ancient historians, the basic truth of their picture is confirmed by the eight or nine temples built between 480 and the end of the century, a number exceeded at the time only by Athens. Selinus, too, witnessed a century of extraordinary architectural activity, and here again exports to North Africa must have been largely responsible. Even if constructed of soft stone and not marble, a large temple was a considerable burden on the resources, and especially the skilled manpower, of an ancient community. The ability to carry off such a project, not once but repeatedly, must be taken as an index of wealth, especially when there were no shrines like Delphi or Olympia to attract rich contributions from outside.

With overseas traffic largely in the hands of foreigners, and with inland trade negligible, there was little scope for a significant mercantile and manufacturing class. The landowning aristocracy itself would anyway not have been averse to dealing directly with foreigners seeking their wheat or other products. Manufacture undoubtedly took the form of handicraft production on a small scale, as everywhere in the Greek world at the time; and it was probably not before the fifth century BC that an occasional entrepreneur developed a relatively large establishment with slave labour.

None of the Greek-style pottery so common on Sicel sites has been found in the Greek settlements, which shows that it was made either by itinerant Greeks or by the Sicels themselves.

Tenure of land was a fundamental question; and again we are faced with a puzzle. It was the rule in antiquity for settlers, of whatever status, to begin by dividing land among themselves; and this certainly happened in Sicily and Magna Graecia. What we are not certain about is the criterion for distribution. Most modern historians argue that, since the colonists came from a world of disparities in property and power, then this pattern was likely to have been reproduced in the new settlement. Though quite possible, one could equally well guess that people who migrated because of inequality would not willingly repeat that condition when they had a free hand. Some support for this alternative view may be seen in the recent discovery that the cemeteries of Megara Hyblaea show no significant class distinctions before the middle of the sixth century.

Either way, the Sicilian communities were soon set in the familiar Greek pattern, with power concentrated in the hands of a group of aristocratic families who had a preponderant share of the land and control of both the priestly functions and the administration of justice. Equally familiar was the endemic malady which the Greeks called *stasis*, a word with a range of meanings running from factional dispute to civil disturbance and outright civil war. The first known instance in Sicily of the class-war type of *stasis* occurred at Leontini around 600 when a certain Panaetius apparently seized power by leading the poorer citizens to victory against the traditional aristocratic cavalry. Panaetius made himself tyrant, and thus introduced the institution round which Sicilian history pivoted for the next three centuries.

Our understanding of what was going on at this time would be greatly advanced if we knew more about the 'lawgiver', Charondas of Catania. Later tradition made him into a Pythagorean philosopher, the architect of a bewildering variety of improbable laws and precepts. It may just be that Charondas was thrown up by the social struggles of the seventh or early sixth centuries and that he prevented outright civil war by compromise, the key to which was a written law code. This, like similar codifications in Greece and early Rome, was an important gain for the common people. As long as the aristocracy monopolized administration, and while the law remained traditional and unwritten, the opportunities for 'crooked judgements' were infinite. A written set of laws was a useful brake.

Tyrants and lawgivers are signs that Sicily had entered the difficult transitional stage from archaic to classical Greek civilization, with its characteristic institution of the *polis* or city-state. In ideal terms, this was a self-governing community, with a rural hinterland, and an urban centre where the main activities of government could be conducted. How a *polis* was ruled was up to a point irrelevant: provided it was free from outside authority, it could be oligarchical or democratic. In addition, it had to maintain a variety of political and property rights. Nowhere, however, was the gap between the ideal of the *polis* and reality greater than in Sicily. Why this should have been so is perhaps the most interesting question in the classical phase of Sicilian Greek history.

CHAPTER 2

Tyranny and democracy

THE FIRST TYRANTS

A growth in population and wealth in sixth-century Sicily was accompanied by a rise in unrest and conflict. The common people clashed with ruling oligarchies; oligarchic factions fell out with one another, as did cities; and in some areas natives fought with Greeks. Energetic individuals began to fish in these troubled waters, and to seize power as tyrants. Though these men appeared early, it was the four decades that ended in the Syracusan revolution of 466 BC that make up the first age of tyranny in Sicily. This was a period that foreshadowed so much of later Sicilian history, with wars at home and abroad, ruthlessness in the struggle for power, and a brilliant upsurge in cultural life. As ever, though, the cost in lives and misery cannot be measured.

Although some tyrants found it useful, especially at the beginning of their careers, to trade on popular aspirations, they themselves belonged to the wealthiest aristocratic class. This at least was the case with Phalaris, that remarkable and perplexing figure of myth, of whom a late writer records that he first seized power at Akragas by misappropriating a large sum entrusted to him for the construction of a temple of Zeus. No such commission would have been given to a commoner. Phalaris then used the money to hire a mercenary force of foreigners and slaves. He installed them in an armed camp on the acropolis, and completed his coup by taking advantage of a religious assembly to carry out a massacre.

Though Phalaris ruled for some fifteen years, we know almost nothing about his reign except that he conducted successful campaigns against Sican communities and that he became a model of monstrous behaviour; he had a gastronomic penchant, we are told, for infant children. His greatest claim to fame was the hollow brazen bull in which he roasted those who earned his displeasure; and his first victim, according to the legend, was the smith who had fashioned the device – 'the only just act which Phalaris ever committed'. The fate of the bull itself is uncertain. It may have been thrown into the sea, or else removed to Carthage in 406 as spoils of war. Either way hardly matters, but the fact that there could be a famous argument about this point among Greek and Roman historians is an indication of how great Phalaris' mystique was.

It is impossible to penetrate to the reality behind the Phalaris myth; and anyway the legend may be historically more important, in that it bequeathed a powerful image of despotism to subsequent generations. For another early tyrant, Cleander of Gela, we know even less than for Phalaris. We have none of the usual stories of his rise to power within the prevailing oligarchic regime or of his career as tyrant. One of the few things to appear certain is that he was assassinated after seven years of rule. His brother Hippocrates then had to engage in a brief civil war in order to succeed him.

Archaeological evidence suggests that Cleander and Hippocrates laid the groundwork for the latter's subsequent conquests in eastern Sicily by erecting fortifications on the northern rim of hills above Gela. They also enlarged the army, placing special stress, it seems, on the cavalry: it is surely no coincidence that the first coins of Gela, struck at this time, featured a naked horseman. There was also an emphasis on mercenaries, and this may in fact have accounted for the introduction of coinage. In hiring troops Hippocrates made no racial distinctions, and his large army included Sicels as well as Greeks. With it he crossed the mountains into Chalcidian territory, and quickly took the towns of Naxos, Zancle and Leontini, which he placed under the rule of vassal-tyrants.

Syracuse presented Hippocrates with a more serious challenge. He had no navy and without one the capture of Syracuse would usually have been out of the question. However, the city was beset with turmoil, and Hippocrates hoped that the lower classes would welcome him as a release from the ruling oligarchy. He was disappointed, and this is presumably why in 492 he accepted the mediation of Corinth. The resulting treaty gave Hippocrates Kamarina, which, as archaeological evidence shows, was now a flourishing community. But though he officially became the city's new 'founder', his life by no means took on a more peaceful tenor. He was soon off on another campaign, this time against the Sicels; and in the course of it he was killed in battle.

In Gela, Hippocrates' cavalry commander, Gelon, immediately assumed the role of protector of the late tyrant's sons. But as soon as he could, he put the boys aside and seized power for himself. He subsequently used the occasion of a revolution in Syracuse to take over there too, and proceeded to make this city both powerful and populous, with an imposing navy and a large army. His methods were simple and ruthless. One of his acts, for example, was to transfer more than half the population of Gela wholesale to Syracuse. Such cold single-mindedness paid political dividends, for in the space of ten years Gelon was able to make himself the most powerful individual in the Greek world, and perhaps in all Europe.

The Greeks were well aware of this. In 481 they sent an embassy to ask for his help against the Persian invaders. Gelon allegedly offered to supply their whole army with wheat, and also to furnish 200 ships, 20,000 infantry, and 5000 cavalry, archers and slingers, on condition that he be made comman-der-in-chief of the coalition forces; but this, we are told, was unacceptable. The account as given by the historian Herodotus is in certain respects implausible. Gelon is unlikely to have responded on any terms to an appeal for Hellenic patriotism against a far-off king who posed no threat to himself: his interests and his problems lay in Sicily and the west. However, the army figures (though not those for the navy) have a chance of being accurate, and if so they indicate a population in and around Syracuse that no Sicilian community was to equal before the modern era.

Gelon's power in the east of Sicily was to some extent balanced by that of the tyrant Theron, in the west; and when the latter took Himera from its ruler Terillus in 483, there were only two independent cities left in Greek Sicily – and the prognosis for them was poor. But Terillus was 'guest-friend' of the Carthaginian leader Hamilcar, and also father-in-law of Anaxilas of Rhegium, who was still in control of Messina. Terillus and Anaxilas decided to ask Carthage for military assistance; and the response was overwhelm-ing. This was the first of many occasions in Sicily's history when internal dissent led to a foreign invader being invited in.

The massiveness of the Carthaginian intervention is not easy to under-stand except by those who believe in a predestined racial war to the death. It is true that the bounds of Gelon's ambition could not be known, and this certainly gave the Phoenician communities in Sicily every reason to feel insecure. But neither this nor any other visible Carthaginian interest in the island sufficiently explains why three years were spent in building up a vast armada – with troops from North Africa, Spain, Sardinia and Corsica – or why the invasion should have been commanded by Hamilcar himself, the *sufet* or chief magistrate of the city. The answer probably lies in the larger issues of western Mediterranean politics. The entente which had been established between Carthage and the Etruscans was losing its force; Rome was beginning to assert itself; and Carthage may have felt it was time to reshape her alliances, even if that meant direct intervention.

Whatever the explanation, the Carthaginians invaded in strength in 480, disembarking at Palermo, and then proceeding eastwards by land and sea under the guidance of Terillus. This was Theron's war in the first instance, but it was Gelon who won it; and his victory at Himera proved decisive. Hamilcar was killed, his ships burned, and many of his men taken prisoner or enslaved. Carthage had to pay a large cash indemnity, which enabled Gelon to increase markedly the issue of coinage. With the spoils he also built temples to Demeter and Persephone in the new quarter of Neapolis in Syracuse, and made a rich dedication in Delphi.

With the battle of Himera, hostilities abruptly ceased. Ten years later in his first Pythian ode, the poet Pindar referred to Gelon's victory in the context of 'gathering back Hellas from the weight of slavery'. That this was the 'party line' in Sicily can hardly be doubted, and it marks the beginning of the myth of a barbarian threat to civilization by Carthage that was to play such a role in the following centuries. The conceit was fostered by the coincidence of a simultaneous Persian defeat at Greek hands. Herodotus says indeed that the victories of Himera and Salamis occurred on the same day; and later writers added that the Persians and Carthaginians had concerted their invasions. The immediate beneficiary of such mythologizing was Gelon. He became a heroic figure, and lived on in the tradition relatively free from the usual stories of butchery and depravity.

The intensely personal and individual quality of the tyrants' actions cannot be stressed too heavily. There was something self-consciously 'heroic' about them, and they possessed more than a touch of megalomania. Adjectives like 'brutal' and 'tyrannical' spring readily to mind; yet such words are insufficient in the face of the rapid destruction and foundation of cities or the repeated transplantation of tens of thousands of people. These men flouted the Greek taboo against polygamy by entering into multiple formal marriages; and what is more their reputations survived it. Equally unorthodox was their constitutional position, both at home and in subject communities. No doubt some sort of governmental machinery existed, including the popular assembly; but in a sense it was irrelevant, and ancient writers understandably showed no interest in the problem.

Moral considerations apart – and not counting the victims – Greek Sicily prospered in this period. Though the tyrants themselves undoubtedly took a substantial slice of the riches, more than a little trickled down, as the persistence of visible wealth after the period of tyranny suggests. Agriculture flourished, fine coins continued to be minted; and the scale and quality of temple-building, as of other public works, remained undiminished. On the material side, it would seem as if Syracuse and Akragas had the necessary conditions to follow in the footsteps of Athens, where tyranny had been overthrown in 508. But though a start was made in 466, the end-product, sadly, proved to be weak and short-lived.

DEMOCRATIC INTERLUDE, 466–405 BC

Such democratic experience as the island had prior to 466 was limited and unpromising. Nevertheless, the normally difficult transition to this form of government apparently required little more than an armed conflict in Sicily against the tyrants and their mercenaries. We have no names of democratic leaders, no innovators or constitution-makers (like Cleisthenes in Athens). There is no trace of resistance by oligarchic factions except in late reference to the great philosopher, Empedocles of Akragas, who is said to have helped break up an oligarchic group known as the Thousand. Yet the fact is that by 466 tyranny seems to have been replaced by democracy almost everywhere.

In its Greek sense, democracy meant direct rule by the whole people. One immediate problem to be faced was who 'the people' of any given community were. Years of mass exile and transplantation had left a bitter legacy on this issue, and once the tyrant's hand was removed, open conflict ensued. In Syracuse 7000 of Gelon's 10,000 mercenary settlers were still resident: when the new regime declared them ineligible for public office, they rebelled, and were forced to leave the city after heavy fighting. Similar expulsions took place in other cities, along with the recall of former exiles.

The shifting of large numbers of people created grave confusion in property relations, since landholdings were confiscated and then distributed or redistributed each time a move took place. There is a firm ancient tradition, still repeated in Roman times by Cicero and Quintilian, that the many lawsuits that resulted led to the development of forensic oratory and the first rhetorical handbooks. Whether the cause-and-effect explanation is correct or not, it is a fact that Corax of Syracuse and his pupil Tisias were the founders of the Greek art of rhetoric at this time and that later in the century Gorgias of Leontini was its most famous exponent in the Greek world.

In Syracuse, the only city about which we have details, the form of democratic government resembled that of Athens. Supreme authority was vested in the popular assembly, and it was here that laws and decrees were passed, foreign and military policy decided, and the state's officials chosen. There was also, in the universal Greek fashion, a council which did the preparatory work for the assembly. However, the council and civil officials were not chosen by lot as in Athens, but elected; and in the Greek view this introduced an aristocratic principle and so a limitation of full democracy. Indeed Aristotle classified the Syracusan constitution as a *politeia* rather than a *demokrateia*, a distinction which is usually, though inadequately, rendered as 'moderate' and 'radical' democracy.

Beneath the political structure, class divisions remained sharply drawn. Though the old ruling aristocracy of Syracuse seem to have disappeared from the historical record, oligarchic sentiment had not, and both political and military leaders were drawn from a wealthy elite. This may have caused a feeling of dissatisfaction; at any rate that is one interpretation of an unsuccessful attempt in about 454 BC to establish a new tyranny with the backing of the poor. Fear of tyrants subsequently led the Syracusans to introduce what they called 'petalism', in imitation of the Athenian practice of 'ostracism' (a device for sending excessively influential people into a form of honourable exile). But according to Diodorus, the unexpected effect was that the better citizens withdrew from public affairs altogether, and as a result, petalism was soon abandoned.

The rapid removal of the tyrants had altered the power structure in Sicily. The island was now at least overtly free from the aggressive domination of the larger cities; and it was this new situation that allowed a Hellenized Sicel called Ducetius to launch a powerful 'national' movement. He began from his native town of Mineo, united the local Sicels into some sort of league, and attacked and destroyed the fortified Greek centres of Inessa-Etna and Morgantina. By 451–450 he was strong enough to invade Akragantine territory; but the following year he suffered a heavy defeat at the hands of the Syracusans and the 'liberation' movement promptly collapsed. The interior of the island was then rapidly subjugated by Syracuse, and though Sicel national consciousness flickered on, as a political force it was effectively dead.

During these troubles, Carthage made no move, partly because she had concerns elsewhere, but partly also because her relations with Sicilian Greeks were friendly. As so often in the island's history, it was internal rivalry rather than external aggression that proved the main cause of instability; and the culprit this time was Syracuse. Though she had defeated Akragas handsomely in the mid-440s, and peace had been declared, a renewed struggle for power now began between the two Dorian rivals. Syracuse took advantage of her solid control over the Sicels – and no doubt of their tribute money too – and built up her forces in a manner that was unashamedly provocative. According to Diodorus, the cavalry was doubled, 100 triremes constructed and the infantry also increased.

What happened in the next decades is unfortunately known to us in the context of Athenian rather than Sicilian history. But given our sources, that can hardly be avoided. Athens began to show political interest in Sicily as far back as the 450s when she signed a treaty of friendship with Segesta. Similar agreements followed with Halicyae and Leontini, as well as with mainland Rhegium. Just what Athens had in mind is far from clear; quite possibly nothing at all. At any rate, Leontini found herself under attack by Syracuse in 427, and in accordance with the treaty, requested help. The Athenians responded with an expeditionary force; and this remained on the island for more than two years until the declaration of peace in 424.

Eight years later, it was the turn of Selinus and Segesta to be at war. Syracuse was supporting Selinus; so Segesta appealed to Carthage. Unfortunately there was no response from this quarter, so she turned instead to Athens, pleading the old alliance, and promising a large financial contribution. The mood in Athens was favourable, partly because of a lull in the Peloponnesian War which had liberated both manpower and resources. But before they committed themselves the Athenians were prudent enough to send a delegation to Segesta to look over the situation. They were elaborately deceived, and the delegation returned to Athens with false but glowing reports of Segesta's wealth. Part of the trick may have been the start of work on the magnificent temple, which in the event was never finished.

After a famous debate in the Athenian assembly, Alcibiades, the main spokesman for intervention, carried the day overwhelmingly; and in the summer of 415 Athens dispatched the most splendid and most expensive armada ever to have sailed from a single Greek city. According to Thucydides there were more than 250 ships, including troop-carriers and supply-transports, and perhaps 25,000 men. But despite this enormous outlay, things began to go wrong almost from the start. There was disagreement and ill-will among the Athenian commanders; Alcibiades was soon indicted in Athens on a complex sacrilege charge; and many months were frittered away seeking further alliances in Sicily or raiding for booty. This gave Syracuse badly needed time in which to strengthen her fortifications and improve her navy.

The war finally centred on Syracuse, as it should have done from the very start. By the time of the last battles in the autumn of 413, Syracuse had gained the advantage, mainly because a Greek citizen militia was not well equipped, materially or psychologically, to campaign abroad for two years. Supplies were uncertain; and when disease struck and morale among the troops began to weaken, the Athenian generals thought it best to retreat. The result was catastrophic. Not only was the army decimated, but 7000 men were captured and imprisoned in the limestone quarries. The generals Demosthenes and Nicias were executed, and an unknown number of soldiers were sold into slavery, branded on the forehead with the mark of a horse. Only a handful of Greeks managed to make their way home, some of them set free according to Plutarch, because they could recite by heart choruses of Euripides; 'for the Sicilians, it seems, had a passion for his poetry greater than that of any other Hellenes outside Greece'.

Syracuse naturally celebrated its success, and a great deal of booty was dedicated to Apollo in Delphi. But the victory brought no peace either to Syracuse or to Sicily. Internal faction, dormant during the period of the Athenian invasion, now flared up again with renewed vigour; and one result was political change. 'The common people,' said Aristotle, 'having been responsible for the victory, now transformed the government from a *politeia* to a full democracy.' Under the leadership of a general named Diocles, they forced through a number of reforms, ironically enough on the Athenian model. The law was codified, and, most important of all, officials were now to be selected by lot.

With the removal of the Athenians from the island, Selinus returned to the attack. Segesta once more found herself in trouble and appealed to Carthage for help, this time with the added inducement that she was willing to become a Carthaginian tributary. For reasons we do not know, Carthage accepted; and in 409 Selinus fell to Hannibal's forces, and was gutted. The Carthaginian commander then marched to Himera and defeated the Syracusans. But rather than follow up his victory, he decided to sail back to Africa and disband his army. Quite why he did this is not clear, but it does suggest that even now no decision had been taken to capture the whole of Sicily. However, when an exiled Syracusan politician gathered an army and started raiding Carthaginian tributaries and dependencies, the Carthaginians returned to Sicily with a vengeance.

Their first target was Akragas, which was now unusually prosperous thanks to its neutrality in earlier wars. After eight months of fighting the city surrendered, and the Carthaginians proceeded to reap their reward in plunder, carrying off many works of art, including – at least according to one tradition – Phalaris' famous bronze bull. One result of this defeat was further political deterioration in Syracuse; and a young man called Dionysius, who was soon to become the most powerful Greek ruler of the age, took advantage of the new situation to get himself appointed to the board of generals, and soon to sole command with plenipotentiary powers.

In the spring of 405 a battle began for Gela. This went much the same way as the Akragantine campaign a few months earlier, and the city was soon evacuated, along with Kamarina. Syracuse should have been next on the list; but for some curious reason the Carthaginians opted instead for peace with Dionysius, and returned home. Diodorus attributes their action to a severe outbreak of plague (which they then carried back to Africa), and though one becomes rather suspicious of the timely intervention of plague in ancient Sicilian history, no better explanation of the Carthaginian withdrawal suggests itself.

The treaty with Dionysius was the first recognition by the Greeks of a Carthaginian *epikrateia* (conventionally, but perhaps imprecisely, translated 'province') in Sicily. According to Diodorus, the agreement stipulated that the Phoenician, Elymian and Sican settlements were to belong to Carthage; the people of Selinus, Akragas, Himera, Gela and Kamarina could return home but on condition that they left their cities unfortified and paid tribute; Leontini, Messina and the Sicels were proclaimed free and autonomous; and Dionysius was recognized as ruler in Syracuse. It was this last provision of the treaty which above all others was to remain in force, and in a manner that no one could have envisaged in 406.

There can be little doubt that it was a combination of the Athenian and Carthaginian invasions that brought tyranny back to Syracuse, and thence in a short time to the rest of Greek Sicily too. This suggests an answer to the question of why the Sicilian Greeks failed to make a success of the city-state way of life. In an essentially alien environment, with powers like Carthage so close at hand, political unrest was almost bound to flourish. Equally, if not more, important was the fact that so much of the population had been uprooted – sometimes more than once – and so many mercenaries infused, that any strong sense of community, so essential to a city-state, was inevitably lacking. Given time, the Sicilian cities might perhaps have recovered from the effects of the first tyrants, and achieved a degree of internal cohesion. But in view of the importance of the island to outside powers, time is something that Sicilians were rarely to be allowed.

CHAPTER 3

Five tyrants

DIONYSIUS I

From 405 until the Roman conquest, which began in 264 BC, the history of Sicily has to be written around the careers and fortunes of five rulers of Syracuse. The sources offer no alternative, and the distortion which results is probably even greater than that produced by the tenacious, though unnecessary, convention of turning the history of the Roman Empire or of England into a succession of individual reigns. Occasionally an archaeological discovery or a rare contemporary document inscribed on stone reminds us that life in Sicily was not all war, rapine and financial extortion by tyrants; but no continuous history can be built out of such scraps.

The first and most striking of these five rulers, the elder Dionysius, became the focus for both contemporary and later moralizing. Fact merged with fiction to the point where his career becomes hard to reconstruct with any reliability. It is a reasonable assumption that he came from an upper-class background, and we know that he first appeared on the scene in the anarchic situation created by the Carthaginian invasion. Though only about twenty-five years of age at the time, he seized his chance with such skill that he had Syracuse in his power within a year or so. Aristotle cites him as an outstanding example of the tyrant who attained power by demagogic appeals to the poorer classes, and the evidence we have suggests this is true.

Personal power at home and abroad was Dionysius' aim, and this provides a key to understanding his thirty-eight year rule. His methods were often singular. He collected the normal revenues of a Greek state but he also resorted to every possible device to raise emergency funds when he needed them, just as he freely commandeered labour for arms manufacture and fortification. In the best Sicilian tradition, he shifted whole sections of the population from one city to another; and though like his predecessors he showed marked unconcern for the mechanics of civil administration, he did alter the former military set-up radically, not only by the injection of a strong mercenary element but also by a new command structure, with the highest posts being given to his kinsmen and close personal associates. The stress on family was to be a *leitmotif* of Dionysius' reign.

All this has a certain intrinsic interest, but it is important too in that it indicates how completely personal the rule of Dionysius was, and was meant to appear. In this respect he created something new in the western world, anticipating the practice of Hellenistic monarchs in the centuries after Alexander the Great. Dionysius had no empire as such: he was not 'king of' any fixed region or people, but ruled wherever his writ ran, so long as he could enforce it. In *de facto* terms, and at its greatest extension, this meant the whole of Sicily (except for the extreme west) and the toe of Italy to the Gulf of Taranto. He had allies in Epirus in north-western Greece, and could count on the support of 'barbarian' Italic peoples of southern Italy, such as the Campanians, Lucanians and Iapygians, who provided his most reliable mercenaries.

Sicily was the heart of his empire, and its incorporation involved him in war with Carthage. Dionysius was clearly a man of prodigious energy, and his passion for fighting was almost limitless. Between 404 and 402 he launched attacks on various Sicel communities, captured Catania and Naxos by treachery, and induced the Leontines to move in a body to Syracuse. He also crushed a mutiny at home and transformed Syracuse into the largest and most heavily fortified of all Greek cities. This would have exhausted many men, but not Dionysius. He now prepared for a major war by modernizing his navy, building siege-engines (including one major innovation, the catapult) and conducting active diplomacy.

His first military objective was the Phoenician settlement of Motya which he captured after a siege which was alleged to have served as a model for subsequent commanders, including Alexander the Great at Tyre. In 396 he took advantage of an outbreak of plague in the Carthaginian army to deliver a crushing defeat, and this left him in effective control of almost all Sicily except for the old Carthaginian sector. But his opponents were far from finished. Fighting broke out once more in 393 and 392, and then again ten years later; and this time it was the Carthaginians who were victorious. Though Dionysius sought to recoup his losses, he died before much could be achieved, and after his death his son made peace. Sicily was now to be free from any serious Carthaginian invasion for twenty years.

The island paid dearly for the privilege of having the Carthaginians driven back in the years after 405. But Dionysius was not a man to baulk at human suffering. His self-absorption was too intense, and his pursuit of power effectively an end in itself. He sought, in contrast to the earlier tyrants, to play a role in the affairs of the old Greek world. Yet, curiously, no material advantage seems to have accrued, apart from some valuable military assistance sent by Sparta in 395; and one cannot take seriously the idea of long-range imperial ambitions in the east. This apparent lack of success, however, need not be construed as failure. His foreign policy could have been inspired simply by megalomania: Dionysius was there to be courted and would flex his muscles or not at will.

The nature of our evidence is such that it is impossible to get any clear picture of what life was like in Sicily under Dionysius. The slaughter of war was undoubtedly very great, but the evidence from the preceding century and the following three hundred years indicates that Sicily had remarkable powers of recovery; or put more crudely, those in the right positions profited from the fighting and grew richer in peace time. It is also interesting to note that Syracuse maintained its reputation for high living. Nor does the island's cultural life seem to have been negligible, though it is curious that Dionysius differed from his predecessors in erecting fortifications rather than temples, theatres, and other civic buildings.

As for those Sicilians who survived without profiting from the troubles, our sources permit only one or two tentative extrapolations. A few years after the death of Dionysius the familiar class-war call for land redistribution was to be heard; and there is little reason to suppose that such features were absent from Dionysius' reign itself. After all, large numbers of mercenaries have invariably been a source of trouble, even when settled on the land and called 'citizens'; and we can reasonably assume that Dionysius' were no exception.

Dionysius was undoubtedly the most powerful figure of his day in the Greek world. He was also a match for any non-Greek in the west. At times he commanded considerable financial resources; and by contemporary standards he had great manpower as well. Nevertheless, he was unable to weld a national community out of his new subjects, even in Sicily. He was not a constructive ruler, and his career has something of the poignant futility of a treadmill about it. Equally dispiriting is the clear absence of any constructive opposition to him in his domain. Whatever spark of popular participation still existed in Sicilian politics at the end of the fifth century BC was snuffed out under Dionysius. Henceforth Sicilians were to be subjects rather than citizens; and all further political action took the form of destructive dynastic struggles, conspiracies and civil wars.

DIONYSIUS II AND DION

Dionysius publicly designated his son and namesake as his heir; and the succession took place without difficulty. The younger Dionysius, however, lacked his father's energy, and opted for the soft life of drunkenness, interspersed perhaps with a little poetry and philosophy. He apparently preferred to live in his mother's native Locri, leaving the cares of the empire to others. Dion – head of the Syracusan wing of the older Dionysius' family

– was a man of very different character. He was educated, haughty, ambitious, and cold-blooded, and within a year he had fallen out with the young tyrant and departed for Greece. Here he remained for nearly ten years, during which time we know hardly anything about him, except that he spent some of the period in Athens in the circle of Plato's Academy.

In 361 or 360 Dionysius felt able to declare his rival a proper exile and to confiscate his wealth. Dion responded by preparing for a coup, and gathered together quite a remarkable collection of supporters, including at least two members of the Academy, Timonides – who kept a log of the venture which he sent to Plato's nephew – and Callippus. Though the motives of this group no doubt differed, there can be little denying the affinity that some men trained in the Greek philosophical schools were beginning to show for tyranny. Only the wise ruler, the philosopher-king, they maintained, could lead the Greek states to virtue.

Dion sailed for Sicily in 357 with a thousand hired troops, and marched on Syracuse, picking up support along the way from several communities that saw a chance to break from Syracusan suzerainty. The city welcomed him, and he was able to enter unopposed. But Dionysius' faithful commander-in-chief, Philistus, moved in to attack, overran Dion's lax defences, and almost succeeded in dislodging him. Only the arrival of twenty triremes and military reinforcements from Greece saved Dion from defeat. The sources disagree as to whether Philistus committed suicide or was tortured to death. At any rate, his dismembered body was dragged through the streets of Syracuse and then cast out unburied.

This act was a fitting prelude to a decade of savage and confused fighting, in which the original dynastic conflict was almost submerged. Dionysius' empire was now crumbling rapidly, and amidst all the confusion the only institution which was not effectively challenged was one-man rule. Though Dion claimed to be a liberator, who had come to replace tyranny with some form of constitutional government, it was widely believed that he aimed to be a tyrant himself; and certainly, by temperament and conviction he was bitterly opposed to popular rule. The lower classes distrusted and opposed him, and they found their own leaders to speak for them, both in Syracuse and elsewhere.

Dion was assassinated in 354 by his erstwhile ally, Callippus. The motive is not clear, but it seems to have been purely personal. Callippus assumed control of the city, but thirteen months later he was driven out by Dion's nephew Hipparinus, and retired to the tyranny in Catania. The situation now went from bad to worse. The east of the island dissolved into shambles, its population sharply reduced, its prosperity gone, and warring factions ready to call in Carthage once again. Unlike the disappearance of the first

Syracusan tyrants, the death of Dionysius I had torn Sicily apart. The process was sordid, and it would hardly deserve a mention were it not for the remarkable saga of Plato's interventions.

The account is contained in a collection of thirteen letters supposedly written by Plato. Though some are undoubtedly false, the story as it stands relates how in 388 or 387 Plato journeyed to southern Italy on a private visit. In Syracuse he met the young Dion, quickly perceived his inner qualities and won him over to philosophy and the life of virtue. When the elder Dionysius died, Dion persuaded his son to invite Plato to Syracuse so that he could be educated in the ways of a philosopher-king. But the visit was a failure, and Plato returned to Athens in despair. Five years later the ageing philosopher was again invited to Syracuse, but once more to no avail.

Despite the air of unreality that pervades the tale – and a number of discrepancies and improbabilities – most modern historians accept it as substantially true. But so far as the history of Sicily is concerned, it really makes little difference whether we believe it or not. The episode only really has any bearing on judgements of Plato's practical sense, and the political teaching of the Academy. It might also affect our assessment of Dion and his plans, though we would do well to remember that Dion was not in power long enough to accomplish anything, whatever his intentions. Events in Sicily took their own turn, with or without Plato's intervention; and the saviour was a man of military action from Corinth, and not an Athenian philosopher.

TIMOLEON

Though Dionysius II managed to return to Syracuse briefly in 346, it was clear that political behaviour in Sicily was no longer possible. The continuing strife between 'aristocrats' and those clamouring for land redistribution created the illusion from time to time that an adventurer had acquired a basis of support; and such an illusion might be strengthened by an occasional meeting of the popular assembly or an election. Real power lay with mercenaries, whether Sicilians or outsiders, as it was they who guaranteed effective control. But even here things had changed, for mercenary forces were smaller than before, a sign not only of the break-up of the old concentration of power but also of a considerable drop in both population and financial resources throughout the island.

With the situation unresolved there was inevitably an appeal to Carthage; and despite difficulties at home, Carthage responded favourably, perhaps in the belief that it was to her advantage to keep the island disunited. The old pattern seemed about to repeat itself. But suddenly a new twist developed.

Hiketas, a former follower of Dion, begged Corinth for help, and the mother-city, which had never before interfered in the domestic affairs of Syracuse, now broke a precedent of centuries and sent a small army commanded by Timoleon. The rationale behind this is wholly unclear. Corinth was a shadow of its past self, and with domestic problems of its own, it could surely ill afford men and resources. Equally opaque is the choice of Timoleon, a man of relatively advanced years, and undistinguished past, whose only memorable act had been the assassination of an older brother.

When Timoleon landed on the beach of Tauromenium in 344, he was greeted by an understandable lack of enthusiasm. His only significant support came from Andromachus, the father of the future historian Timaeus. Timoleon's force was small; he had little money, and his goals were at best ambiguous. Yet within six years he had defeated and destroyed all opposition and was master of the island. Dionysius II was the first to yield, and he was allowed to retire to Corinth. The Carthaginians were then smashed at the Crimisus River – which is perhaps to be identified with the Belice near Segesta – and made peace more or less along the lines that existed in the days of Dionysius I, withdrawing to the *epikrateia* west of the Halycus River.

Despite his success Timoleon had no legitimate authority in Sicily. Indeed were it not for the myth that grew up around him, he would be known primarily as a tyrant; and rightly so, for he had seized power with a mercenary force, and was autocratic, ruthless, brutal and faithless, precisely like his allies and opponents. Yet the picture cannot be left at that, for Timoleon was also a reformer, with a programme that aimed to secure the future of Sicily. He removed nearly all the petty tyrants in the island, and then proceeded to a dramatic destruction of the palace-fortress in Ortygia and similar structures elsewhere. In the constitutional sphere, a 'legislative commission' was summoned to Syracuse to revise the old democratic code. He also sought to inject life into the economy by bringing thousands of immigrants from Italy and the old Greek world, and giving them uncultivated land to farm.

Not much can be said about Syracuse because of the difficulties of systematic excavation. But everywhere else the testimony of the spade is conclusive that Timoleon inaugurated an era of urban growth and prosperity. Not only were Akragas and Gela raised from mere squatters' hamlets to large, functioning city-states, but the whole hinterland behind the south coast witnessed a similar development. There was also a revival of monumental building, which had more or less ceased after the Carthaginian invasion at the end of the fifth century; and the funds for this came from greatly increased agricultural production. Sicily, it must be remembered, was basically an agrarian society; and growth or decline in the urban sector was primarily a function of success or failure in the countryside.

When age and blindness forced Timoleon to retire in 337 or 336, class war erupted, and government and social peace quickly broke down. This is not surprising, for the autonomous, self-governing Greek city was beyond redemption even in old Greece; and there could be little hope for it in Sicily, where it never had strong roots. What is puzzling is that this familiar round of Sicilian troubles, between Timoleon's departure and Agathocles' accession in 317, did not seriously disturb the new prosperity. All the examples Diodorus gives of the revival of monumental building in fact date from the reigns of Agathocles and Hiero II. The Castello Eurialo fortification in Syracuse was probably transformed into an independent unit at this time, and at Gela growth was so rapid that the town overran the old cemetery, which had once been outside the city proper.

AGATHOCLES

Ancient writers tended to bracket Agathocles with the elder Dionysius; and thanks to the historian Timaeus, whom he banished to Athens, Agathocles comes out worse. Even Diodorus joins in the general chorus: 'None of the tyrants before him,' he says, 'displayed such cruelty to his subjects.' But to focus on Agathocles' character is to miss the profound change that had occurred in the world outside Sicily, a change to which Agathocles responded and which stamped his career with novel traits. In simplest terms, the new situation was the emergence of Hellenistic monarchy in the eastern Mediterranean and Egypt; and Sicily, like Italy and Greece, could not but be influenced by the strength and ambitions of the Ptolemaic dynasty, and the kings of Macedon and Epirus.

On the death of Timoleon, the young Agathocles threw himself into the ensuing internecine warfare and spent more than twenty years as a *condottiere* in both Sicily and southern Italy. In 317, aided by several thousand veterans and a reputation for defending the masses against oligarchs, he made a successful bid for power in Syracuse. His coup was accompanied by a savage uprising, and according to Diodorus more than four thousand people were slain, 'whose sole offence was that they were of better birth than the others'. Agathocles then called the assembly, and was voted sole command with plenipotentiary powers. He promised an immediate cancellation of debts and the redistribution of land.

Whether these social measures were actually carried out is not known. It is probable that they were, for though we have very little information about Agathocles' domestic activity as ruler, he clearly did not drop his popular

appeal once in power. The fact that he boasted about his skill as a potter may
be indicative in this respect. More importantly, and in contrast to Timoleon,
his reported atrocities were always class based, and were directed at the
wealthy and oligarchically inclined. Such was his popular support, it seems,
that from 305 until his death in 289 he was able to drop terror as an
instrument altogether. His fortifications, significantly, were defences
against external attack, not citadels against revolts.

The archaeological evidence shows that Sicily prospered under Agathocles. But the price, at least in the first ten or twelve years, was a heavy one.
Not only were the oligarchic factions in cities such as Akragas, Gela and
Messina able and willing to resist, but they also had the backing of Carthage,
which was still pursuing its policy of keeping an equilibrium among the
island's forces. The result was a protracted, costly and far-flung war. It was
fought in North Africa as well as in Sicily, and only came to end in 305 when
Agathocles was forced to sue for peace. Carthage, no more interested than
before in expanding her Sicilian possessions, accepted, and the *epikrateia*
was re-established, with few modifications.

Once the struggle with Carthage was over, the rest of Sicily quickly fell to
Agathocles. It was probably now that he assumed the royal title, a move
which all his predecessors had eschewed. Though some historians have
sought complicated constitutional explanations for this development, it is
unlikely that the new title significantly altered anything inside Sicily itself.
What it did do, however, was to bring Agathocles into line with the new
Hellenistic practice, and this must have helped him in the sphere of foreign
policy. He certainly cut something of a figure abroad, for he extended his
domain into mainland Italy, married his daughter to King Pyrrhus of
Epirus, and himself took as his third wife a daughter (or perhaps step-
daughter) of Ptolemy. Such power, however, was more apparent than real.
It lacked solid foundations, and when Agathocles died, his enterprise died
with him.

CHAPTER 4

A province of Rome

BETWEEN CARTHAGE AND ROME

Agathocles was assassinated in 289 BC, the victim, it seems, of family quarrels over the forthcoming succession to the throne. The next decade saw the usual round of strife and anarchy that followed the removal of each Syracusan strong man. Two factors in particular caused unrest. One was the presence of a large corps of Italian mercenaries called Mamertines, who embarked on a career of marauding and banditry from their base in Messina; and the other was the outbreak of war between Syracuse and Akragas. Though this ended in about 280 with the latter's defeat, Syracuse proceeded to make incursions into the west of the island, and Carthage in response sent a major expeditionary force.

It was now the turn of Pyrrhus, King of the Molossians of Epirus in north-western Greece, to make his mark on Sicilian history. He was one of the most remarkable of the post-Alexander generation of Greek adventurers, and was deemed by Hannibal the shrewdest and most professional of all commanders. His career had begun in the troubled world of northern Greece and Macedon; but he failed to achieve here the power to which he aspired. In 280, sensing a new opportunity, he turned to Italy, where he won two sensational victories against the Roman armies. But his own troops were so depleted – hence the phrase 'Pyrrhic victory' – that he welcomed a clamorous invitation to go for easier game in Sicily.

Pyrrhus crossed to Tauromenium in 278 with a large army. The enthusiasm that greeted him was such that he was able to treble his forces and increase his fleet to 200 ships. Success came quickly, and he was soon King Pyrrhus in Sicily, as his gold and silver coinage testifies. (Whether he was King *of* Sicily, as some historians hold, may be doubted.) He defeated the Mamertines in under two years and threw the superior Carthaginian forces out of the island everywhere except at Lilybaeum, which proved impregnable so long as Carthage controlled the sea. He returned to Italy in the autumn of 276, and the following year was defeated by the Romans at Benevento. This put an end to his western adventures.

Meanwhile one of Pyrrhus' Syracusan henchmen, Hiero, seized power in his native city, reorganized the mercenary army, and in time came to an understanding with the Carthaginians. He was then in a position to prepare properly for an attack on the Mamertines, and to this end even enrolled a new citizen force alongside his mercenaries. In 269 he scored a major victory, although the Carthaginians, true to their strategy of keeping Sicily divided, stopped him from taking Messina itself. Nevertheless Hiero now assumed the title of King, and he held it for fifty-four years without serious challenge, dying in 215 at the age of 92.

Kingship was now a familiar and established institution among Sicilians, as among Greeks everywhere. Hiero, however, surpassed his predecessors, not only in his regular employment of the royal title in public documents but also in the use of a crowned portrait on coins. His wife Philistis, oddly enough, figured more commonly on his currency, and this reflects the unmistakable influence of Ptolemaic Egypt. Yet Hiero was not simply an extension of the Syracusan trend; he was a different kind of ruler in important respects. For one thing, he soon abandoned any idea of extending his realm in oriental Sicily, and devoted himself instead to its management. Furthermore, his interests in the eastern Greek world were determined less by power politics and more by a concern with markets for agricultural and pastoral produce, which explains the particular interest in Egypt and Rhodes.

This reflects the entry of Rome into Sicilian affairs. Dionysius and Agathocles had been able to play a role in Mediterranean power politics even in the face of Carthage, but no Sicilian ruler could do so against both Carthage and Rome. Though Hiero initially allied himself with Carthage in 264, he did not wait to be crushed or even to suffer a military defeat before deciding that he had chosen incorrectly; and by mid-263 he had swung and signed a treaty with Rome. This alliance was one of the most long-lived of the period and through it Syracuse and its dependent states escaped the horrors of the First Punic War. It also reinforced Hiero personally, and spared him the usual threats and conspiracies that beset more vulnerable rulers.

The First Punic War broke out in 264 when the Mamertines in Messina suddenly decided, for reasons that are not very clear, to eject the Carthaginian garrison that was protecting them from Hiero, and appeal to Rome instead. The Romans duly invaded; and Carthage, eager as always to retain control of western Sicily (which was essential to her navigation), responded in kind. Military bases were established at Akragas – the greatest city in Carthage's Sicilian 'province' – and Heraclea Minoa; and it was these that Rome attacked first. Subsequently when a Roman navy came into being, the fighting spread not only to western and north-western Sicily, but also to North Africa. It was a war fought without respite for nearly a quarter of a century, with neither side yielding to the other in ruthlessness or determination.

In the course of the campaigns the Sicilians themselves provided victims rather than manpower. Rome took Akragas in 261 after a six-month siege and sold off 25,000 of the inhabitants; Carthage returned seven years later, tore down the walls, and burned the city. In 258 Kamarina was captured by the Romans and most of its population sold into slavery. A similar fate befell Panormus, and then in 250, Selinus. The last act of this cruel drama was played out at Lilybaeum, which the Romans were forced to besiege for ten years – an indication of what this single Sicilian promontory meant to Carthage. It was only in 241 that a naval defeat finally forced the Carthaginians to surrender. They agreed to a large indemnity, along with a total withdrawal from Sicily and a commitment not to make war on Hiero in the future.

Apart from Hiero's dominion, the whole of Sicily was now Roman territory; and this created a new administrative and imperial situation. In the previous centuries Rome's acquisitions had been solely in Italy, and by a series of ad hoc measures, largely in the form of 'alliances' and 'half-citizenship', she had managed to develop a viable power structure. But Sicily was a possession, not an ally, and new machinery was accordingly needed to organize, administer and exploit. Details are almost completely lacking about the first steps taken – the full-fledged provincial system was still some decades in the future – but we do know that Roman officials were installed and an annual tribute exacted, chiefly in corn.

Sicily's new colonial status did not guarantee her peace, for in 218 the Second Punic War broke out; and from the beginning the island was important as a barrier between Hannibal in Italy and his home base in North Africa. The Romans used Lilybaeum and Messina as bases from which to conduct raids and disrupt the main lines of sea communication with Carthage. Hiero helped to supply the Roman forces in Sicily and on at least two occasions he sent substantial gifts to Rome itself. However, not everyone in Syracuse was so cooperative, not even within the ruling family itself. Hiero's son and co-regent, Gelon, was rumoured to be negotiating with Carthage; and his sudden and 'opportune' death might just be taken as confirmation of this.

Hiero himself died soon afterwards and the half-century alliance with Rome came to an end. For a year Syracuse was beset by palace plots and civil disorder while Rome and Carthage carried on complicated diplomacy, manoeuvring for support among the various parties. But with strong anti-Roman feeling now in evidence, Syracuse gravitated to the Carthaginian sphere; and Rome retaliated by invading in force under Marcellus. For two years Syracuse was besieged, but neither superior manpower nor the most sophisticated assault techniques and equipment were to any avail by land or sea. Archimedes was the fertile genius of the defence, and he provided the Romans with a face-saving explanation for their long frustration. In the words of Polybius, the Romans 'failed to reckon with the ability of Archimedes, nor did they foresee that in some circumstances the genius of one man is more effective than any number of hands'.

Sicily was now the key to the whole war. If the Romans had been thrown out, Hannibal could have been reinforced with men and supplies, Philip V of Macedon might have decided to pull his weight, and Rome would have faced defeat. But Marcellus rose to the challenge with vigour and brutality, destroying Megara and following up a revolt in Enna with mass butchery. In 212 Syracuse itself finally fell. The city was given over to the soldiers for looting and Archimedes was killed, though we are assured that this was contrary to orders. Marcellus shipped back to Rome not only the customary booty but also vast quantities of statuary and paintings, some torn from the walls of temples and other public buildings. This earned him the censure of Polybius and the hatred of Sicilians generally.

The Second Punic War dragged on until Hannibal's defeat at Zama in North Africa in 201. It destroyed Carthage as a power and left Rome in control of the western Mediterranean, poised for world conquest. That is the war's place in the history-books. In the process, however, it destroyed Hiero's kingdom, and so put an end to the last vestiges of independence in Sicily; and it also led to inevitable redirection of Sicily's external economic relations towards Italy. Henceforth the island was no more than a province, and its history little more than an appendage of Roman history.

THE FIRST ROMAN PROVINCE

In 70 BC at the trial of Gaius Verres for gross extortion and malfeasance as governor of Sicily, the great orator Cicero declared that the island was 'the first to teach our ancestors what a fine thing it is to rule over foreign nations'. After the opening speech for the prosecution Verres came to the conclusion that defence was futile and he went into voluntary exile. For political reasons of his own, Cicero proceeded to publish a 400-page book in the form of five lengthy court orations, which were neither delivered nor even written for delivery. That book is our main source of information on the internal affairs of Sicily under the Roman Republic; and its limitations as evidence are obvious.

Cicero set out to create the impression of a peaceful, prosperous, and essentially unchanging island that had been ruined by Verres in the space of three years. Yet nearly a century and a half had passed since the capture of Syracuse in the Second Punic War, and much had changed in that time. Perhaps nothing in Cicero's performance is more disingenuous than his self-satisfied claim that the Roman tax system was just a continuation of Hiero's, thereby implying that the fortunate Sicilians were simply paying what they had always paid and had gained the blessings of peace to boot. In fact, both psychologically and substantively, there was an enormous difference between the taxes paid to Hiero – the yield of which was on the whole expended locally – and the goods and money which the Romans carried away without a similar return.

The basis of the Roman tribute system was one-tenth of the wheat and barley crop, paid in kind and shipped straight to Rome. In addition there was also a levy on wine, olives, fruit and vegetables, and a pasture-tax in cash. Rome also reserved the right to take a second tithe by compulsory purchase, at a price which the Senate fixed unilaterally. Further compulsory purchases were exacted – again at unilaterally fixed prices – for the maintenance of the Roman governor and his staff. Nor was the remainder of the crop at the free disposal of the Sicilians: exports were permitted only to Italy, unless a special licence were given by the Roman Senate. No wonder Roman writers loved to quote Cato's dictum that Sicily was the 'Republic's granary, the nurse at whose breast the Roman people is fed'.

Another tax levied by Rome was a 5 per cent *ad valorem* duty on goods shipped in or out of Sicilian harbours. This was purely a money-raising device: no idea of protectionism was involved, and exemptions were given only for the tithes and for personal goods carried by voyagers. The several communities also had to furnish ships and crews for a small navy whose function was to protect the harbours against pirates. This completes the list of contributions exacted by Rome, but it should be remembered that Sicilians also had local taxes of their own to meet, as well as public buildings, water supply, cults, festivals and other amenities, to pay for.

Local administration, like local taxation, was in principle left to Sicilians, for – as elsewhere in the empire – Rome had neither reason nor the resources to take it on. The little information we have about it suggests considerable diversity between communities, the result in each case of centuries of more or less autonomous development. There were differences, in particular, between old *poleis* like Syracuse or Agrigentum and towns such as Panormus or Drepana which had never been properly Greek. As far as private law is concerned, this was left untouched, and there is even a suggestion that communities were allowed to retain the traditional Greek rule that land ownership be barred to non-citizens, including fellow-Greeks from the next town. Everywhere there are signs that councils and assemblies continued to meet and transact business, albeit in a very low key.

In practice, local autonomy meant freedom from interference only so long as it suited Rome. When interventions did occur, they were variously motivated and came in different forms, both legal and extra-legal. The rarest was a general regulation for the province as a whole, such as the law on slaves, known as *lex Rupilia* of 131. More common were specific interventions, for example that of 197 when the Senate instructed the governor to bolster the population of Agrigentum by transplanting settlers from elsewhere in Sicily; and four years later we find another governor promulgating the rules of cooptation into the Agrigentine senate and specifying that representatives of the new settlers must not constitute a majority.

In everyday affairs, Rome was personified by the local tax-collectors, the two quaestors (financial officers stationed in Lilybaeum and Syracuse) and the Roman governor. The latter's term of office was normally one year, though on occasions this was extended: Verres had three terms because his designated successor was tied up with the Spartacist slave revolt in Italy. Various factors entered into the selection of governor, but neither a capacity to rule well nor a knowledge of Sicily was among them. Moreover, a one-year tour of duty was hardly conducive to good administration, particularly if the governor was dishonest.

Only rarely was a Roman of sufficient standing to be a governor brought to trial and convicted for other than political charges. Verres is a case in point. On any reading of Cicero, he and his gang were a remarkable collection of rogues, who cheated, lied, embezzled, robbed, conspired, suborned and terrorised, all in the interests of personal enrichment. They even flogged and tortured Roman citizens publicly. In 72, the second year of Verres' governorship, an influential Sicilian named Sthenius made a personal appeal in Rome. He gained the support of the two consuls and one of the tribunes, and was considered sympathetically in the Senate (in which Verres' father sat); but he left empty-handed. Verres was re-appointed, and it was only when Cicero intervened that his luck turned.

The Romans repeated in Sicily the practice they had developed on the mainland of confiscating the landed property of declared enemies in the name of the state. Sometimes whole communities were involved, as at Leontini, though more often it was a question of specific individuals or families. This *ager publicus* was then given to deserving individuals, or else leased in large allotments for somewhat nominal rents. How much land the state acquired in Sicily in this way is unclear; but we do know that by some means a number of Romans and south Italian 'allies' and 'half-citizens' quickly moved in, as owners or tenants, and occupied large and profitable holdings in fertile plains and in the extensive pastures of the interior.

Cheap slave labour poured into Italy and Sicily in the second century BC, encouraging the wealthy to increase their holdings in farms and pasture. Sicily was now well on its way to becoming the classic land of large estates, or *latifundia*. But some caution is needed here, as the term *latifundia* is bound, in this period, to be somewhat imprecise: these estates were not so much large single units, as the concentration of a number of separate farms in the possession of one man. Such accumulation often took the form in Sicily of tenancy rather than ownership. Indeed Cicero explicitly says this was a custom among rich Sicilians, who used it as a way of increasing their holdings.

The list of Verres' victims (or alleged victims) reveals that the Roman–Italian takeover did not give the new settlers anything like a monopoly of the *latifundia*; and many Sicilian landowners enjoyed an equal degree of prosperity under Roman rule. As far as the mass of the population were concerned, the tenor of life was no doubt harsh; but at least there seems to have been some security. One test is the absence of serious emigration, despite frequent and often savage warfare. We certainly hear of exiles fleeing to Carthage and elsewhere, and of Sicilians living in Rome for one reason or another. But in general it is remarkable how few Sicilians tried to make their fortunes abroad in an age of mobility.

The vaunted peace that Rome brought to Sicily evidently had the beneficial effects claimed for it. Though the Romans took a heavy tribute under the Republic, they did not pauperize the island. Furthermore there is no contradiction between the idea of an economy dominated by slave-worked *latifundia* and Cicero's statement that the multitude of Sicilian farmers were smallholders for whom a single yoke of oxen sufficed. In a population of, say, half a million on the land, 3000 holdings of 500 *jugera* and more would account for the bulk of the agriculture and pasture, especially on the best acreage, and still leave place for Cicero's little men. These are notional figures but they serve to illustrate what has often been the landholding balance in this kind of economy.

Yet the precise economic position of the mass of the free population is unknown. We lack visible signs of discontent, but this silence might indicate no more than hopelessness arising from fear of Roman power. By contrast, the slave population did protest, and the two Sicilian risings in the latter part of the second century BC were, together with that of Spartacus in Italy, the greatest of their kind in antiquity and perhaps in the whole of history. These revolts suggest that fear alone is an inadequate explanation for passivity. Equally important must have been Rome's well-tried policy of winning over key sections of the subject population.

Modern estimates of the total population of Sicily in Cicero's time range between 600,000 and 1,000,000. There is no way of dividing the total among the urban and rural sectors. The 10,000 citizens of Centuripe included the farmers in its territory as well as the city-dwellers. Panormus, Catania and Syracuse were certainly larger, but on any count no city was comparable to the Syracuse of Dionysius I, and some – Gela, Selinus, Himera – had effectively ceased to exist. On the other hand, population was now thicker on the ground in the interior and in districts – such as the extreme south-east – that had previously been sparsely populated.

Archaeology, as well as literary references, indicates that the still heavily wooded island was very well cultivated, with market gardens, orchards and small allotments filling in the spaces between the *latifundia* and the sheepfolds. Inland communication was adequate, and it is reasonable to assume that the Romans improved the main roads. On the urban side, there was some geographical redistribution. The north-western area, especially Panormus, became much more heavily settled, and it is tempting (but no more than that) to attribute this development to the economic progress in Spain and France under the Romans, which opened a new field for Sicilian trade.

Whatever the influence of Rome on Sicily, it must not be forgotten that Italy continued to be in many respects a foreign country. Language was the obvious test of this. Most Sicilians, regardless of their distant origins, spoke Greek as their mother tongue; and it was Latin that was intrusive, at least down to the end of the first century BC. The Romans accepted the fact, and made no attempt to impose Latin even for administrative purposes. Hence we find that Verres had to employ interpreters. As far as culture is concerned this too was predominantly Greek. Sacred heralds toured the island and summoned representatives to Delphi and other pan-Hellenic shrines; public buildings remained essentially Greek in style; and an occasional Sicilian still turned up among the victors at the Olympic games.

THE GREAT SLAVE REVOLTS

The story of the great slave revolts begins in the Hellenistic East in the second century BC. Greece itself had already fallen to Rome, while in Asia Minor, Syria and Egypt the political system created by Alexander's successors was in a state of ugly dissolution. The immediate beneficiaries of this were the ubiquitous slavers. They bought up war captives and political victims, as well as seizing free men, women and children by the thousands. The majority of these chattels were then sold to eager buyers in Italy and Sicily, and as a result there was a sudden concentration of new slaves, many of them educated, some of high birth, and nearly all of them Greek-speaking.

The newcomers were thrown in with an already sizeable and mixed slave population. At one extreme of this large social group were herdsmen and shepherds – rough men of solitary and brigandish ways. More numerous were the agricultural workers, who ranged from chained labourers to the privileged, but still servile, bailiffs. There were also the urban slaves, craftsmen and domestics, the latter a rapidly increasing and on the whole more favoured group, catering to the growing demands of luxurious living. How these categories differed in their behaviour during the revolts is not easily determined, though it does seem that the pastoral and agricultural slaves provided the mass of the insurgents rather than the leaders.

The first revolt probably began in 139 BC in the region around Enna. This area had a particularly high concentration of slaves mostly employed on *latifundia*, and their misery seems to have been extreme. The spark was ignited on the estates of the wealthy Damophilus – a man, we are told, 'who surpassed the Persians in the sumptuousness and costliness of his feasts' – and the leader of the rising was Eunus, a new slave, of Syrian extraction. We are not told what duties he performed, but we hear much about his reputation as a magician, miracle-worker and prophet. His charisma evidently made him a natural leader; and when Damophilus' slaves rose up and murdered their master, Eunus was proclaimed King with absolute powers.

His first task, after bestowing the title of Queen on his Syrian mistress, was to decide the fate of the slave-owners. He drew a simple distinction: those that could be usefully employed in manufacturing arms were put to work in chains, the rest were summarily executed. Meanwhile a companion revolt had broken out in the Agrigentine district, led by a herdsman named Cleon. He agreed to join Eunus, and with pooled forces of some 15,000 men, the two slave leaders set out on a campaign that led to the capture of Morgantina and Tauromenium, and presumably of much of the territory in between. Success increased their following, and at one stage the army is alleged to have reached 200,000. This is a very improbable figure, but the revolt did acquire sufficient momentum to continue until 132, when it was suppressed by the consul P. Rupilius.

Perhaps the most remarkable aspect of the whole affair is the way Eunus sought to create a carbon-copy of the Seleucid monarchy. He called himself Antiochus (the most common name in the Seleucid dynasty), wore the diadem and other insignia, and minted copper coins bearing the head of Demeter and an ear of corn. Cleon held the title of *strategos*; there was a royal council and a bodyguard, and when it was all over, and Eunus was

found hiding in a cave, he had with him his court butcher, baker, bath
attendant and buffoon. None of this should be dismissed as mad farce. The
slaves were out to liberate themselves, take revenge, and live as free men in
the kind of state they knew best, namely a Hellenistic monarchy. There is no
evidence that they aspired to social revolution. In fact Eunus gave specific
orders to his men not to burn down farmhouses, or destroy agricultural
tools and crops.

The revolt ended with the execution of thousands of the insurgents.
Vengeful punishment, however, could not go too far, for the compelling
reason that Roman society required slaves in order to function. Whether
anything positive came out of the rising seems unlikely. Rupilius' law of 131
did not, as far as we know, tackle any of the fundamentals. The slave
latifundia were left unchanged, and were soon restored to their normal level
of production and profit, with new owners or tenants replacing those who
had lost their lives in the rebellion. No Roman had any intention of
legislating against the free use of one's wealth or the maximum exploitation
of one's slaves.

A generation after this first rising, probably in 104 BC, the Sicilian slaves
struck again. In response to a complaint by a client king, the Senate had
ordered the release of any 'allies' who had been reduced to servitude, and the
promulgation of this decree led to immediate chaos in Sicily. So many slaves
appeared before the governor in Syracuse to demand their freedom that,
after granting it to some 800 of them, he called a halt to proceedings and told
the rest to return to their masters. But instead of obeying they raised the
banner of revolt. For the second time it was new slaves who were the
initiators of a major uprising.

The insurrection of the east of the island found an immediate echo in the
west. Once again two leaders emerged, a man called Salvius in the region of
Halicyae and Heraclea, and the Cilician Athenion between Segesta and
Lilybaeum. Salvius – who may not have been a slave himself – was an expert
at taking auspices and possessed considerable military skill, more indeed
than any other slave commander in either revolt. He was the dominant
figure in the rising, at least at first, and assumed the title of King with the
Greek name of Tryphon. Later on he gave himself a Roman aura, donning
the purple toga, and appointing lictors with fasces.

Although the rebels were fewer than in the first revolt – 40,000 is the
maximum figure recorded – they were probably better equipped and better
trained. Unfortunately for them, however, the Romans were this time well
prepared, and did not repeat the casualness they had displayed in the first
outbreak. Though the fighting ranged widely over the island, the insurgents
were unable to capture a single major city, and when M' Aquillius took

charge of the Roman forces, the revolt was quickly brought to an end. Aquillius was rewarded with an ovation, as a formal triumph would have been considered too great an honour for a victory over slaves.

This time there was little question of what to do with the surviving rebels, since most of them had died in the fighting – 20,000 allegedly in one engagement. Replacements for the lost slaves were soon found, and the only preventive step we know the Romans took was to prohibit armsbearing by those of servile status, a measure as unenforceable then as at any other time. The damage caused by the revolt cannot be estimated, but it is reasonable to assume that it was less than that of either of the two Punic Wars. The island's powers of recovery were anyway soon in evidence, for when Verres arrived in 73 BC, twenty-six years after the end of the second rising, he found a rich land ripe for plunder.

CHAPTER 5

Sicily under the Roman Emperors

THE AUGUSTAN SETTLEMENT

Once Verres had been dealt with, Sicily returned to its normal place within the Roman dispensation. Though it was little disturbed by the civil war between Caesar and Pompey, everything changed with Caesar's assassination in 44 BC. Pompey's son, Sextus, organized an army and a fleet, selected Sicily as his base, and proceeded to take the island with little trouble. Within a few months he had become a major force in the civil war between Brutus and Cassius and the triumvirs – Antony, Octavian (the future emperor Augustus) and Lepidus – not least because all shipments of corn from Sicily were now ended and Italy was blockaded against seaborne supplies from elsewhere. Even the armies of the triumvirs fighting outside Italy were threatened with food shortages.

At a conference held in 39 BC the triumvirs reluctantly agreed to recognize Sextus Pompey's authority in Sicily, Sardinia and Corsica. For his part, Sextus promised to lift the blockade and to resume shipment of the tithe. There was probably little good faith on either side. At any rate war soon broke out, and the destruction in Sicily, despite the short duration of the fighting, was perhaps comparable in scale to that of the Punic Wars. Nor did it end with the defeat of Sextus in 36; for in merciless fashion Octavian levied a 1600-talent cash indemnity on the island, and severely punished those cities that had resisted him. Tauromenium suffered particularly badly, with its entire population being deported.

The Battle of Actium in 31 BC left Octavian in sole command of the empire. Peace was urgently needed in Sicily, as the island was once again in bad shape. Many men had been lost, both in the countryside and in the cities, and a great deal of land was lying idle. Augustus quickly set to work to distribute and rebuild. He kept a large slice of territory for himself and gave another substantial tract to Agrippa, the architect of so many of his victories. Smaller holdings, scaled according to rank, were given to discharged Italian veterans of Augustus' legions. These men then performed a double function, on the one hand replacing some of the destroyed manpower, on the other providing a loyal leavening in the population, particularly in the areas around the chief northern and eastern ports.

On this base, and as part of his reorganization of the empire, Augustus erected a new administrative superstructure. Its precise character is not altogether certain; nor is the date of its introduction. In the end, though, six cities – Tauromenium, Catania, Syracuse, Tyndaris, Thermae and Palermo – were given the status of Roman *coloniae*. This usually implied a substantial influx of Roman veterans, and that is almost certainly the case here. Messina, Lipari and possibly a few other towns became Roman *municipia*, differing in status from the *coloniae* only by being somewhat less honorific. The rest continued as before, allowed to run their own domestic affairs as 'peregrine' communities, subjects of Rome.

One important aspect of the Augustan settlement was a basic reform in the tax system. The tithe was now abolished in Sicily and replaced by the *stipendium*, a levy probably assessed in money on landholdings (and possibly also a poll-tax). Augustus' reasoning was in part purely administrative, but it may also have been a response to a new situation in cereal production. The steady growth in the rural economy of North Africa, and the acquisition of Egypt, provided new sources of corn for the populace in Rome. Sicilian grain seems in consequence to have become somewhat less indispensable to Rome, at least for a period.

SICILIAN SOCIETY UNDER THE EMPERORS

Our knowledge of ancient Sicily is reduced to casual references for most of the next six hundred years. In the two centuries after Augustus, the island experienced only minor administrative changes that are scarcely recorded in the surviving documents. Later reforms in the imperial system, such as the extension of Roman citizenship to virtually all the free population in 212 AD, naturally included Sicily too; but in effect the island had lost all but its geographical identity, at least to the outside world. One contributory factor in this was that Sicily gave no more trouble to Rome. There is only one isolated reference to an outbreak of 'banditry' in the 260s. This apart, the island seems to have been peaceful; and until the Vandal troubles, no legions had to be stationed here and no naval force.

To the emperors, as to the aristocracy, Sicily became simply an outlying district of Italy. Senators were permitted by Augustus to visit the island without first obtaining his permission, a privilege presumably used by absentee landowners to have an occasional look at their estates. Otherwise Mount Etna and Syracuse were tourist attractions of some importance, the latter one of the *villes d'art* of the western Mediterranean, despite all the depredations. Few emperors, however, had much to do with Sicily, apart from Caligula who seemed to enjoy Syracuse, and Hadrian, who spent most of his time travelling in the provinces, and the African Septimius Severus, who was governor of the island before he became Emperor in 193.

In the fifth century AD Sicily returned for a time to the mainstream of imperial history, as a result of the division of the Empire and the barbarian invasions. In 429 a relatively small but mobile and well-organized Germanic tribe, the Vandals, conquered North Africa. Eleven years later they raided Sicily for the first time, and finally asserted a degree of control over it in 468. A few years after that, the German Odoacer, who had gained the throne in Italy, bought it back from the Vandal King. An important period of peace ensued, briefly interrupted in 535 when the eastern general Belisarius captured the island for the Byzantine Emperor in Constantinople; and thenceforward until the Arab conquest Sicily was a province of Byzantium.

Throughout the imperial age Sicilians showed little interest in advancing themselves in Roman government or society. Even in the early Empire, when opportunities were numerous, hardly anyone from the island joined the legions or entered the imperial career service. No Sicilian is known to have attained the rank of Roman senator until the end of the first century. The contrast with southern Gaul, Spain, North Africa or Asia Minor is striking. Yet there was no lack of prosperity among the middle and upper classes, as the theatres, amphitheatres, aqueducts, baths and other urban amenities indicate.

Behind this urban affluence there lay, as always in antiquity, profitable exploitation of the land. This in turn created a foundation for export activity, service trades, and a variety of specialized industries, including – at least in Catania – shipbuilding. Agrigentum, furthermore, was the centre of a new sulphur industry, which was apparently an imperial monopoly worked mainly through concessions. As for the countryside, archaeological evidence suggests that it was well-populated, with clusters of villages, hamlets and larger farm-complexes. There is nothing to indicate that Sicily began suffering from the abandonment of arable and pasture – as happened in some of the most productive regions of Italy in the later Empire – or from deafforestation. On the contrary, there seems even to have been an upsurge in Sicilian agriculture from the third century on.

As regards Sicilian trade, our evidence is somewhat scarce. However, many African pottery lamps have been found in the island covering a period of several centuries, and a few wine-jars from Pompeii, Africa and elsewhere are labelled *vinum Mesopotamium*, a Sicilian vintage from the south coast. There are indications, too, of commerce with Spain and Gaul: a mid-second century inscription to a wealthy citizen of Narbonne mentions that he had been honoured by Syracuse, Thermae and Panormus, presumably because of his role in the trade between Sicily and south-western Europe. Such data are important pointers, but no more; they cannot reveal the scale of production and trade nor the conditions of labour and enterprise.

Precisely how large or populous the cities were in this period, either absolutely or in relation to earlier times, is uncertain. A curious poem by Ausonius, called *Ordo urbium nobilium*, in which he lists the seventeen most celebrated cities of the Empire, puts Catania and Syracuse thirteenth and fourteenth respectively. Syracuse is called 'quadruple', which might just indicate expansion in Ausonius' time; in other words, the late fourth century. That Catania was now a major city is demonstrable archaeologically. So too is the expansion of Palermo, and from the evidence of their cemeteries, Messina and Agrigentum were clearly well populated.

In the countryside there was a clear tendency towards the consolidation of holdings into great continuous tracts. The Vandal invasions did not disrupt this process. On the contrary, barbarian control of North Africa may have restored Sicily to its old role as the 'nurse', to use Cato's word, of the Roman populace; and this could have been one reason why Theodoric the Goth (who ruled most of Italy before the conquest of Belisarius) left property undisturbed in Sicily, while confiscating perhaps a third in central and northern Italy. Another factor was that large areas of Sicily were now owned by the Roman papacy. Indeed when Gregory the Great became Pope in 590, the 'patrimony of St Peter' in Sicily probably exceeded the imperial domain.

Sicilian estates were also in the possession of the sees of Milan and Ravenna, and of local bishoprics and monasteries. These concentrations, like those belonging to the popes (and unlike the imperial holdings), were normally not broken up. Otherwise there was considerable movement in land, through purchase, gift, dowry and bequest; and this fact indicates the existence of a class of large private *latifundia*, normally the property of absentee owners. The extent of these holdings is not easily ascertained. In the later Empire the regular term for an estate was *fundus*, and a consolidated group of *fundi*, a *massa*; but these words were not always used consistently, and in any case they give no indication of actual size.

Archaeology, however, can provide some clues. The so-called Antonine Itinerary of the third century refers to the Massa Calvisiana, which was presumably named after the man who first assembled the estate. One main farmstead-complex of this property has been excavated on a low hillock at the mouth of the Gela River. Scores of tiles have been found, bearing the legend CAL or CALVI, and their distribution could indicate that this one estate extended, on the eastern side of the Gela River, some ten miles north by east to Niscemi. None of the Calvisiana finds, however, can be dated much later than the middle of the fourth century, and we have no way of knowing whether the *massa* was subsequently broken up, or even if it continued as a single holding for any length of time after it had been assembled.

As everywhere in western Europe, the imperial age in Sicily saw a change in the labour system. Slaves continued to be numerous, though on the large estates they were steadily being replaced, from the early Empire on, by tenant-farmers. Some absentee owners put agents in charge, as was the case with the papal *rector*; others dispensed with this intermediary post altogether. Either way, the normal procedure, at least by the late Empire, was to lease the land in large units to entrepreneurs, who then sub-let to the working peasants, the *coloni*. In general the owners and tenants-in-chief did very well out of this system; but the peasants seem to have been badly off. Not only were they required to pay both rents and taxes in gold (with perhaps some commutation in kind), but they were also subject to various perquisites (such as fines on the marriage of a son or daughter) and to unceasing attempts at extortion.

If a degree of poverty was a hallmark of this island, private wealth was by no means inconspicuous. The most spectacular example of this is the villa (or hunting lodge) in the wooded valley at Casale, near present-day Piazza Armerina. Erected on four levels, as required by the terrain, the villa had nearly fifty rooms, courts, galleries, baths and corridors, arranged in four complex groupings approached by a monumental entrance. Relatively little remains of the marble architectural elements, the sculpture and the murals; but the prime attraction was surely the mosaic pavements. They cover some 400 square metres of floor space, and far outdistance in scale (and therefore in financial outlay) anything else of their kind known today.

Nothing points conclusively to the owners of the building but they could only have been from the senatorial class and among the richest men in the empire. The villa was a pleasure dome, not a year-round residence, and its original inhabitants were pagans, and ostentatiously so. It was occupied until the Arab conquest and again for a time under the Normans when it was destroyed by King William the Bad late in the twelfth century. Despite frequent alteration and rebuilding, the villa, rather curiously, seems to have retained its pagan quality. Although the date of its construction is still being discussed, the early decades of the fourth century look increasingly certain.

The Piazza Armerina mosaics were almost certainly the work of craftsmen imported from North Africa, but the style cannot be called anything but Roman imperial. Sicily in the period developed no distinctive culture of its own, unless at the village level about which not enough is known. The marble portrait-busts of Greek philosophers, Roman emperors, or local dignitaries, are exactly like those in Italy or southern Gaul. Many of the hundred or so known marble sarcophagi, mostly of the third century, were imported from Italy, and they are indistinguishable in style and themes from sarcophagi discovered elsewhere, including Rome itself. Their generally poor quality reflects not 'provincialism' so much as the great gap in wealth between the middle-class families who headed the social hierarchy in the Sicilian cities and the absentee senatorial aristocrats.

Only with respect to language may one speak of cultural divergence, even competition. It was never part of the Roman programme to Latinize the Greek-speaking provinces, and Sicily was no exception. Yet the extensive colonization by Augustus introduced a concentrated Latin-speaking element into the island for the first time and this undoubtedly had an impact, at least at the level of official communication. However, the bulk of the population remained Greek-speaking, and the large majority of epitaphs and dedicatory plaques, pagan and Christian alike, continued to be inscribed in Greek. It was only the administrative and educated classes who were Latin-speaking or, more correctly, bilingual.

CHRISTIANITY

The religion of Roman Sicily was syncretic, like that of the rest of the late Greek or Hellenistic world. The worship of such eastern divinities as the Syrian Atargatis (once patroness of the slave leader, Eunus), or Cybele, or Isis and Serapis from Egypt, had been adopted and harmonized with traditional Greek beliefs and practices. The more Romanized Sicilians joined in readily, and this probably meant there was no real dividing-line between lower and upper classes. At Tauromenium there was a temple dedicated to Isis, while at Lilybaeum we find funeral monuments from the late Republic and early Empire still bearing Phoenician symbols.

Jews began to migrate to Rome and other Italian towns and cities before the Christian era. One might reasonably assume that Greek Sicily was no less attractive to them; and certainly by the time of Gregory the Great at the end of the sixth century there were established Jewish communities in Sicily, not only in such larger centres as Messina, Palermo and Agrigentum, but also in villages and *massae* of the interior. The common view, however, that Christianity first took root among the Jewish communities in the eastern cities of Sicily, though plausible, must remain speculative.

The early centuries of Sicilian Christianity are sparsely documented. In time, Sicily produced hagiographies and martyrologies enough, but they have been called, with justification, 'among the most imaginative in the world'. In the seventh century there were claims that the Sicilian church was founded by one of the original Apostles; but these were certainly false. Christian burials cannot be dated much before 200, and there are no authentic Christian personalities before St Marcianus of Syracuse and St Agatha of Catania in the mid-third century. It was only after Constantine lifted the prohibition in 313 that Christianity began to advance rapidly in Sicily, both in the countryside and above all in the cities.

The process of paganism's demise cannot really be traced. It might help if we had a more precise idea of the dates when pagan temples (and public baths) were converted into churches. The practice is attested in Agrigentum, Segesta, Himera, and Tauromenium (where a temple of Isis was turned into the church of St Pancratius), in rural districts, and of course in Syracuse. Here the temple of Athena went through at least two transformations in ancient times, first into a church and later into a cathedral. Yet even in this instance, where the transformations are most clearly evident, we cannot say more than that it was first consecrated before 600, and that it became a cathedral in the seventh century.

The pace at which Christianity grew is dramatically demonstrated by the catacombs, cemeteries and private burial-grounds. Sicily has been called 'the classic land of early Christian funerary architecture'. In quantity, scale and, eventually, in richness of layout and embellishment, the most grandiose of the catacombs in Syracuse rival those of Rome. The oldest, known as S. Lucia – all the names are modern, taken from the churches or other landmarks with which the catacombs are geographically associated – was in continuous use for at least a century during the period of illegality, before Constantine. After his Edict of Toleration, it was greatly enlarged, and new catacombs established. That of San Giovanni was of great complexity, and included variations to cater for class distinctions.

Outside Syracuse, sizeable catacombs existed in the regions of Akrai, Ispica and Modica, and in the west of the island in Agrigentum, Lilybaeum, Carini and Palermo. These are all probably post-Constantinian. Their distribution puts paid to the idea that this Sicilian institution was due either to the needs of a crowded urban centre or to the geology of Syracuse. Elsewhere in the island we find small subterranean burial-grounds, usurped pagan cemeteries, and a wide scattering of private tombs. The ruins of small chapels and troglodytic sanctuaries keep turning up everywhere; but they are hard to date precisely, and this reduces their value as a guide to the development of Christianity in Sicily. At least they attest the populousness of the Christian communities in all parts of the island by the fifth century.

The eastern Emperor Justinian converted Sicily into a Byzantine province in the years after 535. Though Gregory the Great, like the more energetic of his papal predecessors, did what he could to Romanize the church, in liturgy, doctrine and organization, he was under considerable pressure to maintain a *modus vivendi* with the Byzantine provincial administration in Constantinople. This task was made more difficult by the inevitable involvement of the church in secular matters after the effective disappearance of the old community framework. Gregory attempted to deal with this problem, and within six months of his election to the papacy he sent instructions that local bishops were not to meddle in secular litigation except in defence of the poor.

In addition to concern over the division between Rome and Constantinople, the papacy also directed its attention to the problem of heresy in Sicily; but there was never any real call for alarm. The fundamental controversy over the nature of the Trinity saw Sicily firmly in the Athanasian camp. There were presumably some Arians, but they are unlikely to have been as numerous or as vicious as later chroniclers made out. There were also Manichaeans and other heretical sects; but violent disturbances arising out of doctrinal disputes, common in certain other provinces, were apparently not a factor in Sicilian Christianity before the final Byzantine take-over.

Though the emperors in Constantinople showed no apparent concern about Roman influence and authority over the Sicilian churches – partly because they had more pressing problems to contend with – that does not mean there were no strong feelings on this score among Sicilians themselves. The question, however, is perplexing and controversial. On balance, the answer seems to be that the persistence of the Greek language was a symptom of a closer affinity with the culture of the Eastern empire in general. This contention seems to be backed up by what we know of Sicilian monasteries. The isolated location of many of them, the appointment of abbot Theophanes of Syracuse to be Patriarch of Antioch, and the absence of Benedictine monasteries before the Norman period, all argue for an Eastern orientation.

However one interprets the earlier situation, the popes eventually lost. By the second half of the seventh century the Sicilian church was Eastern in every important respect, including the liturgy and ceremonies. There is no need to seek in explanation of this – as some people have done – a new Hellenic infusion through migrations. Greek speakers always constituted a majority of the Sicilian population; and all they needed was a new twist in the perennial political and military struggle between Rome and Constantinople. When this came, the Eastern triumph in Sicily was so complete that even the educated and politically influential minority abandoned the Latin language and returned to Greek.

CHAPTER 6

Byzantium and the Arabs

BYZANTINE RULE

Sicily fell to the Byzantine general Belisarius in 535. There was little resistance, a fact which might indicate a desperate hope on the part of the Sicilians for less oppressive rule. Whether they got it we cannot say, for we know almost nothing about the way Byzantine administration was carried on in Sicily. One remarkable and largely unexpected gain, however, was peace. Whereas the next century saw Italy and North Africa beset by continued and ruinous warfare, Sicily was spared – apart from a brief pillage in 500 by the Ostrogothic ruler of Rome, Totila. This was a rare experience for the island in its long history at the busy crossroads between Europe and Africa.

Although the Byzantine state was at first reasonably solvent, much of its available resources had to be spent on the armies defending the frontiers in the east, and when Justinian died in 565 he left an empire which was financially and economically in ruins. His successors were unable, and probably unwilling, to cut their losses; and they soon had to contend with a new menace, the Lombards, who swept over the Alps and quickly established themselves over most of Italy. Meanwhile, the Moors created difficulties in North Africa, and the Visigoths began their ultimately successful campaign to win back southern Spain. Sicily however was untouched.

In these circumstances the western Pope and the eastern Emperor needed each other's help. This explains both the care that Gregory the Great took with imperial matters, and also the freedom he was given in administering his Sicilian possessions. But soon theological disagreements arose which were so intense that Church and Empire were driven apart. The culmination came in the middle of the seventh century, when the Emperor Constans had Pope Martin arrested and tried on a charge of high treason, for allegedly plotting against him. Martin was convicted and banished to the Crimea, where he died a few months later. This was a hollow victory for the Emperor, as the Italian clergy, as well as Martin's successors, remained hostile and intractable.

In the meantime Constans was taken up with growing difficulties at home; but in 660 he made a sudden and unexpected decision to transfer the capital back to the west after more than three hundred years in Constantinople. This move is hard to evaluate, given the hostility to the Emperor in our sources: they present his departure from Constantinople as an expulsion, the result of popular discontent. But it may just be that Constans was hoping to carry on Justinian's dream of a revived Roman Empire from a central base. Whatever the truth, Syracuse now became the capital of the Byzantine Emperor for the next five years.

If the Sicilians had a momentary vision of glory and material benefit, they were quickly disillusioned, for the financial burden of harbouring the Emperor and his retinue proved intolerable. So too did Constans' tyrannical behaviour; and in 668 he was assassinated. A secessionist rebellion ensued, and a young Armenian aristocrat was made Emperor, to popular acclaim. The revolt, however, was short-lived, and early the following year the murdered Emperor's son – who had been left in command at Constantinople – appeared at the head of an army. The rebellion collapsed, and Constantinople was restored to its position as capital of the Empire. This left Sicily painfully exposed to the forces of Islam.

The Arabs were advancing with almost breathtaking speed, and were now the most dynamic factor in the struggle for the Mediterranean world. From 673 to 678 they kept Constantinople under blockade, while in Africa they advanced westward from Egypt, and in 689 reached Carthage. Soon they would proceed to Spain. Around the turn of the century they took the island of Pantelleria, and for the next fifty years Sicily was to be subjected to repeated raids. Then came a half-century of immunity, with the Arabs of Africa consumed by their own internal troubles. Indeed, were it not for the disunity that had already developed within Islam, it is possible that neither the Eastern Empire nor the Western would have survived at all.

With the Arab advance, Sicily became important not only strategically but also doctrinally. Three of the four patriarchates were set in Islamic territory, and as a result the so-called Greek 'nations' – Syria, Greece proper, and Sicily – became the principal bastions of orthodoxy. Between 678 and 751 all but two popes were 'Greeks', of whom four were Sicilians either by birth or upbringing. This temporary 'Hellenization' of the papacy did not mean an end to conflicts with the Emperor; and the militarization of Sicily by Justinian II toward the end of the seventh century may partly have been intended to intimidate the Church – though its main purpose was clearly to counter Saracen pressure from Africa.

The presence of a military force in Sicily was one factor in the relative passivity of the island during the imperial campaign against religious images in the eighth century. Another was the threat of the Arabs, for while the evidence suggests that Sicilians had little love for Byzantine rule, they were unlikely to rebel with Islam poised to pick up the pieces. Precisely how much Sicilians feared the Arabs, though, is hard to judge. The damaging piratical raids of the first half of the eighth century had ceased, and an uneasy truce prevailed. In 805 the governor of Sicily signed a treaty with the Aghlabid rulers of Tunisia, probably without consulting Constantinople; and another followed in 813 which included an agreement to examine mutual trading interests. Already Arab merchants were living in Sicily.

The situation by 800 was reminiscent of the old days of Carthaginian power. So too was a new fact that changed everything. In 827 the Emperor ordered the arrest of an admiral, Euphemius; and Euphemius in retaliation instigated a popular revolt, defeated the governor, and declared himself Emperor. One of his deputies promptly rebelled and Euphemius appealed to the Aghlabid emir for help, offering Sicily as a tribute-paying province on condition that he be appointed governor. The response came immediately. An elite army of more than 10,000 men – Arabs, Berbers and Spanish Moslems – landed at Mazara, and another conquest of Sicily had begun.

All previous assaults had been piratical raids, but the Arabs now set out to take the island and colonize it. In the event, the task proved very difficult. Constantinople, despite its internal weakness and its many enemies, fought hard for its last western outpost, and the war as a result dragged on for fifty years, destroying men and resources, and afflicting the island with famine and plague. Palermo fell in 831; and twenty years later the Arabs were in control of all of western Sicily. But still the fighting continued, and fortresses such as Enna and Cefalù had to be fought over for years before they were finally lost.

Although Taormina was not taken until early in the tenth century, and Rometta in the mountains west of Messina till 965, the fall of Syracuse in 878 marked the effective end of Byzantine Sicily. Its population was massacred, and the booty taken, according to one of the few survivors, was fabulous. For fifteen hundred years Syracuse had been pre-eminent in Sicily, and for a time it was the richest and most powerful city in all Europe. Its primacy in Sicily had survived the conquests of Rome and Byzantium, just as it had survived the conversion to Christianity. But Syracuse was now compelled to give way to Palermo, just as Christianity had to yield to Mohammedanism, and the Greek language to Arabic. With these changes, Sicily began to move out of the ancient and into the medieval world; and nowhere, arguably, was the dividing line between the two so sharply drawn.

THE ARABS

By the end of the ninth century, the Byzantine forces had almost entirely withdrawn from Sicily. Their departure, so far as we can judge, was not wholly unwelcome, after centuries of autocracy and taxation. Obviously the conquest brought destruction and disorder; possibly some areas became entirely deserted. Once established, however, the new masters of the country were lenient. Some towns were left virtually independent with not even a garrison. The new regime may well have seemed less oppressive than were the Christian Lombards or Franks on the mainland, and less religiously intolerant than the iconoclastic Church at Constantinople. Local institutions were often retained; and though many churches became mosques, in general Christians could live by their own laws, provided they paid the requisite tribute.

Naturally, a subject population suffered some penalties. How far the regulations were enforced, though, is difficult to say. Both Christians and Jews were required to wear distiguishing marks on their houses and clothes; they paid more taxes; and though they could practise their religion, they could not ring church bells, carry the cross in procession, or read the Bible within earshot of Moslems. They were forbidden to drink wine in public, and were expected to rise when Moslems entered the room and make way for them in the public road. This was harsh, but it hardly amounted to religious persecution. If the majority of Christians eventually gave up practising their faith, this was due to a natural process of change rather than to the oppressiveness of Arab rule.

Above all, an enlightened economic policy helped to reconcile the subject population. Taxation seems to have been lower than under Byzantium, perhaps in part because it was allocated and collected more efficiently. The new rulers removed the tax on draught animals which had hindered agriculture, and instead used a land tax which made it disadvantageous to leave fields unproductive. Islam also had a more sympathetic attitude than Christianity to slaves, and preferred labourers with a positive interest in increased production. Commerce flourished, because Sicily once again had the benefit of a central position in an immense economic commonwealth which stretched from Spain to Syria.

Palermo, the Arab capital, grew to be a great city. Theodosius, in the ninth century, already found it magnificent, and he had known Greek Syracuse. Visitors were impressed to find a population which included Greeks, Lombards, Jews, Slavs, Berbers, Persians, Tartars and blacks from Africa; and Arabs came from Spain, Syria and Egypt. Ibn Hauqal, a Fatimid missionary from Baghdad, admired the market gardens; and there were hundreds of mosques in Palermo, more than he had seen in any town except Cordoba. He criticized the dirtiness of the people and their excessive onion-eating; and yet this Palermo was indisputably becoming one of the great cities of the world, surpassed by Baghdad but by few other towns. Its population is almost impossible to estimate, but it was probably greater than any Christian town except Constantinople.

From Ibn Hauqal and later Moslem writers we learn of abundant springs and an excellent irrigation system. The Arabs had learnt in the desert the vital importance of irrigation, even if it were only a mule or stream turning a water wheel; they brought certain hydraulic techniques with them from Persia; and they must have profited from observing the relics of Roman engineering work in North Africa. With their new technology, they planted lemons and bitter oranges. They also brought the knowledge of how to cultivate sugar cane and crush it with mills. So far as we know, they introduced the first cotton seeds, the first mulberries and silkworms, the date palm, the sumac tree for tanning and dyeing, papyrus, pistachio nuts and melons.

No doubt there was some poetic exaggeration in Arab descriptions of Sicily as a garden paradise. Nevertheless, a degree of economic advance is incontestable. Reservoirs and water towers from this period continued to exist for many centuries, and can still be identified today. In the non-agricultural sphere, there was a vigorous fishing industry, and perhaps an altogether new and elaborate technique of catching tunny. Silver, lead, mercury, sulphur and naphtha, vitriol, antimony and alum were produced, Sicilian salt became well known abroad, and salammoniac found near Mount Etna was exported to Spain. The art of silk manufacture and weaving was soon to play a substantial part in the economy.

Not all, however, was gain. The Arab conquest of the island caused extensive damage, as did subsequent quarrels over land and spoils. By the 880s, for example, we hear of strife between the local population and North African settlers. Berbers, it seems, settled predominantly in the south-west near Agrigentum (which was now to be called Girgenti), and soon there was some kind of rivalry between this area and Palermo. Such internal differences were compounded when a further wave of newcomers arrived from Africa to share the fabled riches of Sicily, only to find the plunder already exhausted. An invading army thus did tremendous damage in the south-west between 938 and 940.

Apart from the disruption and devastation caused by the conquest, there are other conjectural qualifications to be made on the negative side of the balance sheet. During their invasion, and in the process of clearing land for settlement, the Arabs evidently set fire to crops and woodland. Cargoes of timber were carried overseas because Africa lacked supplies of hardwood; and the shipbuilding necessary to maintain maritime domination of the Mediterranean probably led to the more accessible areas of the Sicilian forests being cut down. Olive-growing was largely abandoned at some time between 400 and 900, and North Africa took over production of the oil which had once been such a source of wealth.

The pattern of landholding under the Arabs is not easy to determine. The great historian, Michele Amari, thought that small farms were the rule; but to say that the *latifundia* disappeared and then returned in the twelfth century would be to oversimplify. A territorial nobility existed and was presumably endowed with large estates. Yet Moslem succession law did encourage the sub-division of properties among younger sons, and the survival of a large number of Arabic names for small places and farms suggests a fragmentation of property. The existence of intensive cultivation near the cities, replacing the extensive type of cereal cultivation peculiar to the *latifundia*, also indicated the spread of smallholdings and either secure leaseholds or actual peasant proprietorship.

Moslem Sicily was at first a dependency of the Aghlabids, but early in the tenth century a civil war, complicated by the advance of the heretic Shiites, overturned this Tunisian dynasty. Their successors, the Fatimids, then moved eastwards and in 969 set up their capital in Egypt. Sicily was left much more independent, and by the 960s the Kalbid family had established themselves as the effective rulers of the island, binding the military nobility to them by ties of interest and patronage. Greater independence, though, was scarcely a gain. The move of the Khalif to Cairo was followed by the break-up of the North African civilization to which Sicily had belonged. The island was thus isolated, and Christian Europe at last had a chance to counterattack.

An early sign of this was in the 1030s when the Kalbid Emir, confronted with rebellion, made a treaty with Byzantium. Local Moslem support was therefore forthcoming when George Maniaces, a Byzantine general, landed near Messina with a large force that included several hundred Norman mercenaries. These latter no doubt observed the richness of the country and propagated among their friends the idea of further piratical raids. Maniaces occupied much of eastern Sicily for several years and did much damage. But this was the last serious attempt by Byzantium to recover Sicily, and court intrigues at Constantinople soon forced Maniaces' recall. The Mediterranean balance of power had swung against both Constantinople and Cairo. Western Christendom was now on the offensive, and when Roger the Norman landed near Messina in 1060, the days of Moslem Sicily were numbered.

The contribution of the Saracens to Sicilian history is difficult to assess. Their occupation lasted over two centuries. They brought with them their religion and laws, their literature, arts and sciences; and so doing, they made Sicily part of a splendid civilization. Like the Greeks before them, they came to settle and not just to rule and exploit. They probably arrived in greater numbers than any other conquerors of Sicily before or since. They settled more densely in the western and south-eastern provinces, but elsewhere too there must have been a considerable immigration as well as substantial conversion of Sicilians to Islam. Their repopulation of the Sicilian countryside was an important fact.

There are few tangible remains of this Moslem occupation, though some are still uncovered from time to time. Many Saracen buildings were destroyed during the civil wars or as a result of the Norman conquest. Writing materials, just like tufa building stone, perished easily. A little poetry was preserved in Spain and Damascus, but it is hard to discern any single individual of note in Sicilian-Arab culture before the arrival of the Normans. African chroniclers sometimes wrote about Sicily before 1060, and Amari was able in part to reconstruct the period from later sources, but the picture still remains vague. The Moslem legal system left few relics, since subject communities were allowed to keep their own laws.

The Aghlabids had been orthodox in religion and culturally conservative, while the Kalbid emirs lacked the power as well as the organizing ability and enlightened interest necessary for productive patronage. Furthermore the Christian chroniclers were ignorant and prejudiced about this period, and understated or omitted to note its achievements. Hence the known memorials of the Arabs in Sicily are mainly relics of the later Norman-Arab civilization. The Normans, however, depended heavily upon Arab craftsmanship and governmental traditions, both native and imported; and this acknowledgement of the past is convincing proof of its quality.

As a language of government, Arabic proved very durable and lasted for over a century after the Norman conquest. Such was its impact that many linguistic traces can still be observed today. In the topography of Sicily, Gibel and Calta are familiar Arabic formations. Among many changes of place name, Enna became Kasryanni and so Castrogiovanni. Lilybaeum was altered to Marsala, the harbour of Allah or of Ali. Still today, after nine centuries, some hundreds of Arabic words and expressions are in currency, and only the arrival after 1060 of another invader speaking a Latin tongue can have prevented Sicily from being left with a language close to those of Malta and North Africa. It was the Norman invasion which took Sicilians back permanently into the orbit of Europe.

CHAPTER 7

The Normans

THE NORMAN CONQUEST

Early in the eleventh century, there were several groups of adventurers from northern France earning a profitable living as professional soldiers in southern Italy. They included half a dozen sons of a certain Tancred de Hauteville, one of whom was Robert Guiscard, 'taller than the tallest', enormously ambitious and the most dedicated fighter of them all. Guiscard with his youngest brother Roger staked out a territory in Calabria and Apulia. Occasionally these two brothers fought against each other, but usually they were in league; and as they had a real genius for both fighting and administration, they were able to accumulate, by one means or another, the fortunes on which a famous dynasty was to be built.

In 1059, Pope Nicholas II authorized these warlike if not very obviously Christian freebooters to govern as much of southern Italy as they could conquer; and Guiscard in return agreed not to recognize the religious authority of Constantinople. The papacy had developed a specious claim to feudal lordship over Sicily, basing this on the multiple fiction that first Constantine and later the Carolingian kings had owned the island and later 'given' it to the Pope. As a result the Normans had to accept feudal investiture not only for Apulia but also for their further conquests in Calabria and across the straits in Sicily itself.

This was a weak moment for the Sicilian Arabs. Different families were trying to establish independent emirates in the island, and little support could now be expected from North Africa. Just as some Christians had effectively invited the Arab invasion of 827, so one Moslem group now turned to the Normans for help, and so doing set in motion a process that was to lead to the island's subjugation. By agreement with Guiscard, the conquest of Sicily fell mainly to Roger, and after defeating the Greeks of Calabria, he crossed the straits and captured Messina. By 1064 Roger had mastered the north-east, and brought back much booty to divide with his elder brother. Experience gained in this operation was to prove valuable two years later in the Norman Conquest of England.

During the 1060s the Normans built up their fleet, because it was clear that further advance depended on command of the sea. In 1071 Guiscard arrived in front of Palermo with mercenaries and siege engines. After a blockade of five months the inhabitants surrendered. In return for the payment of tribute, they received an acknowledgement of their religion and some autonomy. In other places, Guiscard's men were more patently ruthless, killing prisoners and selling women and children into slavery: the expectation of acquiring slaves was one of the inducements by which the Normans persuaded other freebooting adventurers to join their army.

Guiscard had to return to defend his possessions on the mainland and so left Roger, as Count of Sicily and Calabria, to complete the conquest and set up a government. Roger saw the advantage of offering generous terms so as to be able to employ Moslem civil servants and accountants who understood the existing administrative machinery. There was no massive invading population, so existing farmers had to be courted: many Arabs were therefore allowed to keep their goods and land, sometimes even their castles. Equally important, Moslem soldiers, without abjuring their faith, were from the very beginning an important nucleus of his army and were even used against Norman and other Christian enemies. Roger in 1075 made a treaty of friendship with the Zirid ruler of Tunis, and sent Sicilian grain to Mahdia.

The last stage of the conquest was slow. Roger had to return frequently to Calabria to support his brother and raise more troops. In his absence his own followers would rebel and plunder his estates. Though the Moslem castles fell one by one, fortune changed frequently and there were perhaps more military setbacks than the official chronicler, Malaterra, cared to record. Only in 1088 did Castrogiovanni fall, the one key strategic point of the interior. Three years later, it was the turn of Noto, the last major stronghold of Moslem Sicily. As can be imagined, the process of conquest was highly destructive: 'there is an enormous ruin of castles, villages, and Saracen palaces', recorded one contemporary, 'and it is this vast damage that we now have to repair'.

Although the conquest was violent and often cruel, it was quickly followed by conciliation. There was surprisingly little friction between the Normans and their new subjects, and Sicily was far more submissive than the mainland provinces. Arabs and Jews had to pay a special tax, and yet Norman charters, following Arab precedent, ensured that 'Latins, Greeks, Jews and Saracens shall be judged each according to their own law' and by their own judges. Many Moslems must have emigrated, for all round the Mediterranean there can be found family names which show a derivation at some time or other from Sicily. Others must have fled to the hill country of the interior to escape the brutalities of the conquest; and yet great numbers stayed and proved industrious, orderly and obedient. The army, navy and civil service all gained enormously from their cooperation.

The Normans had an impact on Sicily altogether disproportionate to their number. Theirs was not to be a settlement *en masse* like that of the Arabs. Their influence came from a quite unusual adaptability and political skill. Recognizing that Sicilians possessed a superior culture and administrative system, they adopted both, and added an efficiency and sense of direction hitherto lacking. The Arab division of land was in part preserved, and business relating to tenure and finance continued to be transacted by the pre-existent office of the *dîwân*. It was the ability to absorb and mix different traditions, Arabic and north-European, Roman and Greek, that was the hallmark of the Norman achievement in Sicily. By skilfully using these traditions, Count Roger turned himself from a poor landless adventurer into one of the most successful rulers in the world.

It was in particular the Byzantine element which distinguished Roger's government. Though he came from feudal northern Europe, he learned to combine the aristocratic relationships of feudalism with the eastern idea that a ruler was not the first among equals, but sovereign and even divine. Court ceremonial and protocol were taken from Byzantium; so were many formulae used in his Chancery; but more important was the fact that, whereas the Norman King of England depended on feudal dues and a temporary feudal army, the Norman Count of Sicily could afford permanent mercenaries and one of the strongest fleets of the time.

While restoring Greek traditions of government, Roger simultaneously began a decisive process of Latinization by introducing a new ruling class. His Greek subjects were not elevated to the aristocracy or endowed with fiefs. None of the chief landowners, bishops or leading abbots, seem to have been natives of the island. To fill the main positions of responsibility Roger used trans-alpine Normans and Frenchmen, as well as Italians or 'Lombards' from the mainland. In return for military service they were given land, and sometimes they preferred to bring with them colonists from their home territories. The extent of this immigration can only be guessed, but it would explain how a mainly Arabic-speaking country had by 1200 become largely Latinized in speech.

The new arrivals found very little public law in Sicily, and in this sector, Norman feudal practices tended to prevail. Feudalization, however, was not nearly so complete as in northern Europe. For one thing, the Count was in a strong position by right of conquest and able to keep a very large personal demesne. For another, the shortage of labour after the destruction of the invasion must have acted as an inducement to leave existing landowners undisturbed. This resulted in much property remaining outside the feudal system and free of any obligation to the new nobility. On the mainland, Guiscard and Roger had to concede more to the baronage, but in Sicily Roger ruled as a conqueror and with fewer obligations; and many of the grants Roger made did not carry the right of hereditary succession.

In origin, therefore, and by design, Sicilian feudalism was a reinforcement of the ruler's authority. Similar concerns are evident in Roger's attitude to religion. The surviving Christians were Greek orthodox and Roger endowed more Greek monasteries in Sicily than Latin. The archbishop of Palermo was also a Greek at first. No doubt Roger took into account that the Patriarch of Constantinople was more distant and ineffective than the Pope and so would be less intrusive as a religious supervisor; no doubt too he appreciated the caesaro-papist tradition of Byzantium which gave more weight to the secular power; and probably he also saw in this judicious balance of patronage a useful pressure on Rome.

Roger did however grant favours to Latin Christianity; but on his own terms. The Roman liturgy was introduced, and by 1083 he had appointed a Latin archbishop at Palermo. He decided, entirely on his own initiative, the area of each diocese and how many dioceses there should be; they were privately endowed out of his own purse, and he himself selected the bishops. For the most part he chose French ecclesiastics, though English and Tuscans were also included. Likewise the cathedral chapters were recruited from overseas. This was the time of the great Investiture Contest when, over most of Europe, the Church repudiated any interference by the civil power in choosing bishops; but Sicily was different. Here the Church remained part of the royal prerogative, and the King enjoyed the title of 'Apostolic Legate'.

Roger's success with the Church, and the absence of any serious resistance to him, show how far he had succeeded in pacifying Sicily and Calabria before he died in 1101. Fortunately for the country he had not shared Guiscard's ambitions in eastern Europe. He was able to give large dowries to his daughters, one of whom married Karloman, the King of Hungary, and another Conrad, the son of the Western Emperor Henry IV. Yet though he was renowned through Christendom for his wealth and power, the Norman state lacked a feeling of permanence. Roger had been a nomadic ruler like his Viking ancestors, and spent his time travelling from one province to another with a mobile administration and treasury. He chose to be buried not in Sicily but at Mileto in Calabria; and it was left for his successors to organize a stable kingdom based on the former Arab capital of Palermo.

THE *REGNUM*

At Roger's death, his third wife became Regent. Precisely when her son took over the government is not certain, though it was evidently before 1113.

Roger II was one of the most remarkable rulers of the European Middle ages. He successfully challenged the Pope, and both the Eastern and Western Emperors. He acquired a North African empire, and even aimed at the imperial throne of Constantinople. His kingdom came to include not only Sicily and Calabria, but also all of southern Italy as far as the Papal States. He was a man of insatiable ambition, with a great appetite for work, a remarkable head for details, and a powerful intelligence. The chronicles were probably right however in saying that he was more feared than loved.

Roger's kingdom moved away from models familiar in northern Europe. His teachers in youth must have been Greeks. He spoke Greek and probably Arabic too. He was reputed to keep a harem, and a special part of the palace was reserved for his women and eunuchs. His chief minister, a veritable Grand Vizier, held the splendid title of Emir of Emirs and Archonte of Archontes. By about 1125, this post was occupied by George of Antioch, an orthodox Greek Christian who had learned the art of politics in North Africa. It can have been no accident that such a prominent schismatic was at hand when Roger undertook his fight with the Pope, nor that a man trained in the precepts of Justinian helped to change a count into a king.

Arab, Byzantine, or even Anglo-Norman traditions have been traced as the main constituent element of Roger's administration, but George's contribution was probably decisive. Though many of the lower bureaucracy were Moslems, the chief officers of state were often Greek. Above all, the concept of royal authority was modelled on that of Justinian to the point where Sicily appeared more exotic in western eyes than even the crusader kingdom of Jerusalem. The illusion was even created that Roger was a priest-king whose authority came from God alone, so that rebellion against him would be sacrilege. Court ceremonial prescribed that Roger's subjects, including bishops, should prostrate themselves in reverence before him. His seals show him dressed as an eastern *basileus*, and a mosaic at Palermo depicts him with the imperial cloak, and receiving the Greek crown, not from Pope or Emperor but directly from Christ himself. The laws of the kingdom, too, clearly show an eastern provenance.

As well as a King, Roger was a feudal overlord. Unlike his father, he did not always lead his forces in person, but the feudatories were not allowed to use this fact to assert their own leadership. Moreover their authority was made less by the presence of a strong professional army alongside the feudal levies. The existence of an able class of bureaucrats entirely dependent on the King obviated the need to allow the barons much political power; and in keeping with this, Roger's *curia* was essentially an emanation of the royal will. Furthermore, the development of feudal justice was checked by provincial justiciars who travelled on circuit and enforced the King's law. By the Roman-law concept of *laesa majestas*, full allegiance was owed to the sovereign and not to any intermediary overlord.

A ruler with this degree of power was not likely to have much trouble with the Church. Roger was excommunicated on a number of occasions, but this meant little to him. He took advantage of a divided papacy to obtain the approval of an anti-Pope for his kingship, and then captured the legitimate Pope, Innocent II, when a papal army took the field against Norman aggression; so doing, he won recognition and a withdrawal of excommunication. In return, Roger accepted papal investiture, though in practice he went on electing bishops whether they were confirmed by the papacy or not, regarding the regulation of Church affairs as a royal prerogative in virtue of the hereditary Apostolic Legateship.

Roger's foreign policy concerns were far-ranging and ambitious. He showed considerable interest in the crusading movement. In North Africa, he successfully exploited discord among the Moslems, and soon had control of all the coast from Tripoli to Cape Bon and inland to Kairouan. There was a large element of risk in this policy, for it meant giving up his father's project for peaceful trade. No doubt, however, it was a calculated risk, and it gave political recognition to the fact that in some years many African cities relied on Sicily for imports of food. Roger encouraged the emigration of Sicilians to Tripoli. He even called himself 'King of Africa'.

Inside Sicily itself an efficient government tapped the potential sources of wealth in a way which no subsequent ruler could quite emulate. An abundant currency was again supported by African gold, and the ducat now made its first appearance in history. A merchant marine grew up on royal subsidies, while the navy kept command of the seas and levied a tithe on ships passing through the Mediterranean. The silk industry received an impetus from skilled immigrant Greek labour and the requirements of court ceremonial. The mining of salt and sulphur was carried on, and coral fishing was already a Sicilian industry. Agriculture, too, seems to have flourished.

Perhaps no other king in Europe had such a large revenue as Roger, and his income from Palermo reputedly exceeded what his Norman cousins collected from all England. In part this was because royal authority was strong enough to insist that taxes were paid. In addition, the King engaged in commerce on his own account. His income from agriculture must also have been considerable; and as local government had not yet been taken over by the feudal aristocracy, Roger retained the profits of justice. As he was able to insist that laws were respected, private citizens were not so prone as they later became to taking justice into their own hands. Visiting foreigners noted that no other prince had so peaceful and flourishing a realm as the King of Sicily.

The Sicily of Roger and his two successors was above all a great meeting place of cultures. But as the educated Arab classes left, and the Greek community got submerged with the passage of time, it became clear that these cultures had mingled but never completely fused. By the 1150s, there were already signs that the religious tolerance that had permitted this admixture was wearing thin. Norman-Arab art was an artificial creation of enlightened despotism, not a true interpenetration which was viable on its own. The lack of any true synthesis rendered this culture vulnerable and transient, so that gradually the influence of France and Rome predominated in art as in religion and language.

Norman-Arab art and architecture did, however, exist as a vivid cultural phenomenon for most of the twelfth century. Woodwork and mosaic, coins and vestments, sculpture and lettering, show how a heterogeneous admixture of styles could in effect constitute a style of its own. The same too goes for architecture. With its five red cupolas, St John of the Hermits seems as much a mosque as a Christian shrine. The church known as the Martorana had the words of a Greek hymn in Arabic lettering round the bottom of the dome. Roger's palatine chapel in Palermo is perhaps the most beautiful example of the composite style, with its stupendous Arab painted ceiling, its Byzantine cupola, and interior decoration of coloured marble and mosaics. The latter must have been designed by Greek craftsmen, and they used Greek as well as Latin iconography.

The court of Roger was a centre of science. The King took a special interest in astronomy and astrology, and had a water clock built by an Arab craftsman. Latin translations were made in this period from Plato, Euclid, and Ptolemy, and Al-Idrisi's work on geography, in which Roger himself had a hand, became famous in Moslem Africa. The first translation of Ptolemy's *Almagest* was made at Palermo. In literature and scholarship this achievement was less impressive. There were some writings on science, medicine, jurisprudence and Koranic studies; and a document of about 1150 lists over a hundred poets from Sicilian-Arab families. But little of their work has survived.

Sadly, we do not know much about the French *jongleurs* who came to Roger's court with tales of Roland and the paladins of Charlemagne. The Carolingian legends were at some point transposed into a Sicilian setting, and the popularity of the cycle suggests that this was not merely a superficial culture: Gervase of Tilbury knew that King Arthur was still alive and recovering from his wounds on Mount Etna. These Breton tales later disappeared, though Morgan le Fay remained as *Fata Morgana*, a mirage in the straits of Messina; and after eight centuries, the paladins are familiar heroes in Sicilian legend. The vigour of Palermo court poetry, both French and Arabic, must have been a stimulus to the dramatic new vernacular Sicilian literature which began to appear late in the twelfth century.

THE DISINTEGRATION OF NORMAN SICILY

The test of Roger's success came under William I (1154–66). It is not easy to penetrate through the strong hostility shown to this king by the contemporary historian, Falcandus; but though William was a brave fighter, he must have lacked the application and the strength of character of other Norman rulers. Roger signed almost all the acts which came out of the royal chancery, but his son showed far less interest in government; he preferred to put off decisions and rule through ministers, while living apart in the oriental splendour of his pleasure palaces outside Palermo. Because Falcandus and most of the barons were against him, he has always been labelled 'William the Bad'.

He came to the throne at a difficult time. A certain restlessness during the last years of Roger's reign indicate the growth of both feudal opposition and social tension. Though Sicily remained prosperous, the Western and Eastern Emperors and the papacy were ready to exploit baronial opposition at home. At the same time the Sicilian foothold in North Africa was collapsing before the advance of the Almohads from the mountains of Morocco. In 1156 there was a defeat at Sfax; then Tripoli fell and in 1160 Mahdia. The resources of this small island could not simultaneously withstand a strong challenge in Africa along with treason at home and war with both the Pope and Byzantium.

In 1156, by the concordat of Benevento with the English Pope Adrian IV, William neutralized one possible opponent. He agreed that bishops should be elected by the clergy, and recognized the Pope as feudal overlord of his mainland territories. In return, Adrian confirmed the Apostolic Legateship in Sicily. The barons however were a more difficult problem; economically and socially strong, they also aspired to political power. They grumbled that law, administration and the army had, under Roger, been in the hands of low-born professionals; and they resented the fact that Roger had countered opposition by banishment and confiscation of property.

The more ambitious of them now took advantage of a less popular and less efficient King to shift the internal balance of power. In this, they could exploit racial intolerance and the grievances of certain towns at Roger's centralized and paternalistic rule. A prime target was William's chief minister, Maio of Bari, one of the palace professionals who caused such offence to the feudal aristocracy. The barons called him the upstart son of an oil merchant, a would-be usurper of the throne, and a seducer of young girls. A rising broke out against this man in 1155 coupled with a riot in Palermo; but the King responded with exemplary severity.

Aristocratic opposition, however, continued to exist in Calabria and the Lombard settlements of Sicily; and five years later one of the barons, Matthew Bonellus, organized a more successful revolt in which Maio was killed and the King captured. The Arabs, too, came under attack: their shops were pillaged, the palace eunuchs slaughtered, and the women of the harem shared out; land was seized from Moslem proprietors, and rural settlements were destroyed. Much of eastern Sicily was now cleared of Arabs and other North African settlers. Probably it was after these events that most of the remaining Arab intellectuals left Sicily.

The barons had killed the last great minister of Norman Sicily. The administrative class of bureaucrats however still included many other southern Italians as well as individual Greeks, French and Englishmen. Norman England and Norman Sicily remained very close. Richard Palmer, friend of St Thomas Becket, became Bishop of Syracuse; another Englishman, Walter, became Archbishop of Palermo, as did his brother Bartholomew. These newcomers not only proved a strong support for the barons against the professional lay bureaucrats, but also reinforced the growing shift from Greek to Latin culture that is detectable in Sicily at the time.

William I died in 1166, and according to one partisan observer only the Moslem women wept. His son William was just thirteen; and until he came of age Sicily was ruled by his mother, Margaret of Navarre. Her regency was marked by factionalism and baronial unrest to which she responded by turning to her relatives for help. This only aggravated the situation, and in 1168, her cousin and chief minister, Stephen of Le Perche, was forced to flee the island in the face of a general insurrection. The Englishman, Walter, then seized power and used the Palermo mob to make the canons of Palermo elect him Archbishop.

Though William II came of age in 1172, he did not dare to challenge the Archbishop openly; and Walter remained at the centre of power for twenty years, along with his brother Bartholomew and a third Englishman, Bishop Palmer. For Sicily this was a comparatively tranquil period; and that is one reason why William earned himself the epithet 'the Good'. More important though was the fact that the barons and the chroniclers approved of him; and because of their uncritical support, his personality is difficult to grasp. He had the reputation of being just, lenient, and without avarice. In common with his predecessor, he lived like an oriental sovereign: he patronized Arab poets, his concubines were Moslems, and he kept a bodyguard of black slaves.

Moslems continued to be heavily represented in government during William's reign; and at a time when western Christianity was becoming increasingly intolerant, there were still mosques in Palermo. Nevertheless, the Christianization of the country was proceeding, and the Cluniacs and Cistercians were accumulating large endowments for this purpose. William's greatest act of patronage was to build the immense Benedictine abbey of Monreale. Probably the King intended to create a rival institution to the archbishopric of Palermo, held by Walter: the Abbot of Monreale was made Sicily's second Archbishop even though his see was based only five miles from Palermo.

The building of this huge abbey, as well as the Arabic-type palaces called the Cuba and the Zisa with their artificial lakes, to say nothing of a new cathedral in Palermo, indicates the considerable wealth of Sicily and the concentration of this wealth in the King's hands. Probably this was the most affluent period in the century. But William was living on capital. At a time when the maritime cities of mainland Italy were accumulating new fortunes, Sicilian trade stagnated. There were already signs of political opposition from the commercial centres, Messina and Palermo; and elsewhere too, resentment was felt at the lack of municipal self-government.

William died in 1189, aged only thirty-six. He had no children, and this was fatal in a society which depended on a strong leader and an uncontested succession. The official heir was his aunt Constance, who had married the Hohenstaufen, King Henry of Germany, who later became the Emperor Henry VI. The barons had initially accepted Constance, but subsequently some of them rallied round William's illegitimate nephew, Tancred, who was 'chosen' King by an assembly of prelates, nobles and people. Even his opponents agreed that there was a popular element in his favour. He had the advantage of being a local man. In addition, Palermo had risked losing its central position in government if a German king succeeded. Perhaps most material, though, was that Tancred was the preferred candidate of the Vice-Chancellor Matthew.

Two problems soon confronted Tancred. The first was a civil war against the Moslems in 1189. This resulted in another migration to Africa, and further agricultural depopulation. Though some of the refugees eventually returned and even obtained jobs under Tancred, confidence between the races never recovered. The second was the arrival of Richard Coeur-de-Lion of England at Messina in 1190, together with the King of France and an army of crusaders. Richard brusquely demanded payment of a legacy made to him by William II; and when friction arose between the crusaders and the local population the town was sacked. Tancred was obliged to buy peace, for he wanted English help against his German rival; while Richard, suitably mollified, gave King Arthur's sword Excalibur to Tancred and set out on his crusade.

These enforced concessions show how much Norman authority had been reduced in the *regnum*: the King of Sicily could no longer speak on equal terms with England and France. Something of a vicious circle was set in motion. To ensure Church support, Tancred was forced to renounce more privileges of the Apostolic Legateship, and generous grants had to be made to the religious orders and the towns. His coronation was itself another concession to the elective principle and hence marked a further stage in the acquisition of power by the baronage.

Meanwhile Henry VI coveted the wealth of Sicily as a way of extending his ambitions into southern Europe and the Mediterranean. This had long been in the mind of the Western Emperors, and the marriage with Constance provided a pretext, as an alliance with the naval powers of Genoa and Pisa provided the means. In 1194, Henry arrived in the straits of Messina. Tancred was by now dead, and had been succeeded by his son William III, who was only a boy. What was left of the Sicilian fleet, perhaps outnumbered by the Pisan and Genoese ships, made no attempt to stop Henry, and Messina welcomed the Germans with enthusiasm; so did the Christians in Catania. Most of the nobility hurried to submit, and on Christmas Day, 1194, Henry crowned himself King of Sicily.

To Henry, Sicily was merely an appendage of Germany, the most remote corner of a large empire. He did little to placate his subjects, and gave the impression that he had come solely to gather the spoils of war. He used his soldiers to collect tribute; his German generals were given Sicilian fiefs; and the knights of the Teutonic Order obtained confiscated Cistercian land. The local nobility soon turned against him, and rebellion broke out. The Emperor responded brutally: his cruelty, it is said, did not spare clergy, women, or many people who could not possibly have been associated with the rising. But in 1197, in the middle of this repression, the Emperor himself died. His body was taken to Archbishop Walter's new cathedral at Palermo, from which Tancred's remains had been sacrilegiously cast out.

CHAPTER 8

Hohenstaufen and Angevins

STUPOR MUNDI

The death of Henry was followed by a period of anarchy. The new King, Frederick II, was only three, and though Innocent III was his appointed guardian very little could be done to defend the interests of his ward. A succession of German barons, enriched by grants from the deceased Henry, defied the papal troops and took possession of Palermo and the young King. Confusion was increased by another outburst of race riots in 1197. The Moslem population, such as it was, responded, and marauding bands were soon engaged in stealing food and trying to recover property; and as their rebellion gathered strength, castles and villages were captured. These bandits were exploited by German barons who thrived on chaos.

Frederick was absent from Sicily for twelve years. When he returned in 1220, he set about establishing his authority with a vengeance. He opened a full-scale war in the interior of the island, where the Moslem leader, Ibn Abbad, was acting as an independent sovereign. He also dealt with the barons and brought them to heel. He ordered the destruction of private castles built since 1189, restated precisely the Norman laws on feudalism, and restored the royal demesne. He also resumed the rights of justice, and barons were once again restricted in alienating or subletting their fiefs.

Nowhere else in his empire was Frederick so imperious and authoritarian, for whereas in Germany he was a feudal sovereign, in Sicily he lived up to his titles of Augustus and Caesar. Here even his coins were named *Augustales* and their design was copied from those of ancient Rome. When he summoned a parliament in 1221, the country felt a directing authority reminiscent of King Roger; dice and other games of chance were forbidden; citizens had to return home before the third evening bell; Jews had to wear a specified dress; prostitutes had to live outside the city walls and not attend public baths with honest women. Here was a totalitarian desire to regulate even private behaviour, and these were laws which Frederick meant to be observed.

Whereas Roger I had allowed Lombards, Greeks, Arabs and Franks to be judged each by their own laws, Frederick wanted a more unified system. In 1231 the *Liber Augustalis* was promulgated. Significantly it was in Latin, and was drawn up by the famous jurist, Peter della Vigna, logothete and protonotary of Sicily. These laws, particularly in their concept of royal authority, illustrate the singularity of Sicily in western Europe. The *regnum*, they declared, was held by the Emperor from God himself. Clerics were not to interfere in secular matters. Criminal justice was reserved to the sovereign despite any apparent concession to the contrary, and though prelates and barons could exercise minor jurisdiction with permission, appeals should lie to the King's court. Such an affirmation of royal authority was a severe rebuttal to any claims of municipal autonomy.

Sicily was still a fairly rich country, and one might have expected a vigorous town life. In fact there was never anything like the independent communes of northern Italy. This may have reflected a lack of civic enterprise, but in large measure it derived from the fact that the Norman monarchy was too authoritarian and too strong to need to encourage the towns against the baronage. Each city was dominated by a royal castle, and Frederick built other fortresses at strategic points inland. These were not residential castles, but military. Apparently French engineers and stone-masons were imported to build them, and northern influences can still be seen in the castles of Ursino in Catania and Maniaces in Syracuse harbour.

More than any other Sicilian town, Messina had experienced some degree of independence. Messina possessed interests which differed from those of agricultural Sicily, and her contacts with the outside world made her more restive. The Messinese had rebelled against William II in 1168. They rebelled against Tancred in 1194; and, in return for supporting the German invasion, Henry allowed them to have a free port with preferential customs duties. Genoese, Lombards, Pisans, Florentines and Catalans took advantage of this to open or re-open warehouses there. As a result, Messina had come to develop a fairly strong civic consciousness and a class of merchants who could sometimes act in concert and carry political weight.

Frederick revoked many of the supposed privileges of Messina as inconsistent with his notion of central authority. This led to a revolt by the city in 1232, which Frederick ruthlessly suppressed. Frederick's subjection of the towns helped to ensure that there was never a class of merchants or civic officials independent and vigorous enough to offset the landowning nobility; and this lack of challenge to the aristocracy was to be a fundamental factor in the political, cultural and economic decline of Sicily. Whenever strong government failed, it was the nobles and not the local cities which filled the vacuum of power. Furthermore, it was foreign towns – Pisa, Genoa, Venice, Amalfi, Lucca – that dominated Sicilian commerce, and the profits accordingly left the country without fertilizing local enterprise.

The Emperor no doubt intended to be helpful towards trade and agriculture, though one suspects that he encouraged them mainly to obtain increased taxation for his imperial policy; and this taxation then counter-acted any tendency towards economic growth. On the other hand royal revenue did help to maintain law and order, and this was a boon to the economy. Beneficial too was his attempt to tidy up the diverse systems of weights and measures: even neighbouring villages had utterly incompatible metric systems, owing to their multifarious racial and historical origins, and this had been a great obstacle to trade. He also tried to limit usury, which had always been a great burden on Sicilian agriculture.

The Sicilian economy must have partially run down in the years 1190 –1220, and Frederick's legislation was an over-optimistic attempt to intro-duce order into chaos. To try and stimulate agriculture, uncultivated land was given out with the peremptory obligation to clear it and sow wheat; and Frederick ordained that peasants should not have their animals or agricul-tural implements taken for debt. He encouraged the silk and sugar industries, and was the last Sicilian sovereign for many centuries who possessed the authority, the resources, and the technological curiosity to develop the methods of irrigation from which prosperity had once derived. He may even have tried to build an artificial lake a few miles from Augusta.

Frederick's ruthless adventurousness was reminiscent of the ancient tyrants. He re-peopled Malta, and brought Lombards and Greeks to settle in under-populated areas of Sicily. He built villages with the same ease as he obliterated them for punishment. Most cruelly of all, he transplanted thousands of Moslems to the mainland and set them up in a military colony at Lucera. This, and other operations against the Moslems, must have done considerable harm to Sicily: it left society more homogeneous, but only by destroying a class of small traders and an element in agriculture which was impossible to replace.

Frederick turned against the Sicilian Arabs not for religious reasons but because they were rebels. He continued to maintain cordial relations with the Moslem states of North Africa, just as he continued to keep a retinue of Saracen pages, and a *seraglio*. No wonder popes referred to him as a baptised Sultan. Their pique though was not just at his secular life style. Frederick was also their most dangerous political enemy, since his empire encircled the Papal States. He was repeatedly excommunicated and verbally deposed. Yet he did not serve the Church too badly. He reduced the residual authority of Islam and Byzantium in southern Italy. He went on a successful crusade and became King of Jerusalem. He set up the Tribunal of the Inquisition in Palermo, against the Waldensians, the Paterines, and many other specified brands of heretic; and though he resisted attempts by the papacy to intervene in temporal affairs, he meddled less than Roger in Church government.

In his personal patronage, the Emperor inclined more to science than to art. He was interested not only in technical questions like the draining of marshes or making machines of war, but also in abstract problems of physics. He was fascinated by animals, and his zoo included lions, panthers, monkeys, a giraffe and an elephant given him by the Sultan of Egypt. In addition, he was a great patron of Sicilian vernacular poetry, the pre-eminence of which was admitted by Dante and Petrarch. It was written in a dialect not unlike that of today. To some extent it was the deliberate creation of a royal patron who not only wrote poetry for his own pleasure but deliberately tried to make the *regnum* a single community with its own distinctive culture and literature.

Frederick died in 1250. He could claim to be the most remarkable ruler in medieval Europe. Yet his success in Sicily was personal, for it was largely imposed, and was neither moulded by enduring forces nor genuinely accepted by his subjects. Few of his positive achievements long survived his death. He had made many enemies, and Sicily was to suffer as a result. The jurists who were the backbone of his administration did not form an enduring class, and as he needed the support of a feudal army he had not challenged the social foundation of aristocratic power. The feudatories were overawed while he lived, but were able to undo his handiwork afterwards.

Though Frederick said he loved Sicily above all his other possessions, the centre of gravity of his kingdom had in fact shifted away from the island. Few, perhaps surprisingly few, of his ministers were native Sicilians; and Frederick himself came to prefer residence in the royal hunting castles of Apulia. This reflected a fundamental change. Henry and Frederick had brought with them a European policy, and this condemned Sicily to a subordinate role and increasing poverty. While it belonged to the world of North Africa and the Levant, the island had been rich; but when forcibly attached to western Europe it lost many of the advantages of its geographic position. After 1194, Sicily was one small peripheral region in a succession of large empires, and her wealth expended on projects in which Sicilian concern was minimal.

THE SICILIAN VESPERS, 1282

The year 1250 began a long period of decline for Sicily, decline in power, prosperity and security. Central authority was now defective, and in the absence of a guiding hand the economy deteriorated. The community spirit was lacking which might have produced a city-state civilization as in northern Italy, for although some Sicilian cities did try to assert themselves in the years immediately after 1250, they were too riven by internal factions. Government weakness encouraged people to ignore the law and resort to private justice; and so, at the very moment when feudalism showed signs of declining elsewhere, Sicily experienced the defeat of both royal authority and civic autonomy at the hands of an unruly baronage.

The Emperor's death was followed by fifteen years of civil discord and family vendettas in which rival contestants fought for what was left of Norman Sicily. The Popes strove hard to assert their feudal supremacy, and eventually sold the crown of Sicily to the King of England's eight-year-old son, Edmund of Lancaster. A papal Legate formally invested this English prince with the kingdom, and for ten years he styled himself 'King of Sicily by the grace of God'. He even sent the Bishop of Hereford to collect taxes from his new subjects in order to make up the purchase money. But the prospect of having to conquer a recalcitrant people was daunting; and the barons in England, by threatening civil war, forced the Pope to think again.

France not only possessed far greater resources than England, but some of its people also nurtured strong Mediterranean ambitions. In 1261 a Frenchman became Pope and deposed Edmund for not having paid the agreed price; instead he chose Charles of Anjou, brother of the French King, St Louis. As a scion, Charles was here being given an unexpected chance to acquire a kingdom. He had little interest in Sicily itself, but promised he would no longer claim the rights of Apostolic Legateship. A holy war was declared, and in 1265 Charles set out to take the island from Manfred, the Hohenstaufen champion, who had occupied the throne since 1258.

Manfred was to become a legend in folk memory, as the blond, tragic hero who stood for Sicily's independence against the Pope and the French despoilers of Sicilian wealth. At the battle of Benevento in 1266, he was defeated and killed, leaving his nephew, the fourteen-year-old Conradin, as the last hope of the Hohenstaufen. Two years later there was an even more decisive battle: the Angevins almost lost the day, but Conradin's army scattered too quickly in search of plunder. The unfortunate boy was taken prisoner and publicly beheaded. The Pope's campaign to exterminate the 'viper's brood' had almost succeeded.

Like every invader of Sicily, Charles found a degree of local support. Resentful of government and of taxation, there were invariably some Sicilians ready to invoke foreign help against their rulers, until a new master tried to recoup himself for the expenses of his invasion and set in motion once more the cycle of vengeance and rebellion. Almost invariably the population was divided against itself; and individual cities or families were likely to use any change of dynasty to assert their private interest. In this case Messina and Syracuse, the same towns that had once rebelled against Frederick, now helped the French to subdue the island.

Charles came as a usurper, and ignored the precedent of Tancred whereby a king of Sicily could be elected at Palermo by barons and people. His army was made up largely of adventurers whose first aim was land and plunder, and, as participants in a punitive papal crusade, they were under little obligation to respect persons, property or tradition. The invading generals were more cruel than cruelty itself, said one chronicler; and when the town of Augusta remained loyal to the Hohenstaufen, the French, aided by the Messinese, razed it to the ground, and slaughtered the survivors. Many Sicilians took advantage of the invasion to settle old scores or to set themselves up outside the law; and for some years a state of effective civil war prevailed.

To pay his knights, Charles confiscated many large estates, and those of the old aristocracy who kept their lands often did so only through bribery. French barons were appointed to control the cities, and most of the higher royal officers were Frenchmen, or else Italians from the mainland who were equally unpopular. Angevin feudalism, as a result, came to resemble a military garrison in a resentful province. The old nobility was particularly aggrieved, as Charles sought to reconstitute the royal demesne at baronial expense. He also refurbished royal taxation, and was more favourably disposed towards the cities than Frederick had been. Particularly galling was the fact that Charles centralized public life on Naples. To him, as to Frederick, the mainland provinces were more pleasant to live in and therefore received a larger share of his patronage.

Charles promised to rule by the good laws of William II, which implied that he would be less extortionate and less totalitarian than Frederick. In practice, however, he resorted to forced loans and frequently imposed *collecta* without parliamentary consent. He was precluded by his submission to the papacy from adequately taxing the clergy; yet the conquest of Sicily had been expensive and someone had to pay. The same went for his ambitious foreign policy. Perhaps he and his Tuscan bankers shared the common illusion that the south was inexhaustibly rich; but in fact this fabled wealth depended on good government, social harmony and an abundant labour force interested in agricultural productivity. Such conditions no longer existed. Sicily simply could not carry the weight of Charles's extensive ambitions, and the result was the most notable rebellion in Sicilian history.

The opposition to Charles centred on King Peter of Aragon. By amalgamating Aragon with Catalonia, Peter acquired in Barcelona one of the great ports of the Mediterranean. The bankers and merchants of this town coveted Sicily as a source of food and an outlet for the growing textile industry. In 1262, Peter married Manfred's daughter Constance, the last heir of the Hohenstaufen, and this gave him a claim to Sicily. He also found that the younger sons of the Spanish feudal aristocracy could be tempted by the prospect of obtaining principalities in this distant island. There was also a straight commercial rivalry, for the Catalans were competitors of the Tuscan bankers and merchants who had underwritten Charles of Anjou. Unlike Tuscany, however, Catalonia had a fleet, and history had shown that control of Sicily depended on sea power.

To the Hohenstaufen party in Italy, Peter of Aragon was the leading representative of the anti-papal ghibelline tradition. Another of its exponents was John of Procida, Chancellor of the *regnum* under Manfred, who had gone to live at the court of Aragon after having his possessions confiscated by the Angevins. Stories were told of how John subsequently visited Sicily in disguise to prepare a revolution; and of how he brought together the anti-papal forces of Europe, even persuading the Eastern Emperor to help finance a Sicilian revolt. Some such conspiracy undoubtedly did exist, though the stories have never been fully authenticated. In the event, though, the population of Palermo rebelled ahead of time and defeated the Angevins on their own.

Since about 1500 this rebellion has been called the 'Sicilian Vespers'. There was probably no connection with any evening hour; but the name has remained as a permanent symbol of the desire for Sicilian independence. On Easter Monday, 1282, people were gathered outside the walls of Palermo. French soldiers were searching people for arms. One soldier was apparently suspected of taking liberties with a woman, something which in this society was a greater offence than political persecution. In a moment of impetuous anger he was killed. This touched off a revolt that may possibly have been organized, but which has a much closer resemblance to one of those improvised explosions of popular vendetta and social revolution familiar in later Sicilian history.

The most violent feelings of xenophobia were involved, even if they lacked constructive aim. Every stranger whose accent betrayed him was slaughtered; and several thousand Frenchmen were said to have been put to the sword in a few hours. Monasteries were broken open and monks killed; old men and infants were butchered. Even Sicilian women thought to be pregnant by Frenchmen were ripped open. This was not a feudal revolt but a popular revolution, and for that very reason its immediate success was astonishing. It was an episode of singular barbarity; and only subsequent political developments made it possible for a horrible massacre to be magnified into the most glorious event in Sicilian history.

Some of the leading citizens of Palermo at once called a 'parliament' and the city was declared an independent republic, which suggests they may have envied the growth of municipal autonomy elsewhere in Italy. Armed bands were despatched to organize the rising on a broader front. 'Captains of the people' were elected or self-elected in villages of western Sicily; and, inspired no doubt by a variety of motives, the revolution spread. Within a few weeks, Sicily had been cleared of Frenchmen. As success came, the initial frenzy died down. The Hohenstaufen baronage, who must have been astonished by the whole episode, now tried to hijack the movement in order to prevent it from developing in undesirable directions; and their success meant that the revolt was to mark yet another stage in the victory of feudal aristocracy over centralized monarchy.

The Sicilian Vespers was subsequently made out to be the very archetype of a patriotic rebellion; but it was more complex and protean than that. It was first an *émeute* and a *jacquerie*; then it seemed a movement for municipal autonomy; and finally it developed into a feudal revolt against a strong state, or even a struggle of one baronial group, the Hohenstaufen landowners, against another, the French. In addition it formed part of a war in which Catalans and Neapolitans – such as John of Procida – were using the Sicilian baronage for a much wider scheme of power politics against Anjou.

Quite when and how Aragonese influence became dominant is uncertain. Some people had an interest in maintaining that John of Procida and Peter of Aragon had been the chief actors all along: the Angevins needed to ascribe their defeat to more than a civilian mob, and it suited the Aragonese to take credit for everything. But the revolt broke out long before Peter could have been in a position to help, and its first leaders did not invoke Aragonese help. Only when he had made closer touch with the Sicilian barons and heard that Charles's ships had been destroyed did Peter act; and, spurred on by a formal request for help from a group of Sicilian notables, he landed at Trapani on 30 August, five months after the original outbreak. A few days later he was acclaimed King at Palermo, and in the now traditional formula he undertook to safeguard the liberties of Sicily as established by the good King William a century before.

The Pope and Charles of Anjou desperately promised reforms in the hope of retrieving their fortunes. But these were no more than a confession of failure; and they came too late. The Palermo massacre had effectively weakened the papacy and ruined Charles's hopes of a Mediterranean empire. The *Regnum Siciliae* was to all intents severed at the straits of Messina, with the incidental consequence that Calabria, which for centuries had been closely identified with Sicily, now became attached to the Kingdom of Naples. These 'two Sicilies' were not only divided at the straits, but their rivalry was quickly developing into a central fact of Mediterranean history.

Though Sicily gained in one direction from this severance, she lost in another. The island had already been deprived of the stimulating connection with Greece and Africa which had almost seemed a condition of her past greatness, and now her links with Italy were curtailed just when Italian history was entering the golden age of Dante and Giotto. She was cut off from the university of Naples and the professional jurists who had been the backbone of the Hohenstaufen monarchy. Messina lost many of her natural economic connections. For a century Sicily remained under the ban of Rome, her leaders excommunicated and her churches under interdict; and for four hundred years she was attached not to the Italian but to the Iberian peninsula.

CHAPTER 9

Rule by Aragon

THE NEW FEUDALISM

Sicilians submitted without difficulty to rule from Spain. Their capacity to initiate a war of independence had not been matched by an ability to agree among themselves on a formula for home rule. This indicates that the rebellion of 1282 cannot have been against foreign domination *per se*. Perhaps some of them hoped that a distant King in Aragon would leave them more to themselves than the meddling and in many ways anti-feudal governments of Frederick II and Charles. If that was so, they were soon disillusioned. Though Peter convened parliaments, and agreed that the island should continue as a separate kingdom, he too imposed frequent *collecta* and sometimes ignored feudal privileges. Furthermore, a new Spanish feudal aristocracy began to receive land in return for military service, and naturally it was these men who were closest to the King.

Peter undertook that after his death the crowns of Sicily and Aragon would never be held by the same member of his family. This promise was not observed. James, who succeeded Peter, insisted on remaining King of both Sicily and Aragon, and Sicilians had to go on providing grain, soldiers and ships to the common fund. Indeed, far from allowing Sicilian autonomy, the interests of Aragon eventually convinced James that he should make peace with the Pope and surrender this distant island to the Angevins. Return to Angevin rule might have been no bad thing for most Sicilians, but, as it threatened the property and even the lives of some of the chief landowners, the King's plan met stiff opposition.

James had appointed a younger brother, Frederick, as his Lieutenant at Palermo. This Frederick had been brought to Sicily as a child and had grown up a Sicilian. Perhaps he also had ambitions of his own. In 1295 he summoned a 'parliament' to debate his brother's decision regarding the surrender of the island; and, in a remarkable move, the barons appointed him king of an independent Sicily in place of his brother. So began a forty-year reign that has sometimes been extravagantly described as a noble period of warfare against Angevin Naples, during which the heroic Sicilian baronage became a symbol of patriotic independence; but, in fact, selfish interests predominated in this war, and nothing was achieved by it except destruction.

Details of the fighting are unilluminating. Enthusiasm flagged as the to and fro became more and more pointless. The barons were reluctant to fulfil their obligations of knight service, and Frederick had little enough money to hire soldiers. Certain Sicilian feudatories, out of personal interest or vendetta, joined the Angevins and helped foreign armies to sack neighbouring Sicilian towns. At Messina, too, the mercantile classes showed some readiness to restore the Angevin connection, which to them meant the defeat of Palermo, as it also meant food supplies and trade with Calabria and Naples. As for the common people, one may guess that their chief sentiment was a desire to end the war either way and in the meantime to avoid commitment.

A decline in the cohesion of Sicily was accompanied, and not accidentally, by a growth in baronial pretensions. The nobles were in fact emerging as the chief victors in the revolutions of 1282 and 1295–6. At his accession James had had to undertake not to use the emergency *collecta* tax too frequently; and, in his law *Si aliquem*, he allowed childless barons to bequeath fiefs to collateral branches of their family, so making it much less likely that feudal estates would ever devolve to the crown. In 1296 Frederick had to grant a charter of liberties that included the promise to summon an annual parliament and not leave the island or declare war or make peace 'without the full knowledge and consent of Sicilians'. The problem for Frederick was that he was a usurper, and as such was heavily dependent on the nobility.

The feudal character of society had become much more marked than in Count Roger's day. Feudal tenures now covered a large extent of the island as successive kings built up a following by grants of land to friends and servants. Many other royal prerogatives, including castles, forests, tunny fisheries, salt pans, tithes and the farming of taxes, had been given out as feudal concessions, and gradually these grants were being thought of as providing revenue and power for the baron rather than military service to the King. Feudalism, instead of reinforcing central authority, as under Roger, was thus coming to represent a principle of disorganization and a diminution of royal rights.

The feudalism of the fourteenth century was a burden on society. If only, like the king-makers of 1296, the feudatories had continued to see their own advantage in pressing for an annual parliament, this at least might have allowed the common interest to be discussed, and so associated private individuals with the promotion of general welfare; but nothing more was heard of annual parliaments. The barons now had easier means of making their interest prevail. Though they were uneducated and illiterate, administration fell increasingly into their hands. Criminal jurisdiction, for example – the right of *merum et mistum imperium* – was now regularly granted to the senior counts and in time became inheritable; its sinister manifestation was the gallows raised outside any village where the baron's word was law.

The years after 1350 witnessed a general dissolution of society. Envy of the newly enriched nobility from Spain led to friction between 'Latin' and 'Catalan' factions. The chief division was between the Chiaramonte and d'Alagona families, both of which had acquired large estates from the dispossessed French barons after 1282. The Chiaramonte offered their services to the Angevins; and with German and Neapolitan troops they utterly devastated the coastal territories along southern Sicily. Their opponents, claiming to be the champions of Frederick IV and Sicilian independence, similarly extended their own power in the north by deliberately starving whole areas into submission.

Peace was eventually reached by simple exhaustion. In 1372 Naples agreed to accept Sicilian independence on condition that Frederick style himself 'King of *Trinacria*' and pay an annual tribute. The Papacy likewise agreed to peace, though Frederick had to acknowledge the feudal overlordship of Rome. How much ninety years of warfare had cost is impossible to assess. The damage, though, was considerable. The enemy had often landed large forces to burn forests and farmsteads, to cut down trees and vines; for their best hope was to exhaust the island, to stop commerce, ruin the tunny fisheries and bring agriculture to a halt. The chronicler Villani spoke of each side acting 'like savage beasts'; and there was mention of 'innumerable victims' dying of famine.

Armed adventurers from as far away as England made a good living in this world of civil strife. Rarely were there pitched battles, so it was not the soldiers who chiefly suffered: armies learnt to feed off the country. Peasant families fled from the coastal territories, to the great loss of agriculture; some emigrated to Calabria and Sardinia and increased the depopulation which Moslem evictions and the Black Death had already caused; others took to military life in brigand gangs. It is possible, however, that the chroniclers exaggerated the human tragedy. So long as merchants and bankers still existed, foreign ships came, men wore gold, and ladies had hairstyles like towers and battlements, then clearly all was not lost.

THE END OF INDEPENDENCE

When Frederick IV died in 1377, he left a young daughter, Maria, in the care of Artale d'Alagona, leader of the Catalans. Who this girl married was obviously of crucial importance. For some years the island was administered by d'Alagona and three other leading barons, but the mutual jealousies of the 'vicars' made this experiment relatively short-lived. In 1390 Maria was abducted from Catania castle, taken to Barcelona and married to Martin the young grandson of the King of Aragon. Two years later Martin invaded the island. Two of the four vicars joined him. A third, Andrea Chiaramonte, was besieged in Palermo for a month. When the city fell, Chiaramonte was executed and his vast estates bestowed on the leading Spanish general, Bernardo Cabrera.

Though Martin's concession of land to foreign adventurers was little liked by existing feudatories, they gradually submitted. In the first place, he was obviously winning; and secondly, he showed himself ready to confirm the usurpations of crown lands and revenues. As it happened, though, he could do little else, for after many decades of anarchy, registers had been lost and earlier traditions of government forgotten. As a result, and in contrast to the Norman and Hohenstaufen period, the barons were permitted to keep a strong hold on public life. Martin's power was also limited in another respect, for Sicilian independence of Naples was possible only because of an increasing dependence on Aragon; and this second Spanish invasion now brought a substantial new wave of landowners from Spain who before long dominated government and administration.

After a lapse of half a century, parliament was summoned once again. In keeping with Aragonese tradition, a degree of initiative and discussion was allowed. The plea was made for fewer Catalans to be appointed to government jobs, and the King was asked to apply only Sicilian laws, and 'live of his own'. At the same time the bold suggestion was made that members of parliament should be represented on the royal council and even given some executive powers if the King were absent. For a brief moment, parliament seemed to be approximating to a pattern made familiar in England; but Martin rejected this last proposal, and the parliamentarians were in practice too divided to acquire much authority unless he wanted it.

Martin I remained strongly under the influence of his father, and the latter, who was now King of Aragon, watched over every detail of Sicilian administration. It was the King of Aragon who financed the troops in Sicily, who appointed to jobs and fiefs, and decided about desmesne lands and ecclesiastical policy; for the Aragonese regarded Sicily as their advance guard in the Mediterranean. Thus, at a time when other countries in Europe were growing in cohesion, Sicily was losing its political personality and its potential as an independent State; and when Martin died in 1409, he donated Sicily to his father, like any other item of personal property.

Too many members of the ruling class were either Spanish by origin or bound by material interests to the Spanish dynasty for serious protest to arise. There was no outcry when in 1412 a member of a cadet branch of the house of Castile was appointed King. Though Ferdinand proclaimed himself 'by the grace of God, King of Sicily', the islanders had not even been consulted. There was some controversy when parliament met in 1413; but it was mainly over who should have the honour of carrying to Ferdinand a message of humble submission. The King was petitioned to keep the administrative and legal system of Sicily separate from those of his other dominions and appoint local people to government offices. Nevertheless, there was no power behind these requests, and in fact the Castilian dynasty was to apply local laws with considerable latitude.

Sicily was no longer a residence of kings. For four hundred years it was to be administered by viceroys, a centre less of politics than of administration, and with none of the perquisites pertaining to a major focus of government. The term 'Viceroy' was at least an acknowledgement in theory that here was a distinct kingdom; but, of seventy-eight successive appointees, very few were Sicilians by origin, and none at all after the first fifty years. Short of a revolution there could be little hope of secession. When the first Viceroy was appointed, a group from Messina misread the situation and asked him to become an independent King of Sicily. He refused, and few such proposals were ever heard again.

ALFONSO AND THE ECONOMY

Sicily's loyalty and her dependence on Spain were confirmed during the forty-two year reign of Alfonso of Aragon after 1416. The local nobility served him faithfully in his dynastic wars, largely because he rewarded them handsomely for doing so. Estates or privileges held by a baron for thirty years were allowed to become his by law even if illegally acquired; and thereby both the King and the towns lost many rights of taxation and property. The barons were allowed to administer oaths of allegiance to their own tenants as well as to impose private taxes on them; and when the nobility grumbled that the royal courts were too expensive, they were allowed to hear more cases in their own courts.

Alfonso's reign has been described as the period when Sicily emerged from the Middle Ages; and certainly in his affectation of humanism, as in his conduct of war, Alfonso seemed a new kind of sovereign. He was a generous patron of the arts and was given the appellation 'Magnanimous' by his Spanish and Neapolitan subjects, though he hardly justified this title in Sicily. He re-established a school of Greek at Messina, and set up the first Sicilian university at Messina. But his reign seems culturally interesting only by comparison with the desert of the two preceding centuries. In fact Sicily contributed few names to the Renaissance except Panormita, the humanist scholar, and Antonello da Messina, the painter, and both these were expatriates who spent their lives in Naples, Venice or Milan.

Alfonso liked the reputation of being a great patron, but in practice had little money for the arts. His sources of revenue were still much as under the Normans. He had the income from the somewhat diminished crown estates; there were the royalties from the valuable tunny fisheries; and above all there were the duties on exports. But all this was inadequate to his considerable needs. Hence he resorted to borrowing from barons and towns. He also imposed a regular 'donativo', the Spanish name for the *collecta*, and this, without anyone realizing it, soon became the largest single item in the regular revenue, even though each grant was thought of at the time as an emergency once-for-all measure. That of 1446 was still being paid in the nineteenth century.

These grants did not however stop Alfonso's continued alienation of crown property and prerogatives. No crime was so great that a criminal could not buy a pardon; and new offices and taxes were instituted simply so that they could then be sold. This was the improvidence of a sovereign who had other things in mind than local welfare or prosperity. In consequence, he was prepared to give up prerogatives which had once been thought indispensable for the public weal. Efficient administration would be impossible as soon as barons knew that they could compound by money for any illegality, and a planned budget was out of the question when the very sources of revenue were sold outright to produce current income.

It was Alfonso's foreign policy that was the greatest drain on resources. After capturing Naples, he embarked on an adventurous series of wars against Florence, Genoa, Milan and Venice. Sicily contributed to these on a more generous scale than some other parts of his empire; and the consequence for the economy in general was disastrous. This was a period in Europe when great fortunes could be made. Equally it was a time when lack of capital and enterprise were heavily penalized; and though some Sicilian nobles did take advantage of the speculative possibilities offered by Alfonso's wars, on the whole neither capital nor enterprise was forthcoming.

Not all the blame should be attributed to Alfonso. A more fundamental fact was that an independent middle class had never emerged. The prejudice of the nobility against trade seems to have been particularly acute in Sicily; and this infected the aspirations of the rest of society, which continued to see in the acquisition of land the highest social attainment. Equally the lawyers remained dependent on aristocratic ducats, and so failed to become an innovative and independent force; and this was one reason why parliamentary institutions took a different path of development from those in England.

The most significant failure, perhaps, came with the towns. If the baronage was growing stronger in Sicily, it was at the expense of urban autonomy. Palermo and Messina alone had much civic freedom, and even this was largely an illusion. Control by either the government or the landed proprietors had left little scope for a municipal third estate to develop with interests distinct from those of the baronage, and in fact the cities never formed a strong and independent force in parliament. Perhaps the continuous squabbling between various towns, to say nothing of faction fights inside them, made civic freedom seem less attractive than a government which could guarantee order, justice and effective administration.

A symptom of the lopsided development of Sicilian cities was the predominance of foreign merchants in their economies. Catalans, not surprisingly, formed a particularly important group, and they traded above all in cloth. There were Genoese, who, as bankers as well as merchants, provided Alfonso with what he needed at Naples in return for special privileges in Sicily. Tuscans and Venetians were also in evidence. So too were English merchants; and, in the sixteenth century, there was an English consul at Trapani, and another at Messina (where the word *ingrisi* came to mean 'foreign' or 'incomprehensible'). These diverse connections at least helped to keep Sicily from being too exclusively absorbed into the world of Spanish culture.

A PROVINCE OF THE CASTILIAN EMPIRE

In 1458 Alfonso died, bestowing Naples on his illegitimate son, but leaving his other kingdoms to his brother John. Sicilians were given no say in the matter. The straits of Messina once again became a barrier, and John divorced Sicily still further from the rest of Italy by proclaiming that the island should never again be a kingdom separate from Aragon. There seems to have been no active resistance to this revolutionary and wholly 'unconstitutional' proclamation. If there had been, John could hardly have overcome it, for he had no available forces to spare and his authority was gravely threatened in Spain itself.

This lack of political initiative in Sicily was fatal. In 1479 John was succeeded by Ferdinand and he, through his wife Isabella, united Aragon with Castile. The Spanish peninsula was becoming a single nation, and in the rapidly enlarging Spanish empire Sicily was inevitably condemned to take a small and diminishing place. Local interests were considered less and less, even though local taxes went on increasing. The conquest of Granada and war against the Turks both made demands on Sicily, and African gold which arrived in payment for Sicilian wheat was used to pay for military provision. Ferdinand also decided to conquer southern Italy from his cousin, and hence Sicily had to aid yet another invasion of Naples.

Another sign of subservience was the introduction of the new Spanish Inquisition. From 1487 onwards the notorious Torquemada was sending Inquisitors to Sicily, and soon a permanent institution was properly organised with its headquarters in the royal palace at Palermo. Naples successfully resisted the introduction of the Holy Office; but in Sicily, though there was some initial opposition to it, to be enrolled as an Inquisition official was soon regarded as a great privilege by the Sicilian nobility. The chief Inquisitors, with their devoted intolerance, helped keep Sicily orthodox and eliminate 'racial' minorities; but, at a time when the civilization of the Renaissance was advancing elsewhere in Europe, the country was insulated from much of what was most challenging in contemporary culture.

Also damaging and equally indicative of Sicily's subordination to Spain was the expulsion of the Jews in 1492. Although the citizens of Palermo protested that trade would be damaged, the orders from Spain were firm. How many Jews now emigrated and how many were 'converted' and allowed to stay cannot be said. But even converts forfeited much of their property, and probably a good deal of their wealth was taken out of Sicily. Though the impact of the expulsion may in the past have been exaggerated, the country certainly lost some industrious citizens and no doubt a lot of capital too; and this lack of craftsmen and of organised credit were to rank among the chief weaknesses of the Sicilian economy.

Though a number of insurrections occurred in Sicily between 1510 and 1525, it is hard to ascribe them, as some historians have done, to a resurgent national consciousness. They more likely derived from a temporary disquiet among the barons who for 250 years had held the upper hand in their dealings with the crown. Now, however, the growing demands of the state for revenue, together with new ideas about royal sovereignty, and the need to make Sicily a strong military bastion, induced the authorities to reassert central controls. One sign of the new situation was that the baronage was increasingly subject to the jurisdiction of the royal courts.

The most serious rising in this period occurred in 1516. The Viceroy had summoned parliament and asked the already disaffected barons for money. When news arrived of the King's death, a number of them seized the initiative, claiming that the Viceroy's authority had automatically been abrogated. Meanwhile, a popular revolution had broken out at Palermo. According to the Viceroy, this was organized by nobles with criminal gangs in their employ. Similar stories were told about every Sicilian rebellion from the Vespers on, no doubt with considerable justification. But it is also the case that it suited the authorities to make these allegations; for political and social problems thereby became much more tractable.

The 1516 rising – which lasted for a year – provided an inauspicious start to the reign of the new King, Charles V. Charles was the grandson of Ferdinand. He was an Austrian Habsburg who also happened to rule Spain; but it was a Spain which no longer meant Aragon and Barcelona. The centre of gravity had shifted to Castile and Cadiz; and the Mediterranean would soon be less important than the Atlantic. Sicily was to be deprived of its privileged position on the main trade route of the western world. Once again the island was being pushed further to the periphery, and some painful adjustments were required. Despite this, Sicily was to prove one of the most loyal provinces of the Habsburg empire.

CHAPTER 10

Spanish administration
1500–1600

GOVERNORS AND GOVERNED

Spanish rule has sometimes been blamed for corrupting Sicily, for causing economic decline and social maladjustment, for perverting a healthy baronial class, setting Sicilians against each other, and giving an example of idleness and political apathy. But like all such historical accusations, the charge is not easy to prove or refute. It can be admitted that, as Spanish monarchs ruled Sicily for more than four centuries, the influence of Spain must have been extensive. Nevertheless, many things ascribed to this alien influence were experienced in other countries which were quite outside the orbit of Spain, and that vague complex of qualities named pejoratively as *spagnolismo* sometimes seemed to characterize the Sicilian ruled more than their Spanish rulers.

Spanish policy admittedly aimed at conservation rather than improvement, and in this long period a great number of things changed surprisingly little. The viceroys were not charged with devising fundamental reforms. They were chiefly concerned to keep the country quiet. But Sicily was not an easy place to govern, and few Spanish viceroys survived without stirring up some kind of criticism. Almost all of them were faulted for being either too strong or too weak. Even honest efficiency was disliked; and no credit was given when, at the end of the sixteenth century, a viceroy decided to be firm about appointing officials on merit and to make them keep fixed hours and work in proper offices at the royal palace.

Though corruption was common to all European states, the Sicilian government seems to have been particularly prone to it. Such a malady was widespread in a society that continued to regard public office as predominantly a source of private advantage. Rich Sicilian aristocrats could apparently hire the Great Seal to authorize some private malpractice; a scrupulous viceroy might find that the Treasury had big gaps in its accounts; money could buy liberation from prison or the imprisonment and torture of a private enemy; and we have confirmation from parliament in 1523 that judges were purchasing their jobs and then selling justice to recoup the expense.

Successive viceroys, Italian as well as Spanish, were fond of expatiating in their reports on the character of the natives. Whether or not they copied from each other, the general conclusions remained much the same and received general confirmation from other visitors. There was admiration for a subtle inventiveness and sharpness of mind, as there was only praise for the loyalty to Spain, the friendliness to foreigners, and the readiness to obey really firm government. Yet Sicilians were criticized for being the most vengeful and passionate people in the world. Their capacity for false witness and bribery was notorious, as was their selfish concentration on their own good without consideration for the common weal.

Many Sicilians were equally explicit about their own limitations, and hence they were grateful to Spain for providing a workable structure of administration. Some Neapolitan writers were later to lament the arrival of the Spanish in Sicily on the grounds that this island was thereby divorced from the Italian mainland with which she rightly belonged. To Sicilians, on the contrary, the Vespers and their invocation of Spain in 1282 became the very symbol of local liberties against the desire of Naples to dominate and exploit. Any government tended to be disliked and criticized in Sicily, but animus was directed much less against Spain than Naples.

Successive Spanish administrators realized that the cheapest way to hold the island with only a small garrison was to introduce few changes; local susceptibilities or privileges were best left unchallenged. Social reforms, therefore, even where recognized as desirable, were renounced in deference to baronial interests. Social revolution could be exorcized by providing cheap bread; and the government merely had to perpetuate among other classes the illusion that their parliament and privileges saved them from Spanish exploitation. Far from being oppressive, indeed, Spain could more properly be accused of being too lax, too respectful of the antiquated feudal parliament and of the privileged immunities of nobles, clergy and the town guilds.

In the absence of a vigorous middle class and any strong political consciousness, resistance to Spanish rule was slight. Even in the most obstreperous moments of opposition, Sicilians carried the royal flag and burned candles before the King's picture. If they rebelled, it was against individual afflictions – hunger, the aristocracy, badly distributed taxes, or a viceroy whose fount of patronage was running dry. There was nothing in Sicily remotely comparable to the patriotic revolt of the Netherlands against Spanish rule, or to the rebellions of Catalonia, Portugal and Lutheran Germany.

One notable feature of Sicily was the strength of sectional interests and loyalties, that easily overrode any feelings of common nationality. Some people relieved themselves of responsibility for the internal rivalries by accusing Spain of deliberately setting the barons against the towns and the towns against each other; but Sicilians needed little encouragement in this, and the viceroys were the first to be shocked by the way Sicilians wasted their energies in factiousness. Not only were cities such as Palermo and Messina pitted against one another, but townsmen bickered with the country dwellers on whom they depended for food, and fear of either the town mob or the peasantry kept every other class in willing bondage to the government. Perhaps only the imposition of Spanish rule kept Sicily intact.

THE BARONAGE

The King and his feudatories were only on rare occasions at odds with each other, for they had basic interests in common and yet largely diverse spheres of operation. The King needed Sicily for military bases and for its food supplies, whereas the barons were quite content so long as they controlled local affairs and were taxed lightly. In these circumstances, the aristocracy lacked the will and perhaps the capacity to lead a separatist movement, a fact indicated by their own mutual jealousies quite apart from the often hostile attitude towards them of other Sicilians. Cut off from the ordinary life of the common people, they had acquired more and more of a vested interest in Spanish rule.

Though the nobility had power, it was in important respects circum-scribed. Military service was no longer a privilege but an easily evaded duty, and with their antiquated weapons and armour the aristocracy were far more vulnerable in moments of popular disturbance than their fathers had been: this, no doubt, is one reason why after 1523 they were less willing to rebel. They had no monopoly of the great offices of state; on the contrary, orders came from Spain in 1569 that they were no longer to be given these offices, partly because they were not educated to understand the growing technicalities of administration, but also because it was prudent to concen-trate their energies in local government.

Despite their power, some of the aristocracy were quite poor, and most of them were learning to live on credit. Some were in debt through bad farming, others through inability to administer their large estates, or through the stock family lawsuits which it was fashionable to drag out for decades. Fashion also imposed on those with any social ambition an expensive life in a palatial town house near the Viceroy's court. The consequent impoverishment of some of the old families was a worry to the government. For one thing, it was bad for agriculture. Landowners were sometimes paying well over half their agricultural income in mortgage interest.

Any landowners of moderate ability and industry must nevertheless have survived inflation better than other elements in the community. What they lost in the devaluation of fixed rent incomes they must have regained from the depreciation of their mortgage payments, to say nothing of the still more important fact that wheat prices rose fourfold between 1500 and 1650. Moreover, marriage policy was carefully contrived to keep these fortunes intact: nobles did not scorn marrying beneath them for money, and intermarriage between cousins, even between nephews and aunts, was occasionally countenanced. In addition, the entailment of property was much more common than in Naples. Younger sons might have only a small inheritance which would return to the elder branch at their death; and this expedient helped preserve the *latifondi* during periods when it might have been profitable to divide them up.

Though agriculture was the source of their wealth, the nobles lacked any practical interest in agriculture. Disdaining an active economic role, they became absentee landlords attracted by the glamour of the court and the comforts of Palermo. Once there, according to a Neapolitan observer in the 1590s, they took on the prevalent affectation of indifference to making money, and preferred to mortgage their estates and hand over management to a new class of *gabelloti*. Anyone who remained on his estates and tried to introduce agricultural innovations risked incurring the disapprobation of his peers. The productivity of the soil thus did not go back into the land; it went into the towns, into the building of palaces and churches, while provincial roads were neglected and the farming community was abandoned to malaria and brigandage.

Title and status were something of an obsession with the aristocracy. Alfonso in the fifteenth century had created the first marquis not of royal blood. By 1621 the number of *titulados* swearing fealty to the new King was over double that of sixty years before. Yet the real acceleration in this process was only just beginning: in the course of the seventeenth century, as the fashion caught on, 102 princedoms were created, and this in a population of about a million. Each baron, as he bought his way up this hierarchy, thought himself obliged to make ever greater expenditures on outward show, even though this almost invariably had to be done on high-interest credit. Each new title acquired would bring with it the need for a more numerous body of retainers.

Though viceroys were pleased to indulge the taste for buying titles and privileges – and we know that there was a deliberate policy to bring the aristocracy to Palermo where they could be kept under supervision – the ruinous predilection for excessive luxury was repeatedly deplored by the government. At least three sumptuary laws date from the sixteenth century. But this was a department of life where legislation had minimal effect. Limitations on ostentatious mourning and on dowry payments would perhaps have been welcomed by the nobility if only they could have been enforced; but no one could be expected to stand voluntarily aside from a code of competitive pomp which had become the outward mark of a man's status in life.

The obsessive striving of the elite for status was a major impediment to social progress. Instead of suggestions for improving the economy or making Sicily more self-reliant, the shocked baronial protests smuggled out to Madrid were more concerned with viceroys who did not treat the *titulados* with sufficient respect, or with commoners who used titles to which they had no right. The grandees begged that the Viceroy should be ordered to address them as 'Excellency', and that ordinary barons should not be given the same consideration as themselves. Several times they tried to establish their own precedence over the prelates in court ceremonial.

PARLIAMENT

Sicilians came to boast that theirs was the only parliament apart from that of England to keep its old liberties. Some of them were even convinced that it dated back to the fifth century before Christ. They cherished it as a symbol of Sicilian nationhood and as an instrument whereby Spain was forced to win local collaboration; nor was this entirely incorrect. Viceroys were recommended to respect parliamentary privileges and knew that there might be trouble if they behaved without consideration or did not study the rule book. However, the importance of this institution should not be exaggerated. Despite what later patriots claimed, it was never in the same league as its English or French counterpart.

By the fifteenth century, the Sicilian parliament had come to consist of fairly regular sessions of three separate 'brazos', or Houses. The first of these was composed of the bishops and abbots, a privileged group, which was not always amenable to pressure. The second was the military, or baronial House, and consisted of the island's leading feudatories. As the king's policy was to indulge the nobility in every matter except political power, this House tended to get off quite lightly, and anyway the landowners could always pass on the tax quota to their tenants. The third House, the domanial, contained representatives from those towns which remained directly subject to the king and were not part of any feudal estate. Its members were frequently selected by the government itself and, at least after the fifteenth century, displayed little political awareness.

In time the domanial *brazo* came to be compared to the House of

Commons in England, but in fact the royal cities never stood together as champions of the third estate; they were more interested in trying to diminish each other and curry favour with the authorities. This lack of solidarity is at first sight surprising, as together the royal towns had to pay as large a quota of the *donativi* as feudal Sicily, which by this time was a far more extensive and populous area. Such an unbalanced tax system did great harm to the economy. It could exist only because, in the domanial as in the baronial House, those who voted a tax were quite unrepresentative of the people who would carry the main burden.

Though Sicilians often claimed that parliament defended their liberties, in fact it seems to have been no more of a restraint on the government than was the Inquisition or indeed the Palermo mob. Although it could advise the Viceroy that the country was too poor to pay as much as he asked, it nearly always granted the sum demanded. The Viceroy could anyway make laws on his own with no reference to parliament, whereas parliamentary petitions were frequently refused or given only qualified approval; often such petitions merely repeated requests of past years which, even when granted, had not been observed in practice. In any case parliament had to agree to taxation long before the King's answer to petitions could arrive from Spain, and this was another reason why money grants were never made conditional on redress of grievances as they were in England.

As government grew, new *donativi* were introduced. Their apportionment was unfair, as the government itself sometimes admitted. Poor people in general, and especially in royal towns, were worst hit. Public protests were on occasion registered against the bishops and against Palermo for tax avoidance. Non-residents sometimes took out nominal citizenship at Palermo solely in order to escape tax on their income elsewhere, just as many people made fictitious charitable gifts to the Church so as to benefit from ecclesiastical immunities. Such were the exemptions, in fact, that the suggestion has been made that they reduced the parliamentary *donativi* to a tenth of what they could or should have been.

One body which helped to create and preserve these exemptions was a committee of parliament copied from the Cortes of Aragon. This 'Deputation' was an executive committee which continued in existence during a parliamentary recess and was in theory meant to guarantee the 'fundamental laws' of the kingdom. This function soon became largely atrophied, and in practice the Deputation became more concerned with protecting the privileged classes rather than maintaining Sicilian liberties or enhancing the prerogatives of parliament. It was also responsible for the collection and allocation of the *donativi*. The duties of the Deputation, however, lay lightly on its members. For two centuries, so ran one complaint, not a single bridge was built or repaired in this land of mountains, valleys and torrential streams, and the tax money collected for bridges simply disappeared in accounts which no one could understand.

CHURCH AND STATE

One reason for the placid acceptance of Spanish rule was that Sicilian churchmen were in general submissive and dependent on the crown. Although subsequent popes whittled down Pope Urban's grant of legatine powers to the rulers of Sicily, and on occasion claimed the island as a papal fief, it was the King's pretensions to ecclesiastical authority which generally prevailed. The appointment of bishops was in effect a royal prerogative; Church affairs in general were supervised by a government department; and the Inquisition looked to Madrid and not Rome for its authority. This remoteness of papal authority was one reason why the Church in Sicily was in some ways lethargic, and why so many clergy, for example, were married. It also helps to explain the lack of a special kind of stimulus and conflict which elsewhere contributed to the development of a more sophisticated political system.

Inevitably there were some instances of friction between Church and State. At least three times in the first half of the sixteenth century riots took place against the Inquisition; twice Sicilian rebels were sheltered by the Pope, and more than one viceroy was excommunicated. Pope Paul IV attacked Philip II as a heretic and a 'drain full of filth', and once 'confiscated' Sicily and awarded it to the Venetians. But Philip, for all his piety, resolutely maintained his inherited rights over 'the Sicilian Church'. Most popes, after all, needed Spanish political help too much to question the King's pretensions, and Rome needed Sicily's wheat, which friendly viceroys sent on specially advantageous terms.

Royal control over the Church was made easier by the fact that the more important ecclesiastical posts were not only in the King's gift but were regularly, and for practical reasons, bestowed by him on foreigners. For many centuries it seems that no native-born Sicilian held the archbishoprics of Monreale or Palermo. Naturally there were complaints at this, and not only from frustrated careerists. Foreign clergy, despite many royal promises, were often non-resident; and, quite apart from any religious disadvantages, this resulted in a substantial drain of agricultural earnings overseas. It also meant that the senior member of parliament and some of his episcopal colleagues were shadowy characters who had little interest in Sicilian affairs but a great need for royal patronage. One further consequence was that there was little contact between rich and poor clergy, since so many of the rich were regularly resident elsewhere; and this gap eventually had important social and political results.

The Inquisition was an additional means by which the Church was harnessed to the State; and it became another buttress in the elaborate edifice of checks and balances. The Inquisitors were directly responsible to the King who appointed them, and were sometimes used by him to counteract the Viceroy. There were some disadvantages, however. People at every level of society, but especially the higher aristocracy, attached themselves to the Inquisition as lay familiars; and, among other privileges, they could then claim immunity from the ordinary courts even in cases of murder. Viceroys protested that under cover of belonging to the Inquisition the nobles were arming bands of delinquents who could then break the law with impunity.

From the King's point of view this authoritarian organization, with its secret and even terroristic methods, was very useful in that it helped him to maintain religious and political orthodoxy. It was an ancillary spy system, and its separate police force and prisons were a means of inculcating fear and submissiveness. In a country where the King could afford only a small military establishment but where fear was an essential ingredient of political power, this was a cheap instrument by which he could recruit Sicilians themselves to keep other Sicilians in subjection.

Sicily was a frontier territory very close to areas of spiritual infection in North Africa and the Near East. The fanatical excitement of the Counter-Reformation encouraged the Inquisition to persecute not only the various protestant heresies – which had made their mark at Messina in particular – but even those Jews and Moslems who were converts to Christianity. By trying to eliminate heresy, the Inquisition was helping to attack a dangerous source of independent and sometime revolutionary thought in politics as well as religion. Along with Jesuit control of education, this contributed to keeping Sicily orthodox and obedient. Barely a glimmering of the 'scientific revolution' was allowed to penetrate.

Only this fierce regard for moral and religious orthodoxy could have made successive kings overlook the manifest abuses of the system and allow the Inquisition such power. The Holy Office became extremely rich through benefactions, but especially because it confiscated the possessions of any victim. Such confiscations were, of course, a strong incentive to zealous persecution, and people complained that not even tradesmen who were owed money by a heretic could collect once the Inquisition had marked him for their own. Informers, on the other hand, might obtain one-tenth of the proceeds of any successful prosecution, and, since the anonymity of informers was kept, many people must have found this an effective and profitable means of paying off private scores.

The Viceroy sometimes reached the point of complaining that Inquisitors used their position for personal financial profit and spent too little time on matters of faith. Certainly their wealth was considerable, a fact which facilitated the recruitment of laymen as assistants or familiars. Ferdinand in 1510 had said that there should not be more than twenty of these lay officials in each large city, but in 1577 the Viceroy put their number at over twenty thousand and it was still growing. Obviously far too many people were financially interested in an institution which, once it had got rid of Jews, Moslems and heretics, spent a good deal of time feathering its nest and undermining the Viceroy's authority.

By the 1590s, after a succession of ugly brawls, the King at last realised this. Henceforward the Inquisition's jurisdiction was not to apply to barons. Tax collectors and those who owed money to the state were also excluded, as indeed was anyone involved in public business. The new ruling also covered homicides and cases 'which concern the public good'. Even higher officials of the Holy Office could no longer be protected from the royal courts if they were themselves accused of homosexuality. From this moment onwards the Inquisition played only a minor role in religion and politics.

DISORDER AND BRIGANDAGE

Sicily shared with the rest of Europe the social upsets associated with a long period of currency depreciation and increased prices. Inflation at the end of the fifteenth century was such that Constantine Lascaris, who in 1467 had become teacher of Greek to the Basilian monks of Messina, complained twenty-five years later that the value of his salary had depreciated by a third. The most obvious effect of this inflation on public life was the increasing inadequacy of ordinary tax revenue. Another was the growth of vagabondage. In the worst years many country dwellers were forced into the towns to find food and work, and this caused a problem of urban over-population and a lack of labour on the farms.

Brigandage too seemed to be on the increase, and much began to be heard of it in official reports. Though common all over Europe, the Spanish governors thought it especially characteristic of Sicily, where in many inland areas neither royal nor feudal justice had normally penetrated. Here individual family communities had for centuries tried to maintain their own laws and way of life. The bandits were often no more than these rough mountain dwellers, people who were perhaps descended from the fugitives of some distant invasion; or they may have been shepherds from the hill country who began to clash with the settled agriculturalists of the valleys as increased population meant more arable land and so less winter pasturage in the lowlands.

The life of a predator on society had always possessed certain attractions, and not only for these outlaws of the interior. When a bad harvest meant no food and no money with which to pay taxes, some farmers retreated seasonally into the penumbra of the *maquis*. Since Spanish-speaking officials had virtually no point of contact with the peasantry, and since the legal system was obviously *ex parte*, there were many people ready to develop a counter system of morals and politics. When a baron invoked the hunting laws to exclude shepherds and others from land which he had illegally enclosed, he generated a fierce if usually underground resistance. This is one way in which the notion gained acceptance that to cheat and steal successfully made one worthy of respect and admiration.

The detailed incidence of brigandage is hard to document, but some known examples in the sixteenth century suggest that a pattern familiar in later centuries was already well established. The gang of Agnello in the 1560s had its own flag with a death's head, as well as pipes and drums like the King's army; it was well armed, and could operate right up to the walls of Palermo. Rival delinquents working in Agnello's area without his permission did so at their peril. He could rely on people to tell him of police movements, and no doubt it was for this reason that he saw the propaganda value of giving to the poor as well as terrorizing them; but clearly it was not only the humble who assisted him. The bandit Saponara, who was caught in 1578, died of poison when in solitary confinement, and the authorities were not even very surprised, for they knew that highly placed individuals feared what he might disclose under torture.

One element in brigandage was the revolt of the poor against the rich. Another was the very reverse, when barons gave shelter and protection to bandits in return for their help in keeping the local peasantry at bay. Yet another was aristocratic feuding. Three generations of the di Luna and Perollo families contended for power at Sciacca, supported by private armies of cutthroats and retinues of slaves. In Palermo, where nobles could hire assassins to kill in broad daylight, there were pitched battles in public thoroughfares. The courts were always reluctant to take action where barons were involved, and the government was even asked by parliament to reduce the penalties on nobles who sheltered bandits, on the plea that any landowner risked terrible reprisals if he refused such shelter.

Though strong government action was inhibited by the unwritten compact between rulers and nobles on which Spanish administration depended, honest attempts were made to enforce the law. Malefactors who ran away from justice were declared *banditi*. After another year of evasion they became *fuorusciti*, or outlaws, and could be killed by anyone. A third class was merely kept under surveillance: these were the *relegati*, turbulent characters who took care not to be caught *in flagrante*. They must often have been not so much perpetrators of crime as local bosses. The Viceroy Gonzaga tried the remedy of forcing people in this latter group to live in special places remote from their homes: but the outcry was such that he had to desist, stating that he would never in future use such severity with mere crimes of 'honour'.

More successful was the offer of pardon to any bandit who turned King's evidence: *omertà*, the honour among thieves upon which the underworld relied, was a code in large measure forced on the humble and innocent by the guilty. This made it very hard for the authorities to gather any evidence. Accordingly, the government stipulated that anyone who betrayed a known murderer could obtain not only his freedom but also the highly profitable right to reprieve other criminals as well. Many of the leading bandits in Sicilian history were eventually caught by these means. However, in a society that often regarded false testimony as a legitimate instrument of social and political struggle, the use of informers was bound to be dangerous.

The official Captains at Arms had a mounted force of police to apprehend bandits; and it was found that compelling these policemen to compensate any victims of theft was an effective way of preventing crime and discovering culprits. The nobility objected that the Captains were altogether too intrusive and efficient in doing their job; and without doubt police powers of summary justice must often have been abused. Nevertheless, as the Messinese once informed the King, making secret agreements with a brigand might in practice be the best way for the government to keep crime within bounds. It might even be worth turning a blind eye if the police used their office to take revenge on personal enemies. Rough and ready law enforcement was better than no law enforcement at all, and there were no means of making policemen popular with people who either wanted their jobs or feared their efficiency.

PIRACY AND DEFENCE

The King was mainly interested in Sicily for the help which the local population could give towards Habsburg policy in Europe and the Mediterranean. In 1519 Charles V became Emperor as well as King, and he inherited interests which stretched from Africa to the Baltic, and soon as far as Mexico and Peru. Spain had to fight for long periods against the Turks and

France; and there were shorter campaigns against Germans, Dutch, English, Portuguese and even the papacy. Sicily had no obvious interest in these wars with the exception of that against the Turks; yet she was forced to contribute towards them with huge quantities of bullion and tax-free wheat. In the end even viceroys protested that the country could pay no more.

This military contribution was chiefly needed against the Ottoman Turks, who had annexed Greece and the Balkans and were busy occupying the North African coast. Sicily had once thrived on its African connections, but now found itself caught in the firing line between Christendom and Islam. Ferdinand and Charles used the island as a base from which to establish garrisons along the African coast; and the expense of successive expeditions, as well as payment of the garrisons, fell to a considerable extent on the Sicilian exchequer. This was debilitating enough, but Sicily also had to endure frequent retaliatory raids by the Ottomans. It was little compensation to be referred to as a bulwark of Christendom in the Mediterranean, especially in the light of the awkward fact that Christian France was fighting alongside the Turks against Spain.

By the 1580s Philip had decided to cut his losses and partially to withdraw from the Mediterranean. The decline of Spain had begun. Sicily was now more exposed than ever, and raids on her coast inevitably became more frequent once the navy and the Spanish garrisons had departed. The so-called Barbary 'pirates' proved particularly destructive, and in thirty years over eighty attacks were recorded. These predators, who were often of Christian origin, came in search largely of slaves and food, and no farmhouse within ten miles of the sea was safe. For the next two centuries they were to do great damage to external and even internal trade.

The extent of piracy and privateering, as of internal brigandage, were expressions of Spain's very limited commitment in Sicily as well as the island's inability to contribute much to its own defence. Here was one reason why Messina and Palermo could not compete commercially with northern cities. A siege mentality led to defence expenditure which, even though ineffective, was a hindrance to economic growth. Furthermore, the external challenge did not have the beneficial effect of creating a community sense, a feeling of cooperation in active resistance. Those in danger preferred flight to the interior; and though pious citizens created a charitable fund to buy slaves back from North Africa, there was insufficient communal confidence for the organization of a positive and collective military response.

Sicily was not easily defended; but the Spaniards did what they could afford. Ferramolino of Bergamo, one of the foremost military engineers of the time, was employed to make a thorough survey and build new fortifications in the years after 1535. Large bastions and ditches were constructed in Palermo, and houses and trees were destroyed all round the city to eliminate possible cover for an enemy. At Syracuse the ancient Greek monuments were used as quarries to strengthen Frederick II's fortress of Maniace against artillery, while the Viceroy Gonzaga aimed to build or refurbish a hundred watch towers to warn against attack. Unfortunately this project was hampered by the lack of corporate responsibility: some of these towers were never built at all, others soon fell into disrepair. A more bullying attitude by Spain might not have come amiss.

CHAPTER 11

The economy 1500–1650

ECONOMIC POLICY AND THE REVENUE

Spain both helped and hindered the expansion of the Sicilian economy, but how far it did so and in what directions are questions not easily settled. Nor is it possible to be confident when tracing the fluctuations of growth in different fields. Despite many appearances of decline, one foreign observer in the 1550s described Sicily as the richest of Spain's Italian possessions, and late in the sixteenth century a Viceroy reported that it was flourishing as never before. This must have been either a deliberate falsehood to comfort or deceive the King, or else a mistake by someone familiar only with the subtropical coastline, for the revenue of Sicily was only half that of Naples or Milan.

Sicilian aristocrats notoriously wore fine clothes, but this was not necessarily a sign of economic health. Not every visitor could observe that the nobles were heavily in debt and that this expenditure on foreign luxuries was both a burden on the balance of payments and a loss to productive investment in Sicily itself. It took time before people could make a pattern out of such tell-tale signs as emergency food imports, a regular shortfall in tax revenue, and special measures to relieve poverty; but the indications became increasingly clear after 1535. In a bad year, a Viceroy wrote in 1578, 'there are few kingdoms poorer than this one'.

When things went wrong, one explanation in retrospect was to blame Spanish misgovernment. Even though Sicily escaped the trade monopoly practised in Spain's New World dominions, this was still colonial rule of a kind: commodities were exported raw, navigation was run by foreigners, and agriculture was made to serve imperial policy. Some Sicilians undoubtedly gained from the commercial connection with Spain, yet others lost because Spanish interests caused a decline of trade with Africa and the East, and the result was a shortage of precious metals and a barrier to capital accumulation. But not everything was Spain's fault; and if this plausible alibi had not existed, Sicilians might have had to consider more fundamental factors in the island's economic backwardness, such as land distribution, tax allocation and social inequality.

Taxation was, of course, the chief complaint against the government, but how much was actually collected and how much sent to Spain can only be guessed. Certainly there was often a serious lack of coin, and though much of this can be explained by the import of foreign luxuries, legitimate and smuggled, or by the profit to foreign shipowners, a good deal must surely be ascribed to direct or indirect payments to Spain. One set of figures from the 1590s shows that, quite apart from a good third of Sicily's total revenue being earmarked for defence, another fifth went for emergency expenditure 'on His Majesty's service'.

The sixteenth century brought a crisis in government finance everywhere in Europe; but Sicily had in addition special problems of her own, particularly after Gonzaga's expenditure on rearmament in the 1530s. 'The ordinary income of the government does not cover even basic everyday expenditure,' reported the Viceroy bluntly in 1546. As administration became increasingly complicated, and wars more frequent and expensive, the budget was completely unbalanced; and on one occasion under Charles V, more had to be borrowed in a single year than parliament was willing to grant over three.

One particular problem for the government was that the fiscal system was growing impossibly complex. Taxes varied from place to place and from year to year, and they were collected in many different ways. The dozen or more *donativi*, taken together, were the Viceroy's main standby. Customs and trade taxes were usually the second largest item, followed by the crusade tax. But viceroys frequently complained of the slackness and corruption of Treasury officials and of the many mistakes made over payments. Often it was convenient for a tax to be capitalized by the government, with a lump figure being accepted from a professional tax collector who was then allowed to recoup the sum or improve on it as best he could.

Where public finance bore most heavily on economic life was over the taxation of exports – wine, cheese, meat, silk, but above all cereals. The *tratte* (*ius tractae*) were licences which had to be purchased before selling grain overseas. They could be very remunerative in years of abundance so long as outside demand was maintained; and they had a great advantage in that they could easily be collected at the storage pits or *caricatoi* to which landowners were obliged to bring surplus produce. The government incidentally obtained a bonus of about 2 per cent of these deposits, being the average amount by which humidity expanded the grain between deposit and sale.

Feeding the growing cities was a particular headache to the authorities in the sixteenth century. One emergency remedy for shortages was to place an embargo on exports. Alternatively overseas sales could be discouraged by imposing an additional export tax if wheat prices ever exceeded a certain limit. The government, however, had other interests to consider besides those of the Sicilian consumer. *Tratte* produced revenue, and too many were sometimes sold, with disastrous results. Furthermore, favoured foreigners, including the Pope, were allowed to export wheat without paying duty or observing embargoes. The result was occasional famine, an excessive increase in the cost of living, and riots.

From 1515 onwards there were parliamentary protests that increasing export duties were making wheat less profitable to grow. One result was a great increase in the smuggling of cereals out of the country; and this alone may have saved Sicilian agriculture. More controls were then applied, until smuggling reached the point of being deemed as severe an offence as heresy or treason. Desperate orders were issued to the effect that not even the grower himself should consume his own wheat until it had been declared. But this did not work. In 1541 the Viceroy had to tell Charles V that 'the greater part of this kingdom is dying of hunger'.

Unfortunately the authorities could diagnose only part of the malady; and they had no effective solution to suggest. All over the Mediterranean there was now a pattern of irregular and sometimes insufficient harvests, but in Sicily conditions were made especially bad by the lucrative and easily collected export tax which the King was understandably reluctant to forgo. The Viceroy Gonzaga eventually advised reduction of this tax as the only way to restore commerce and increase revenue, but the King overruled his advice. Such a policy was particularly short-sighted, given that cheap food was a basic necessity for the smooth working of the Spanish administration.

In general the standard of life must have fallen since the later Middle Ages. Food was becoming increasingly expensive; and perhaps there were already more mouths to be fed. This was a world in which hunger riots were never far away, where in the grim months before the harvest people might attack the storage pits, and where emergency bread rationing was often necessary. To economize on wheat flour, the Viceroy tried ordering that fashionable gentlemen should not use starch for their cuffs and collars. Such measures were clearly not the answer. But any more fundamental solution was beyond both the economists and the civil servants.

CHANGES IN AGRICULTURE

Everything in Sicily in the last resort refers back to agriculture, for this sector supplied the raw material for whatever commerce and industry existed. It furnished most of the taxes and far the greater proportion of all personal incomes. It was a factor in foreign policy, as well as providing the basic cause of every political revolt for centuries. The fundamental problem facing governments was how to procure adequate tax revenue and yet encourage wheat growing. The two were not easily reconciled. The export levy on wheat was increased in the sixteenth century, which raised prices and discouraged production; and in 1564 the *macinato* was introduced. This was a tax on the grinding of flour, which was easy to collect and difficult to avoid, and which for three centuries was to prove a grave burden on agriculture and the standard of living.

In the early sixteenth century, Sicily perhaps exported two million bushels of wheat in a good year, and possibly as much again through smuggling. She still had some claim to be what Braudel called the Argentina of Europe. But the increased taxation, together with a growing city population and the cropping of marginal lands, posed a challenge which was too difficult. In northern Europe, the stimulus of increasing population and land shortage eventually led to the discovery of improved methods of agriculture and crop rotation, but in Sicily there were too many physical and social obstacles to overcome.

The cereal areas of Sicily were hot, dry and had a heavy clay soil; hard wheat grew here quite easily, but higher-yielding varieties and more profitable crops would have called for new methods, more labour, and heavier monetary investment. Part of the trouble, so people said, was that rich Sicilians were too rich to have much incentive for the changes which would have been required; or, at least, social custom was against it. Landowners found it socially more acceptable to buy new estates than to improve old ones; for land meant prestige as well as being a hedge against inflation, whereas improvements would have needed thought, work and money, and still would have been difficult to carry out.

The peasants were therefore left to cultivate the land as they always had. Using the most primitive tools, they were accustomed to exploit one area to the point of exhaustion and then move elsewhere. The traditional simple rotation of wheat and fallow resulted in land still being idle every other year, or even two years in three, and the lack of an alternative crop not only brought all the disadvantages of monoculture but meant a gradual lowering of the yield per acre. Moreover, the climate was probably changing, becoming drier and more extreme than it had been in Arab and Norman Sicily. This, along with more predatory methods of agriculture, would help to explain why in the sixteenth century some springs and water courses failed.

Two successive years of bad weather could suddenly throw the whole economy into disarray. High wheat prices would occasionally encourage farmers to plough up soil and woodland, but then a temporary glut would reverse the process, except that goats and erosion prevented the trees from growing again, and the hillsides were left denuded. At the same time a trend towards *métayage*, or share-cropping, discouraged improvements just because neither landowners nor labourers were anxious to invest in the land so long as the other party received half of the proceeds from any unilateral investment. Moreover, this kind of contract could drive a tenant into permanent debt if one bad harvest left him with no margin in reserve.

Agricultural improvements depended only to a small extent on government action. It was easier to legislate against usurious loans than to stop them, easier to penalize cattle thieves than to enforce the penalties. The Viceroy in 1601 did make an attempt to standardize the many different systems of weights and measures which hamstrung inter-village commerce; but it was thought enough just to issue a decree without setting up precise master measures, and in any case there was tremendous and effective opposition to such a revolutionary step. Messina, for instance, could not have endured to change its measurements and adopt those current at Palermo.

Likewise any improvement in communications would have required more local cooperation than was conceivable. The fact that all wheat had to be carried to the ports on muleback helps to explain why other countries increasingly found Sicilian produce too expensive. Far from getting better, it looked as if communications became slower in the course of the sixteenth century. Even the main Palermo–Messina road was dangerous and sometimes impassable, and hence this journey was usually made by sea. One outside observer was surprised to find that the inhabitants of Messina hardly ever ventured into the interior more than a few miles outside the city-gates.

Sicily must have remained well wooded throughout the Middle Ages, but by the mid-sixteenth century deafforestation was showing its usual effects. As the soil dried out, avalanches occurred that occasionally cut off villages or even buried them. Soil erosion gradually began to upset water control, changing the course of rivers and creating regular annual floods. Fertile valleys were being crippled by the spread of marshlands and malaria; and this fact, together with the insecurity caused by brigands and pirate raids, resulted in cultivators being pushed further up the hillsides where steep inclines made the cycle of soil erosion still more severe. Rivers which had once provided irrigation now disappeared for most of the year; in the wet season they became torrents which carried away bridges, destroyed mills and houses, and sometimes broke down city walls and devastated whole areas of Palermo and Messina.

The increasing severity of the environment may well have been a factor in the decline of sugar cane production. About 1410 there had been thirty refineries in Palermo alone, and at Syracuse there was a 'gate of the sugar makers'. The subsequent demise of this trade meant a serious loss of foreign exchange. In addition to climate, several other factors seem to have been at work. Wood fuel became exhausted near the refineries and it would have been too expensive to bring by mule back from more than a few miles away. Perhaps irrigation and water power became too scarce. Clearly production had also become inefficient. This was the kind of industry that needed constant investment, and there was always the temptation to go for immediate profits at the expense of assets. By 1610 it was occasionally cheaper to export the raw sugar and then re-import it once refined.

INDUSTRY AND URBANIZATION

During the Middle Ages, wool, cotton and silk had all been cultivated in Sicily; but it was always hard to create a flourishing textile industry, and by the sixteenth century there were marked signs of decadence. The basic problem was that local money and labour shied away from industrial enterprise. Sicilian wool was probably not good enough for fine cloth, but domestically grown cotton was of adequate quality and yet continued to go overseas for manufacture. Much the same happened to silk. Perhaps silk weaving never recovered from the exodus of Arab workers in the twelfth and thirteenth centuries and of the Jews after 1492. At all events, 90 per cent of Sicilian silk was exported raw.

The government may have been partly to blame for this state of affairs. Some people accused it of deliberately discouraging higher quality textiles that might rival Catalan cloth. Better founded were criticisms of the government's financial policy which taxed manufacture more heavily than exported raw material. But such obstacles were less important than the absence of a true entrepreneurial mentality, or indeed local rivalries: when the duty on exported silk was sharply increased in 1562, Messina resisted this as discriminatory, but then bought a privilege at enormous expense forcing the silk exporters of eastern Sicily to use this one port only. Such restrictionism was bound to harm the industry. The Messina merchants were more concerned with injuring their competitors in Palermo and Catania than improving their own efficiency.

Another important reason for the absence of industrial growth was the large number of landed proprietors in the big towns. This was particularly the case with Palermo, a city that was expanding fast in the sixteenth century. The rich were moving there partly to escape the rigours of rural life, but also to get closer to the Viceroy and obtain favours, pensions and titles. Furthermore, exemption from the census made residence in Palermo a useful means of tax avoidance. As a result, the territorial aristocracy were, except for very brief periods, in undisputed control of the city and its finances. The resulting environment was unfavourable to economic development. Palermo was a parasite town that consumed much of the revenue of the island and yet despised the country districts which made its luxurious living possible.

The drift of the nobility from the land was accompanied by that of the peasantry. This has been variously explained as a flight from brigandage, from feudalism, or from enclosures of land by the baronage. One result was the formation of an urban proletariat in Palermo, and already in the sixteenth century some Viceroys were expressing their horror at the growth of slum conditions. The shopkeeper and artisan classes were also growing. For some time they had been organised in guilds or *maestranze*; there had been more than forty of them as early as 1385. Each was presided over by a consul, and they supervised and laid down standards for each industry, excluding competition, and regulating the admission of apprentices.

As Palermo grew, so the Viceroys took pains to embellish the city. Two of the finest streets in Europe, the via Toledo and the via Maqueda, date from the second half of the sixteenth century. This urban development destroyed much of the mediaeval city and caused considerable displacement. So too did the fact that the several hundred aristocratic families who now converged on Palermo needed room for their *palazzi*. In the interests of security, building was forbidden for half a mile outside the city walls, but the shanty towns in the suburbs were growing faster than problems of overcrowding could be solved. The flight from the countryside soon created a fertile seedbed for plague and revolution.

The expansion of Palermo, and also its great rival Messina, was accompanied by a remarkable development of new towns and villages. One element in this was the arrival of immigrant labour from overseas. In the course of its history Sicily had absorbed many foreign peoples, and the latest were Greeks and Albanians fleeing from the Turkish occupation of the Balkans. Landowners and government alike, recognizing their usefulness as farmers, helped establish these newcomers on uncleared territory. Of seven main villages created by them, the largest was Piana dei Greci which was settled by Albanians in the sixteenth century. These immigrants were mostly Catholics of the Greek rite, and they kept their own priests. Right down to the twentieth century they retained a distinct identity, with their own language, folklore and fashions of dress.

In creating these new settlements, the Albanians gave an impetus to a movement which by 1600 was changing the face of the countryside. Normans, Hohenstaufen and Angevins had all founded new villages in Sicily, and the leading barons followed suit. The Chiaramonte, for instance, had built Mussomeli and Siculiana, and held out inducements to encourage settlers to populate these deserted areas. At least nine new communities were founded in the course of the fifteenth century, and over the next two hundred years about 150 more were established, almost doubling the number of village settlements previously in existence.

One probable reason for this remarkable process was a growth of population which increased the demand for food and so encouraged enterprising landlords to plough up virgin land. Another factor was inflation and the growing need of the barons for money. Founding villages was an obvious solution, as with little expense indebted landowners were able to improve their estates and increase their income. Since the large *latifondi* were sparsely inhabited and thinly cultivated, a landlord who wanted to meet the cost of city life would divide parts of his estates into smaller farms on attractive long-term leaseholds which would appeal to tenant farmers.

The foundation of new villages simultaneously conferred on the baronage prestige and the illusion or reality of power. Social status among the magnates was largely measured by the extent of their territory and the number of townships where they held powers of life and death. There was prestige for the Tomasi family in obtaining the barren island of Lampedusa, and for Requesens in colonizing Pantelleria. Founding a village with more than eighty families usually brought with it a seat in the baronial house of parliament, or an extra vote if its owner already possessed this privilege. In this way the parliamentary barons increased from 72 in 1556 to 277 by 1810, while the other two Houses of parliament remained barely altered. Yet some of these prestige hamlets never grew large enough to carry the expense of public administration and eventually ceased to exist.

ECONOMIC DIFFICULTIES AFTER 1600

The reign of Philip III (1598–1621) was a time of exceptional economic difficulty. New trade routes were being developed elsewhere in competition with those of the Mediterranean, and all over Europe there were continued problems of currency depreciation and government revenue. Prices were rising because of American silver and an expanding population; yet Sicilian trade was simultaneously inconvenienced by a shortage of money. What had once seemed to be a favourable balance of payments was threatened by increasing foreign competition to Sicilian wheat exports and also by excessive spending overseas on the part of public authorities and private citizens alike.

The vicissitudes of trade and currency were compounded by the effects of bubonic plague. The rapid urbanization of Messina and Palermo had made these two cities particularly vulnerable, and in one bad outbreak in 1575 half the population of Messina is reported to have been killed. Another serious infection occurred in 1624, and the whole life of Palermo was brought to a halt. Many people died, including the Viceroy himself; general traffic ceased; so too did wheat exports and the collection of taxes. It was only when the bones of St Rosalia were miraculously discovered in a grotto near the city that the plague abated. St Rosalia was rewarded by being made chief patroness of Palermo, and the annual festivities in her honour henceforward became the greatest event in the city's social calendar.

Though plague obviously had a serious effect on the economy, it was slight compared to the impact of the Thirty Years War which broke out in 1618. Sicily was naturally required to help the Habsburg cause, and complaints soon arose that the country was being exhausted in the service of Spain. The fiscal demands from the government were certainly huge. Sicily had to send 70,000 *scudi* a year to help the Emperor in Hungary, and in 1620–1 the enormous sum of a million *scudi* was allocated for expenses in Germany. Soldiers and galleys regularly went, at Sicilian expense, to fight against the enemies of Spain, and vast amounts of food furnished the Habsburg armies in Lombardy and Alsace.

Such demands, far from diminishing, increased as the prospect of defeat began to loom. Parliaments had occasionally to be called twice in the same year; in 1639, extra stamp duties were placed on official documents and a 2 per cent on leases and contracts of sale. But at this point there was a concerted opposition from rich people, lawyers and clergy, so that these particular taxes had to be withdrawn. The government was getting desperate. Pardon for all crimes except treason was put up for sale on a sliding scale varying with a man's income. But finally the Viceroy reported that no more revenue could be found. Commerce was at a standstill, and the normal taxes were yielding less and less. At last even parliament was emboldened to say that further demands could hardly be met.

Yet despite the fact that many aristocratic families were undeniably living well beyond their means, it is evident that some people still had plenty of money. More and more the towns were forced to pay their taxes by borrowing, but at least there were people to borrow from. Notwithstanding all the complaints of poverty, this was a century of grandiose civic buildings, baroque palaces, and churches. It was a period when scores of new villages were built. Though lack of capital was restricting economic development, more accurately it could be said that what was really lacking was not so much actual money as the habit of profitable investment, and clearly some Sicilians were far richer than the tax collectors were ever allowed to know.

CHAPTER 12

The disintegration of Spanish Sicily

THE PALERMO REVOLT OF 1647

In Sicily, as in many other parts of Europe, the last decade of the Thirty Years War was a time of acute unrest. This was due less to any sense of political injustice than to social upheaval and economic distress. Too much money had been sent overseas to pay for the war. At home, after 1630, there had been cuts in public works and in expenditure on the police: the Viceroy noted with astonishment that once again it was unsafe to travel anywhere without twenty or more companions as an escort. And in 1641 the English ambassador secretly informed Spain that certain Sicilians, with French help, were plotting to win independence. Others were said to be negotiating with the Turks.

Administrative and political grievances certainly existed, but it was not these that would cause revolution. Hunger was the real problem. Two bad wheat harvests in succession were the danger sign, especially as the available storage capacity was not keeping pace with the growth in population. By 1647 the situation was drastic. In February of that year, heavy rains rotted the seed, and sowing had to be done again; but few peasants can have had any seed to spare. A savage drought then occurred in March and April, and, fearing requisition, many growers hid their remaining stocks. In the countryside there was sometimes nothing to eat except wild plants. In the towns there were beggars by the thousand sleeping in the open; disease began to spread, and dozens died of starvation each day.

When finally, in May, the bread ration could no longer be maintained, a procession marched on the cathedral, and a loaf stuck on a pole was thrust insultingly at the image of Christ on the altar. There were shouts of 'Long live the King and down with taxes and bad government'. As church bells summoned people onto the streets, the Viceroy shouted from a palace window that he would lift the food taxes; but the City Hall was already alight, the prisons were being opened and the excise offices demolished. The terrified Archbishop armed his clergy. Some aristocrats tried throwing money to the mob, but most fled to their country estates, so causing additional unemployment and leaving the forces of order leaderless.

This riot was the work of the very poor, and was perhaps instigated by petty criminals. If there was any acknowledged leader it was the escaped convict and murderer, La Pilosa, who seems to have linked the Palermo underworld with that of the surrounding villages. The government and the well-to-do were powerless against such a spontaneous movement, and when the rising was eventually defeated, it was by the artisan guilds of Palermo which represented the privileged working class. These *maestranze* may have included as many as a quarter of the working population. Their members tended to live close to one another in crowded areas in the town, and were usually a law unto themselves. Often no doubt they resented the patrician administration of the city, but most of them depended on the aristocracy for employment and had good reason to fear mob rule; nor had they any country estates to which they might escape.

There is little evidence that the revolutionaries thought of appealing to a nationwide revolt. Some towns remained quiet throughout the rising; they may have had more grain stocks or been less torn by social divisions than Palermo. Far from feeling a common nationality and opposition to Spain, some of them opposed the revolution or treated it as an occasion for private gain. The citizens of Catania seized the opportunity to annex land which they claimed that the crown had wrongfully taken. Messina, faced with social troubles of her own, curried favour with the Viceroy by giving him money and soldiers to put down the Palermo revolt and offering to house him and his court.

Though the insurrection of 1647 understandably caused panic, there was never much danger to Spain. No support came from overseas, and the popular leaders were more concerned with specific grievances than with general political goals. The divisions inside Sicily, geographical and social, went far deeper than any presumed national solidarity, and in the end the revolt was put down largely by Sicilian action. A decisive fact was that the *maestranze*, though possessed of some collective feeling and political sense, were divided; and they were also frightened of losing their own few privileges. Once they agreed to act as a police force against the populace, they destroyed their only leverage on the government.

By September the revolution was over. The city welcomed the Spanish troops back with enthusiasm. The Archbishop of Monreale absolved the people from the sin of revolution and publicly exorcized the demons and witches that had caused them to rebel. To economize on food, everyone who was unemployed or who had lived for less than ten years in Palermo had to depart at once on pain of death; all wheat stocks had to be declared, and rewards were promised to anyone who gave information about concealed supplies. In puritanical reaction against the general laxness associated with the revolution, all gaming was prohibited *sub poena triremium*, and masks were forbidden lest they should become a cover for further misbehaviour.

For all the violence of the revolt, the fundamental inertia and submissiveness of Sicilian society won through; and the established order was restored as if nothing had happened. Since the rising had been against the Sicilian rich rather than against Spain, the nobility were obviously grateful that the King had prevailed and that any promises of constitutional and economic reform had not been seriously intended. The new Viceroy, Cardinal Trivulzio, agreed to let the nobles bring their hired bands into Palermo to garrison the bastions, for it was important to end the existing dependence on the artisan guilds. The popular representatives in the city senates of Palermo and Catania – 'the Greeks call this democracy but I call it government by demons', said one ecclesiastic – did not last for long: it was felt they demeaned the glorious title of senator.

The tax system was also readjusted in favour of the patrician classes. Even the *maestranze* joined in requesting the restoration of the excise duties on food, because the suspension of interest payments on civic loans was causing unemployment. All that Trivulzio could do was to try to insist that the *octrois* be more moderate than before and subject to fewer privileged exemptions. At the same time the rate of interest payments was reduced, to 4 per cent for Palermitans and 3 per cent for foreigners; but, in compensation for their loss of income, the restored *octrois* were to be supervised by nobles and clerics chosen from among the loan-holders.

THE REBELLION OF MESSINA 1674–8

Ten viceroys ruled Sicily in the twenty-five years that followed the Palermo revolt. Constitutional and social issues receded and government again confined itself to little more than the basic questions of supply and revenue. Food shortage became of paramount concern, as the great variety of regulations designed to deal with such an eventuality suggests. During a serious scare, for example, citizens of Palermo had to carry identity cards in order to exclude aliens from the bread queues; litigants got special permission to enter the town, but only if they brought their own food – everyone else was liable to be excluded; and police were sent to ferret out stocks of wheat in the countryside.

Palermo was not the only city to have such problems. Messina, too, was volatile. She had been glad to help Spain put down revolutions at Palermo and Naples in 1647, but her loyalty was conditional on being treated almost as an independent state. The city was now administered by senators elected on a very narrow franchise. The King's powers were exercised by the *strategoto*, who was often a Spanish nobleman; but as a rule he did not interfere too much. Enhanced independence, however, did not lead to sustained prosperity. Exports from Messina started to decline; so did her civic revenue. The silk workers began to emigrate, and by the 1660s the city's population, which had reached about 120,000 early in the century, was falling.

There were a number of reasons for this economic malaise. One was the development of a government-sponsored silk trade in France that robbed Messina of business. Another was the increasing exclusivity of the city's ruling oligarchy, and the accompanying temptation for this narrow group to use the city finances to bolster its supremacy. This intensified the conflict of interest between the nobles and the ordinary people. The oligarchy spent ever larger sums on preserving the city's silk monopoly in the face of protestations and counterclaims by Palermo and other Sicilian towns, and it was the poor of Messina who effectively paid.

A succession of bad harvests after 1671 finally brought matters to a head. People began to die of starvation, riots broke out, and strict food rationing had to be imposed. The *strategoto* blamed the crisis on the speculative profiteering of the rich and tried to restore social peace by enlarging the franchise and giving the nobility only half the seats on the city council. They replied by attacking him for class prejudice. He was even accused of deliberately provoking the riots as an excuse for diminishing the city's privileges. To tide over the crisis the Viceroy suspended the *strategoto*, but the city was also asked to surrender some of its more extravagant pretensions.

In 1674 revolution broke out at Messina. Unlike the Palermo movement of 1647, this was not essentially a hunger rebellion of the poor: prices, indeed, seem to have been steady, and the food shortage had become less acute. This was a revolution by rich people clinging to what they regarded as indispensable privileges. They feared any liberalisation of the constitution as an encouragement to lower-class unrest; they felt threatened by the growing centralisation of Spanish rule; and they were frightened by the hostility of Palermo and the challenge to their rights over silk export. Spain, furthermore, had shown an unwelcome readiness to accept democratic reforms and obviously lacked confidence in the capacity of the merchant aristocracy, so much so that the new *strategoto* was given greater powers to overrule the senate.

In July 1674, therefore, the revolutionary decision was taken at Messina to refuse entrance to Spanish troops and to execute some of the democratic leaders in the town. The rebels immediately sought help from France, ironically the country that had the strongest interest in curtailing the Sicilian silk industry. France was then at war with Spain, and Louis XIV was well aware of Sicily's strategic importance. When Messina appealed to him, he named the Duke of Vivonne, brother of his current mistress, to be Governor of the island; and French troops reached Messina early in 1675.

Once again the internal divisions of Sicily were provoking a destructive invasion and civil war. The Spanish Viceroy called up the militia; but the response was muted, and the government had to fall back on five regiments of Spanish troops and three of German. When France looked like winning, some of the nobles showed signs of changing their allegiance. But there was never any suggestion of a new Sicilian Vespers against foreign rule, not even in June 1676 when the main Spanish and Sicilian fleet was destroyed by the French in full sight of Palermo. Perhaps the loyalty of Palermo was assured by the disloyalty of Messina. At any rate, after three centuries, it was clear that Spanish rule was passively accepted.

Spain had reason to be grateful for Sicily's benevolent neutrality, and repeated orders came from Madrid that undue demands should not be made on the population. France in the meantime retained her foothold in and around Messina; but it was clear that disenchantment with the French was growing. For three years commerce had been interrupted, and the rise in prices was provoking lower-class unrest. Furthermore, France had no more respect for Messina's privileges than had Spain: when the city's ambassadors to Paris called on Louis, they were given only two horses for their carriage instead of the six which protocol required. Suddenly the citizens began to suspect that Louis had never intended more than a minor diversionary campaign in his war against Spain, and this suspicion was enough to paralyse the most fervent rebels.

The French had learnt not to be unduly preoccupied with the interests of Messina. While the city's ambassadors were still at Paris receiving assurances of help, a withdrawal was already being secretly prepared. Louis would not even negotiate a peace guaranteeing Messina against Spanish revenge. Suddenly, realizing the fate in store for them, the leading burghers of Messina fled. A sudden fear spread among those who were left that the peasants and unemployed artisans would use this opportunity to sack the town in revenge for the ruin brought upon them by the nobility. A civic guard was therefore urgently formed. As looting began to spread, many citizens welcomed the return of Spanish troops and shed 'tears of joy at being freed from the tyranny of France'.

THE LAST YEARS OF SPANISH ADMINISTRATION

The revolt of Messina had put Spain to enormous expense, and the city did not get off lightly. The town hall was pulled down, and the site ploughed up and sown with salt. The elective council was abolished. So too was the university, and the money spent instead on a formidable castle that commanded the town. Firearms were confiscated. The royal mint was transferred to Palermo, and property belonging to rebel families was sold off, including fiefs, jurisdictions and sometimes whole villages. Messina became a ghost of its former self, and its population declined by more than half in a single decade.

When the Duke de Uceda arrived as Viceroy of Sicily in 1687, he found a violent and desolate scene. Bandits were being protected by the aristocracy and the judiciary; commerce was almost at a standstill; and the refusal to pay debts was widespread. Not only were labourers often too frightened to leave the safety of their villages, but Palermo itself was again almost out of control. Uceda tried to forbid all weapons without exception, especially the deadly 'Messina knife'; a regulation was even made against soldiers using real arms when they drilled. But at best this was only a holding operation: Spain still had no intention of intruding further into Sicilian affairs than was necessary for certain limited strategic and economic aims.

Demands for taxation went on being dutifully met. The Viceroy had orders to avoid if possible the bother of calling parliaments; and, instead of their meeting every three years, in fact only four were held in the last thirty years of the century; yet the spirit was lacking to protest at the 'illegal' practice of collecting *donativi* in the intervals. Admittedly the general distribution of these taxes was by now somewhat more equitable; but the Deputation, in other words the higher aristocracy, still had wide powers of choice in their more detailed allocation between members of each class; and no doubt this remained an important reason why the taxes were so easily accepted by them.

The Viceroy was warned that parliament might create 'much embarrassment and inconvenience' if he did not take care to supervise the choice of representatives. In practice, however, with the appropriate distribution of favours, the management of parliament proved relatively simple. Moreover, the nation's representatives had virtually given up seeking a share in legislation. To judge by their petitions, they were more interested in asking that the King should intervene with the Pope to confirm their veneration for St Rosalia or to request that more Sicilians be beatified. Once the ambitions of Messina had been tamed, the dominant classes in society showed no sign of wanting to use this moment of Spain's weakness to win even a minor degree of political initiative or autonomy.

Most Sicilians were infinitely less concerned with problems of government than with economic difficulties and natural disasters. No man-made events had quite the impact of the eruption of Mount Etna in 1669 and the terrible earthquake of 1693. Minor eruptions of Etna had been fairly frequent; but that of 1669 was on an altogether different scale. A tongue of lava two kilometres wide flowed for over twenty-five kilometres from the central crater, crumbling the walls of Catania and filling up part of its port. Vast areas of the countryside were sterilized. The Viceroy sent what help he could, though some Catanians feared that this concealed an attempt by Palermo to steal the sacred veil of St Agatha which was their most prized defence against the destructiveness of nature.

The earthquake of 1693 did even more damage. It almost entirely destroyed Noto and Modica, and left Syracuse and Ragusa largely in ruins. Catania was reduced to rubble. Horrified observers told how the earth opened up and swallowed people, how rivers disappeared and enormous waves swamped the coastal villages. The terror of this nocturnal destruction made tens of thousands of town-dwellers flee into the countryside. Perhaps 5 per cent of the island's population died on this occasion, many from diseases contracted in the aftermath of the earthquake. Over a large area the normal workings of society came to a halt; and the only university in Sicily ceased to exist.

The seventeenth century ended with the death of Charles II (1665–1700). His inglorious reign concluded the direct Habsburg line in Spain and Sicily, for he had no son. In accordance with his will, Spain and Sicily found themselves bequeathed, like so much personal property, out of the Habsburg family to a grandson of King Louis XIV of France. Once again Palermo was unmoved. Apparently there was no need for ratification of this bequest by the Sicilian parliament. The Viceroy simply proclaimed three days of festivity in honour of Philip V, and the nobles and populace were said to have joyfully participated in a spectacle more lavish than had ever been seen there before.

Sicily had for years been involved by the Habsburgs in a wearisome war against the Bourbons. Now she was on the opposite side, but still had to fight in the same apparently irrelevant contest. Louis XIV's plans for Sicily were ultimately foiled; but it was not because of local opposition against him. For twelve years a Grand Alliance fought the War of the Spanish Succession to prevent the union of France and Spain. England, Holland and Germany wanted the Archduke Charles, an Austrian Habsburg, to be King of Sicily, and had good reason for seeking to prevent the island from becoming a forward base for a French Mediterranean empire.

In 1707 Austrian forces reached Calabria and prepared to invade Sicily. There were now only three thousand troops defending the island; and some of these were Germans whose loyalty to the Bourbons was suspect. To make matters worse, there was also a revolt among the galley-slaves. As an emergency step, it was decided to use French and Irish soldiers to garrison

Palermo, a proposal which was apparently accepted by the urban aristocracy, but not by the town guildsmen. A riot broke out and once again for a short while the *maestranze* and the town proletariat were at one.

Cannon were trained down the main streets and the arsenal was captured. For a month the Viceroy could not leave the palace; and the French ships standing off the coasts were afraid to act. Some of the nobles tried to counter the insurrection by employing armed gangs recruited in the countryside, but this only enraged the guildsmen, and soon many of the leading citizens thought it best to flee to their country estates. Again, just as in 1647, the *maestranze* were left in a position where they could set up their own kind of civic administration and police force; and for a short time they were remarkably successful. But in the end internal divisions and inexperience exposed them to corruption and weakening of purpose. The government regained control, and many of the rebels were tortured and executed.

At this point the Viceroy decided to brave unpopularity and retire to the more loyal town of Messina. He wrote desperately to Philip that the small Sicilian garrison was not nearly enough to ward off invasion. Isolated enemy landings took place on the coast, and English ships once bombarded Mazara. As war came closer, the German and Spanish troops stationed in Sicily became more restless. In 1711 the Viceroy had to execute a number of officers, and their heads were marinated in brine and exposed publicly at Messina as a warning. But before any invasion or revolution took place, an international congress at Utrecht confiscated Sicily from the Bourbon Philip V and gave it to his father-in-law, Victor Amadeus, the Duke of Savoy. The long years of Spanish rule had suddenly come to an end.

CHAPTER 13

Three experiments in foreign government 1713–65

RULE FROM TURIN

The sudden reversal that removed Sicily from Spanish rule and attached her once again to an Italian power was partly the result of English intervention. The Austrian Habsburgs would have liked to take Sicily for themselves and so restore the *Utriusque Siciliae Regnum*. But England preferred the island in weaker hands, and argued that the Duke of Savoy-Piedmont merited something for having prudently changed sides during the war and helping to defeat his Bourbon relatives. When Queen Anne anachronistically demurred to a country being bartered around without its consent, her ministers pointed out the incidental diplomatic and political advantages. The Duke himself was delighted. He came from an ambitious family which set particular value on territorial acquisition, and it seemed a worthy outcome of a costly war to obtain a regal title and be able to call himself King of Sicily and Jerusalem.

Victor Amadeus was brought to the island by an English ship in October 1713. This was the first royal presence in Sicily since 1535. Six thousand soldiers were also carried from north Italy by the English to replace the Bourbon garrison. The new King stayed for a year, during which he visited the main coastal cities and made an effort to understand local problems. He brought a good deal of cash with him to subsidise the Sicilian budget, and instigated enquiries into most areas of national life. Furthermore, the first attempt in a long time was made to think out a programme of administrative reform.

Improving the economy was made a principal priority. Encouragement was given among other things to a paper factory using local raw materials, and skilled workers were brought in to start a glass industry and improve the quality of local woollens and silks. The King wanted to introduce new types of labour-contract from Piedmont in order to mitigate the problems of urban unemployment and rural depopulation. He was also advised of the need to get landowners to sell off parts of their large estates, and so create many more middle-sized farms. Though such measures were sensible, the Piedmontese were often condescending and critical in their approach to economic problems. Furthermore, a number of vital interests could not but feel threatened, and when northerners were freely chosen to be ministers and judges, the implication that Sicilians were either corrupt or incompetent gave offence.

This five-year experiment in Piedmontese rule showed, among other things, that deeply entrenched methods of thought and behaviour were a formidable obstacle to any serious attempt at reform. One particularly tricky area was pride. Sicilians were accustomed to the pomp of Spanish viceroys and found the frugality of their new masters hard to accept. Victor Amadeus himself did not wear gold and lace, but undyed wool, large boots and a casual travelling wig; and dislike of this somewhat puritanical northerner went so deep that, a hundred years later, children were still playing a game in which stones were thrown at a dummy called Victor Amadeus.

The sense of dissatisfaction was never allowed to reach the point of open revolt. A few barons got jobs after a short list had been drawn up with details of their individual weaknesses; and the rest were allowed to go on enjoying their privileged immunities. The King was quite aware of the economic and judicial disadvantages of unfettered baronial rule, but in practice he could not afford to give more than the most general consideration to feudal abuses. His cryptic advice to Viceroy Maffei was not to set the barons against each other, but to ensure if possible that they were not too much united. Any change in ownership of a fief had to be by royal permission. In 1716 it was ruled that all barons who had founded new villages without first buying a licence should forfeit them; but this was not enforced very rigorously.

Though the reforming zeal of the Piedmontese proved irksome, it was a clash with the Church that probably did as much as anything to undermine the new dispensation. Controversy had been touched off by a minor incident in 1711, when the Bishop of Lipari excommunicated certain local officials who had taxed a consignment of beans without realizing they were episcopal property and so exempt. When the Pope supported the Bishop, the Spanish Viceroy retaliated by pointing out that the Pope's authority in Sicily was limited by ancient custom and would always require validation by the crown. For five hundred years both sides had avoided this kind of jurisdictional conflict, but, perhaps inadvertently, they had now allowed a full-scale battle to grow up out of nothing, with interdict on one side, arrest and deportation on the other.

Victor Amadeus inherited this dispute from the previous administration. Matters were made worse when the extreme papalists used his accession to resurrect the claim that he should first ask Rome for feudal investiture. But the King had sworn to preserve Sicilian privileges and would not submit to this demand; on the contrary, he insisted that, by law and tradition, even

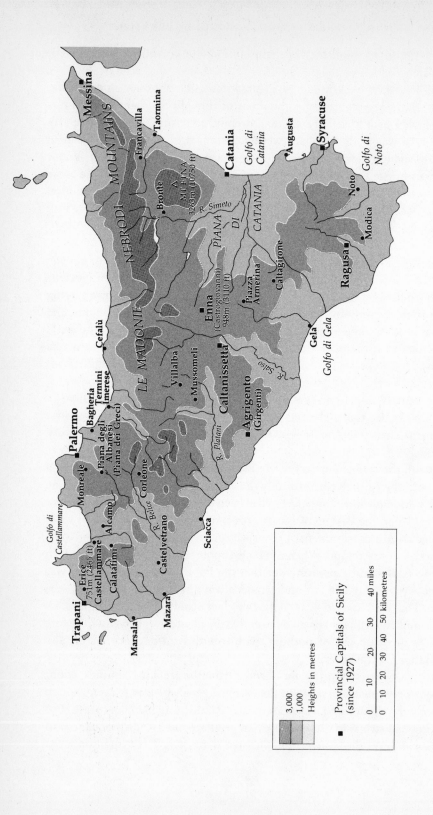

Messina

Taormina

Francavilla

MT ETNA
3263m (10750 ft)

Bronte

R. Simeto

Catania

Golfo di
Catania

Augusta

Syracuse

Golfo di
Noto

Noto

Modica

NEBRODI MOUNTAINS

PIANA DI

CATANIA

Ragusa

Enna
(Castrogiovanni)
948m (310 ft)

Piazza
Armerina

Caltagirone

LE MADONIE

Cefalù

Gela

Golfo di Gela

Termini
Imerese

Villalba

Mussomeli

Caltanissetta

R. Salso

Bagheria

Palermo

Piana degli
Albanesi
(Piana dei Greci)

Agrigento
(Girgenti)

Monreale

Corleone

R. Platani

R. Belice

Alcamo

Castelvetrano

Sciacca

Golfo di
Castellammare

Erice
751m (2465 ft)

Castellammare

Calatafimi

Trapani

Mazara

Marsala

Castelvetrano

3,000

1,000

Heights in metres

Provincial Capitals of Sicily
(since 1927)

0   10   20   30   40 miles

0 10 20 30 40 50 kilometres

papal dispensations for marriages, let alone excommunications, were invalid in Sicily without the royal *exequatur*. He was privately encouraged in this view by the King of Spain, who may not have been averse to creating trouble for his successor.

In 1715, a papal bull was issued declaring an end to the 600-year-old concession of legatine powers to the Kings of Sicily. The Pope also refused to sanction the crusade tax or let the clergy pay their share of the *donativi*. Hundreds of priests were exiled or imprisoned for obeying this papal order, and their goods were confiscated. Bishoprics were left vacant, their revenues declared forfeit, and in many places the public exercise of religion almost came to a halt. Released by the Pope from their allegiance, citizens were encouraged to defy royal authority, and the monks of Girgenti even prepared to repel royal officers with boiling oil from the walls of their monastery. Proud though Sicilians had always been of the Apostolic Legateship, this interdict soured their loyalty to the new regime much more than it did to the spiritual authority of Rome.

RULE FROM VIENNA

Victor Amadeus did not take long to learn how little he could do for Sicily, and soon began to think of exchanging the island for Milan or Florence. With this in mind, he prepared for war against his late ally, Austria. Misguidedly he believed that Spain would support him; but Spain had different ideas and seized the opportunity to invade the island and recover the territory she had lost in 1713. Victor Amadeus desperately called upon the rest of Europe to support the Treaty of Utrecht, and offered to cede Sicily to Austria in return for Tuscany or Sardinia provided that he could go on calling himself a King. The Austrians, however, had already decided to fight Spanish aggression. An invasion force was sent, and for a year the island was ravaged by two large armies, Austrian and Spanish. Their engagement at Francavilla in 1719 was probably the biggest battle fought in Sicily since Roman times.

In February 1720, this War of the Quadruple Alliance ended with Philip's acknowledgement of defeat. The Emperor Charles – the Habsburg claimant to Sicily for over fifteen years – now became King, and the European diplomats drew up the Treaty of London which confirmed his accession. The interests of Sicily bothered no one. Victor Amadeus, now compensated with the kingdom of Sardinia, took away with him some of the Sicilian navy, all the archives of his own reign and some of previous reigns; and a number of the more talented Sicilians went at his invitation to take up jobs in Turin. In the meantime a large Austrian army tried to impose firm government,

MAP 3 Modern Sicily

confiscating weapons and forbidding the Palermo guilds to man the city fortifications.

The lack of resistance did not mean that Sicily would readily accept government by yet another foreign power. The first Viceroy, in all too familiar fashion, outraged the privileged classes by his apparent lack of respect for them, and soon had to be withdrawn. His successor realized that much more tact was needed. Some of the barons were made Princes of the Holy Roman Empire, while the mayor and senators of Palermo were properly recognised as 'grandees of Spain first class'; and any barons accused of harbouring bandits were now treated more leniently than before. The Church, moreover, was pacified to the point where Benedict XIII repealed the bull of 1715 and allowed a modified version of the Apostolic Legateship to be restored 'in perpetuity'; and the Spanish Inquisition, despite complaints at its excesses and a slight curtailment of its legal powers, was now given its head once again in matters of religion.

Even though the Austrians were ready to pay most of the expenses of their invasion, they expected local contributions towards the cost of a garrison and of additional warships to protect commerce. They also wanted 30,000 *scudi* a year for the imperial general, Prince Eugene, as well as money for new bridges. The Austrians, like the Piedmontese, were accustomed to more expenditure and more efficient tax collecting than was the practice in Sicily; attempts were made to make the fiscal system both fairer and less damaging to the economy. In other words, this was in many ways an enlightened administration. Some Sicilians took advantage of the fact to advocate certain particular reforms; but they were a tiny minority, and the general consensus seems to have preferred inaction and low taxes.

TRADE AND INDUSTRY UNDER THE AUSTRIANS

Though the King was able to increase revenue by such means as selling titles and regalian rights, he knew that the profitability of his Sicilian venture depended ultimately on a radical improvement in the island's economy. By now, even merchants in Austrian Naples found wheat cheaper to buy in the eastern Mediterranean, and this fact adversely affected almost everyone in Sicily. Unable to diagnose exactly what was wrong, the government tried as one experimental remedy to make commercial treaties with the rulers of Tunis, Tripoli and Algiers, rejecting what were called 'superstitious considerations of affected Christian piety'; and this *rapprochement* with the Barbary powers may have helped wheat exports as it possibly diminished the privateering which had deterred slower-moving ships from visiting Sicilian waters.

A serious effort was also made to revive the commerce of Messina. Accordingly, the city was granted greater privileges as a free port and its taxes were reduced, and to attract newcomers some immunity was promised for crimes committed elsewhere. But such reforms did not benefit Messina as much as was hoped. Foreigners were not so easily lured back, and perhaps they were now convinced that the Sicilian market was unprofitable. Silk was bought more cheaply in China. The port dues were infinitely cheaper at Leghorn and Reggio, for Messina was so heavily in debt and so restrictionist in outlook that heavy local taxes made its commerce uncompetitive.

One general obstacle to trade was that Sicilians feared to put up risk capital without fairly precise guarantees of success. Above all they required preferential legal privileges. A complex of different *fori* and legal systems had grown up gradually over the centuries. Not only the Church courts which gave special immunity to the clergy, but the Inquisition and the Apostolic Legateship, the Chancellor, the Protonotary, the Royal Mint, the Auditor General of the army, the Admiralty, the tobacco tax collectors, the wheat export council, the crusade tax, the customs, the British and French consuls, even to some extent the *maestranze*, all had a jurisdiction of their own; and members of each *foro* busily tried to establish their own exemption from jurisdiction by the others. As a result, there could be little guarantee that contracts could be honoured or debts paid.

Industry too, like trade, proved hard to galvanize. Sugar production, for example, had been declining fast, though there were still about four factories operating at this time, each apparently with about four hundred workers. The Austrian government optimistically imagined that, with cheap enough credit, at least six more factories could be made economic, and with this aim in view a heavy surcharge was placed on all imported sugar. But before this tax could have any effect, the wealthy few who were the main consumers of sugar in iced drinks and sweetmeats persuaded the government to rescind it, and Sicilian sugar cane soon ceased to be grown commercially.

The Austrians optimistically thought that the raw materials existed for quite a number of other industries, and the presence of so many beggars suggested that labour was abundant. It therefore seemed to them that Sicily was allowing herself to remain poor unnecessarily. Only the coarsest glass, for example, was made locally, yet some of the main raw materials were being exported from Sicily to Venice. Gunpowder was bought in Genoa, though sulphur, saltpetre and charcoal had been exportable commodities in Sicily itself; and shipbuilding was on such a small scale that Sicily possessed only about twenty ships capable of reaching Genoa. But the dearth of local enterprise, while easily observed, was with difficulty diagnosed, let alone remedied.

NAPLES AND THE SICILIAN PARLIAMENT

The governments of Turin and Vienna confronted local problems with some initial enthusiasm, but both of them lacked the patience, the tact and the sheer physical force to make much impact on such a traditionalist and static society. Concessions to Messina did not result in rescuing the town from its depression. Improved methods of taxation could be suggested but not easily applied, nor could economic resources be mobilised in a world where most changes were feared and resisted at many different levels of society. Rulers and ruled therefore became quickly disenchanted with each other. In comparison with Austria or Savoy, Spain could be called decadent, and yet Sicily had become accustomed to the distant and easy-going Spanish government that allowed the nobility a free hand to govern and misgovern their serfs as they wished.

When international tensions momentarily isolated Austria in 1734, another Spanish expedition therefore found it an easy task to retrieve the kingdom which Spain had lost in 1713. There seems to have been no Sicilian rebellion against the Austrians, no organised group which called on Spain for deliverance; but at the first news of a successful Spanish landing, another deputation of nobles from Palermo hurried to meet the invading general and assure him of a welcome. The Austrian army did not put up much of a fight, and what now took place can hardly be called a serious invasion. Sicilians suddenly found their country joined once again to Naples and made into an apanage for Don Carlos, an *Infante* of Spain, who became King with the title of Charles III.

The victory of Charles with so little bloodshed was greeted with what was called 'extraordinary enthusiasm'. It flattered people to have another real King arrive in person and swear to preserve their laws. Palermo was delighted to have him reject the suggestion that he should rightly be crowned in Messina, while the Messinese in compensation were relieved of the last remaining financial penalties imposed in 1679–80. Charles opened up the royal palace, and Palermo half came to life again as the centre of court receptions. After a week, however, he left. All that Sicilians were to see of him in the future was his statue, and this for cheapness' sake was made out of the melted-down bronze from a statue of the Austrian Emperor (and used for previous kings before that). He had not even remembered to call a parliament to confirm his accession.

Even though Sicily was now to be ruled from Naples, the influence of

Spain remained strong until the middle of the century. There had been Spanish viceroys even under the Austrian Habsburgs, and Spanish fashions in dress had again been accepted. Spanish manners and behaviour were still accepted as the outward sign of gentility, and masquerades and carnivals remained a permanent part of Sicilian life; bull-fights, too, were much enjoyed by all classes throughout the eighteenth century and were not unknown in the nineteenth. But a solid undercurrent of Italian cultural influence had always persisted and now became much more marked. Many viceroys even under Spain had been Italians. The architects of the eighteenth-century Palermo villas were mostly educated at Rome, and use of the Italian language had become increasingly common alongside the Sicilian dialect. In 1741 the Viceroy opened parliament with a speech read in Italian, though in 1738 he had used Spanish.

When Charles was promoted in 1759 to the throne of Spain, the rest of Europe would not let him keep Sicily and Naples as well; so he presented these two kingdoms to his son, who became Ferdinand IV of Naples and Ferdinand III of Sicily. Once again the old laws and privileges of the island to which Charles had sworn did not prevent the realm being treated as personal property and the succession being governed merely by dynastic convenience and the balance of power. Some of the Sicilian nobility followed Charles and went to live in Spain. The new King Ferdinand was to call himself an *Infante* of Spain and at first took orders from Madrid; but during his long reign of sixty-six years Sicily more and more developed the links which bound her to Italy.

The Neapolitan Bourbons at first hoped that they might succeed where Austrians and Piedmontese had failed. Charles III, for example, set up a Supreme Magistracy of Trade with wide powers of intervention in economic affairs and with a governing body on which the nobles could be outvoted by merchants and officials. This body had to look after shipping and shipbuilding. It was intended to control the collection of customs duty and internal communications in general, as well as mines, the salt industry and the fisheries. One of the tasks laid upon it was to gather the statistical information on which economic policy could be based. Another was to tackle questions of private indebtedness and insolvency, which were having such harmful effects on trade and the provision of credit.

But instead of welcoming this institution, every vested interest in Sicily was immediately mobilized against it. Parliament repeatedly begged the King to put things back as they were before. So did the Palermo senate. Many private *fori* found their jurisdiction curtailed by it and hence less profitable. So did the main tax authorities. Altogether this institution was far too revolutionary, and after seven years the King decided to take most of its authority away. His experiment in 1740 of letting the Jews return also had to be revoked, as it was thought to be endangering religion. Such experiences destroyed much of Charles's interest in the development of Sicily's economic potential. He decided rather to play up to the barons with a less active and less interfering administration than that of Turin or Vienna, and little more was heard for a time of any serious schemes of reform.

CHAPTER 14

Society and administration in the eighteenth century

CEREALS AND THE ECONOMY

In the first half of the eighteenth century, Sicily in a good year may still have produced twice as much wheat as she consumed. On average, though, the amount exported was declining, and the annual variations in production were enormous and almost certainly much larger than they used to be. After two good harvests in succession, growers might have surplus wheat to feed to their pigs, and the next year would let land go out of cultivation; after a bad harvest, however, high grain prices could lead to more land being ploughed up, herds of cattle being killed off and scrub burned on the mountainside. In very bad years, less wheat was grown than was needed for domestic consumption and supplies would have to be imported.

Many explanations were suggested for why, at a time when agriculture elsewhere was beginning to experience a great development, Sicilian farming remained backward. Primitive methods of cultivation, landlord absenteeism, and unremunerative contracts of labour were given as possible reasons. An increasing intensity of drought was another possible factor. Climatic changes in North Africa were possibly responsible for the fact that great armies of locusts used to descend on Sicily for years at a stretch, clogging the water supplies and leaving not a green leaf anywhere. The Church developed a special ceremony to curse these locusts, and bounties were given for them to be swept up in sackloads.

A population of probably not much more than a million in 1700 was half as much again by the end of the century. According to the Marquis of Villabianca, whose diaries are a major source for the history of these years, domestic food requirements seemed in 1775 to have doubled in living memory; yet production was not keeping pace, and the agronomist Balsamo insisted that Sicilian wheat production even in quite good areas was no more than six times the quantity of seed. The changing distribution of population made things still more difficult, because people were moving into the cities and left the agricultural areas impoverished. Judging by the census returns, some villages lost half their population in the course of a century, and others altogether disappeared.

Though official policy only added to the difficulties, the government could not help interfering. In the first place it needed revenue, and the flour excise was not only the easiest tax to collect and the hardest to evade, but it fell mainly on the poor and so was much more acceptable to parliament and civic authorities than a land tax would have been. One British vice-consul thought this the most fundamental reason of all for the backwardness of the Sicilian economy. Furthermore, the numerous excise barriers and the officials which they required were a potent obstacle to trade. Their collection was leased out to private individuals who bid for them at a certain price; the successful contractors then tried to recoup the cost as soon as possible, and were allowed to enlist private bodies of armed police for the purpose.

The government also took upon itself the responsibility of ensuring that enough food was retained in Sicily to meet any emergency. Every consignment for export still needed government permission, so that sometimes, as Balsamo complained, the Sicilian farmer was penalised rather than rewarded for his pains. The procedure of control had changed little. The 'third part' of the harvest had to be surrendered at a controlled price to local authorities, and the rest had to go to the royal *caricatoi* for storage. Each year in December the *Maestro Portulano* calculated how much had been deposited, how much seed would be needed for the winter sowing, how much flour for feeding the population until the next June, and then he decided how much could be exported.

The chief beneficiaries of this system were the grain brokers at Palermo who sometimes bought a crop before it had even been planted. Occasionally they could raise and lower prices in a single day and so manipulate both growers and exporters simultaneously. These were the people who could afford export licences, and in their hands the *tratte* became a negotiable currency. It was said in 1726 that almost the whole trade was controlled by half a dozen brokers, and their interests were neither those of the consumer nor of the farmer. If they could persuade the *Maestro Portulano* that there was not enough wheat for export, an embargo might be declared, with the result that the price would fall and they could buy cheaply; if subsequently they could give exaggerated reports of the harvest, the government might permit more than the safe amount of exports and the consequent rise in prices was sheer gain.

One effect of artificial prices and controls was to make smuggling highly profitable. Inevitably the evidence for this is more circumstantial than statistical. In 1790, the British consul thought that a third of Sicilian cereal produce was 'occulted by the growers and not reported'; and one estimate suggests that well over a million bushels on average were leaving the island each year as contraband – in other words, as much as might go in legal export. Meat, animals, barley, vegetables, wine and silk were also spirited out of the country to avoid export tax. Moreover, public opinion was strongly behind the smugglers on principle and from economic interest. When the Marquis della Rajata was murdered in church by a smuggler he had punished, the assassin was publicly applauded.

The whole traffic in commodities was under severe strain. One reason was that growers reacted to increasing controls by avoiding, or at least delaying, despatch of their produce to the *caricatoi*. This undermined the whole system, as it upset the calculation of what stocks were available for export. Lying at Palermo harbour in July 1775 were a hundred and fifty cargo vessels hoping for export licences, but after months of waiting they had to depart empty to the Levant with their much-needed foreign currency. For the third successive year, the British consul expressed the disappointment and anger of foreign shipowners with the uncertainty of this system of *tratte*. It seemed to him an obvious reason why alternative markets were gaining ground and why some Sicilian wheatlands were only spasmodically in production.

He might have added that the hard Sicilian wheat was difficult to mill and so was losing favour in overseas markets, while soft wheat, which the arid areas of Sicily could not grow nearly so well, produced far bigger yields in milder climates and could now be bought much more cheaply. Moreover, one main advantage of *grano duro* had been its durability. The soft wheat of the Crimea and northern Europe, by contrast, had been more liable to rot on long sea voyages. But faster journeys and better storage methods were beginning to make this ancient advantage less important. At the same time, the higher costs in Sicily of production and transport, together with the export tax, excises, bribe money and the merchants' rigging of prices, were adding to prime costs and allowing other countries to overtake Sicily.

LAND TENURE AND THE ROAD SYSTEM

Contracts of labour and land tenure were coming to present a special problem of their own for the farming community. In the seventeenth century there had been an increase in the number of *enfiteusi*, the long-term leaseholds or permanent copyholds by which landowners attracted labour to their estates; but this trend was not maintained through the eighteenth century. Absentee landowners no longer had quite the same incentive as before to found new villages or the same interest in attracting labour by granting long leases. On the contrary, inflation was reducing the value of fixed *enfiteusi* rents, and leasehold farms were being divided between heirs to the point where rent collection and good farming were alike difficult or impossible.

The preferred contract now was the *gabella*. This was a form of tenancy whereby an entire estate was leased out, usually for three years, sometimes six, to an individual rentier known as a *gabelloto*. It was a system that had become increasingly common in the course of the seventeenth century. Since it comprised a large area, it fitted easily into a world of fiefs. It was especially attractive now that the barons lived in Palermo, as a *gabelloto* would supervise a large estate, pay punctually, in advance, and relieve the landowner of the bother and indignity of dealing with individual peasants.

The *gabelloto* was sometimes a very rich man, occasionally a foreigner; but usually he was someone who had emerged from the peasantry, either by clever farming, or moneylending, or by using strong-arm measures to assert his authority in a neighbourhood. He may originally have been the head of the force employed by a baron to police his estates: becoming a field guard was a familiar way of acquiring local power and influence. By the 1770s these *gabelloti* were referred to as the new tyrants of the countryside; some were already rich and aspiring to become aristocrats themselves. They had the reputation of being more ruthless than the landlords, more anxious to repudiate the earlier *enfiteusi* contracts, and this helped to reduce the peasants to a status of absolute dependence with a day-to-day or at most a yearly contract.

The *gabella* was usually a short tenancy, and this had the great advantage of allowing the landowner to keep abreast of inflation. But the corollary to this was that few practising farmers would be interested in capital-intensive agriculture, for instance in planting vines, citrus or olives: lacking security of tenure, managers and labourers alike would be avid for quick returns. Being forced to pay rent in advance, a new tenant would be encouraged to slaughter animals and cut down timber, both of which processes had already gone much too far. His interest was in ploughing up virgin soil, overcropping it with wheat year after year, and leaving it abandoned after expiry of his contract. This was the easiest kind of farming on a *latifondo* whenever a landlord had lost interest in developing his estates. It rarely produced more than nine bushels an acre, and, in the absence of proper crop rotation, the land was left wastefully uncultivated every other year.

The famous economist, Paolo Balsamo, lamented the regressive character of the *gabella* contract and the fact that the *gabelloto* himself had as his aim to live as a gentleman capitalist, remote from the land. Thus at a time when English agriculture was being transformed by leaseholds, one could ride through Sicily for hours without seeing a farmhouse, a road, or even a tree, as nearly all the profits of agriculture were spent in the towns where the landlords lived. Here was a fundamental reason why Sicilian agriculture was becoming uncompetitive. The rents taken by these absentee landlords ought either to have been invested productively or else reduced by half; yet either alternative was, for social and political reasons, unacceptable.

Towards the end of the century, a small class of intellectuals was beginning to recognize this impasse. Nevertheless, the *latifondisti* could argue – with some justice – that drought, as well as the absence of roads and capital, made extensive farming the most appropriate kind of agriculture for Sicily; but in part they were merely trying to justify a way of life they preferred. Longer leases and greater security of tenure could have increased productivity at little cost to anyone, and this would not have been incompatible with the system of *latifondi*. A simple change by which beans were planted every third year could have had important results, but it would have also needed a radical change of outlook. The Austrians in the 1720s had concluded that Sicily was poor when there was no reason for it to be; and now men such as Balsamo confirmed that Sicilian agriculture should be giving four times its present yield.

Better roads and bridges would have been the first requisite of a prosperous agriculture. Communications were probably not as good as they had been in Roman times. Except for a few miles of paved road outside Palermo, the only means of travel by land in 1700 was along circuitous mule tracks or *trazzere*, the wide sheep runs used by wandering herdsmen. As a result the cost of transport was high; and this was a major reason for the increasing uncompetitiveness of Sicilian wheat as well as for the enduring poverty of the mass of the population. With transport so expensive, the peasants had little incentive to grow a marketable surplus and often no choice but to sell their produce to the local boss. Furthermore, the condition of the roads meant they usually had to waste up to six or seven exhausting hours a day travelling over bridle paths to their work, and could carry with them only the most primitive and ineffective kind of plough.

A proper network of highways would have done more to change economics, politics, and even morals than any other reform, and the Marquis Giarrizzo thought over-optimistically that with good will it would take only five years of serious work to achieve. But for social as well as financial reasons, the good will was lacking. Proper roads would have been expensive, given the nature of the country; they would also have demanded a much greater efficiency and honesty from the barons of the parliamentary Deputation who supervised the tax money allocated to public works. Realistically, a proper road system could only have come about with a reduction in parliamentary privilege and an altogether more forceful attitude by the Viceroy. It would have needed either more private enterprise by individual landowners, or at least the much readier acceptance by them of communal responsibility and higher taxation.

In the 1770s road construction did become a question of serious public interest and the King ordered a Neapolitan military engineer, General Persichelli, to draw up plans for a main road inland between Palermo and Catania. Obstructionism, however, made Persichelli's job impossible. Towns and landowners sometimes fought each other over alternative routes, and created trouble over any project which was not to their advantage. One observer remarked that you could deduce from the routes chosen the names of the landowners serving on the Deputation. Even the basic difference between those who wanted a coast road and those who preferred Persichelli's scheme was not resolved. Once again the Viceroy's authority was insufficient to carry out government policy against local non-cooperation, and the century ended without Sicily having any roads worthy of the name.

THE NOBILITY

Baronial influence was as strong in eighteenth-century Sicily as anywhere in Europe. The barons owned most of the land even though they paid only a fraction of the taxes. They possessed feudal lordship over about 280 out of 360 villages, so that most Sicilians lived under their direct jurisdiction; while the minuscule middle class relied utterly on them and seldom showed much independence. At the end of the eighteenth century the titled aristocracy consisted of 142 princes, 788 marquises, and about 1500 other dukes and barons, quite apart from the boasters of pretended titles that were sufficiently common to be legislated against. About twenty families among this nondescript proliferation possessed overwhelming economic power.

Although for convenience one may speak of 'the aristocracy', this was naturally not a homogeneous group. The owners of new creations, for example, were still divided by a special degree of snobbery from older titles, and viceroys disregarded this difference at their peril. Some nobles were very rich indeed; most were poor. A very few were cultivated *grands seigneurs*; many more were entirely illiterate. There was a down-at-heel provincial nobility who failed to afford life at Palermo, as well as a new and more mercantile aristocracy in the growing town of Catania. Most prominent of all, however, were those who lived grandly in the capital and were the petty sovereigns of some feudal estate which they perhaps never visited.

The general impression given by the baronage as a whole is one of fecklessness and inadequacy, and singularly few of these leaders of society left a name behind for the admiration of posterity. There were a few exceptions, however. The Prince of Niscemi in the early eighteenth century was a hard-working man of affairs; the Baron of San Giaime e Pozzo produced a manual of agriculture in 1735; and Prince Biscari at Catania not only had a reputation of being benevolent to his servants and tenants, but built up one of the finest private museums in the world. He introduced foreign artisans to encourage linen and rum manufacture, and in one emergency, at his own expense, he virtually fed the whole town of Catania for a month.

Most nobles were heavily in debt, partly through improvidence, though partly no doubt through the declining profitability of cereal farming. The increasing resort to *gabelloto*-management may well have led to a decline in production, as short leases inevitably diminished incentive. Moreover, landowners in time found the *gabelloti* to be somewhat intractable subordinates, and the difficulty of compelling them to pay their rent was given by the Deputation as one reason why creditors went unpaid. Any increase in agricultural incomes now had to be filtered through this new managerial class who, legally or illegally, sometimes took a good 50 per cent of the profits for themselves. Costs also increased in proportion as more marginal land was cultivated and distant fields came into production.

The complaint of personal impoverishment, however, was no doubt deliberately exaggerated in order to keep taxes low and creditors at bay. Sicilian economic backwardness cannot simply be explained by poverty, for the extravagant rebuilding of Catania, Noto and other towns after the earthquake of 1693 tells a more complicated tale. In the mid-eighteenth century, the parliamentary taxes were estimated as being under 1 per cent of the declared value of property and even less of its real value. Parliament in 1754 thought that a subsidy of 80,000 *scudi* would be very high. Yet in the 1720s the Prince of Valguarnera paid 180,000 *scudi* for his villa in Bagheria, and the Prince of Palagonia, who had recently been fleeing from his creditors, was thought to have paid 200,000 for his. Plenty of money seems to have existed somewhere; the important fact was that it was spent on prestige rather than productive investment.

Keeping up appearances was a costly and time-consuming activity. A carriage, or preferably two, was obligatory, and by the 1740s this fact was causing serious traffic problems in Palermo. Balsamo vainly wished that the nobles would occasionally ride through their own farms on horseback instead of taking their daily journey along the marine front with their liveried equipages; but appearances were everything and the afternoon drive was mandatory. When Marquis Regalmici was detailed to carry urgent relief to areas damaged by an earthquake, he insisted on waiting until he could leave with appropriate dignity, accompanied by a large and brilliant cortege; as a result he arrived a fortnight after the disaster.

The fact that the Sicilian aristocracy consumed much and produced nothing was a fundamental reason for the island's backwardness. To some extent, however, their social preponderance and their extravagant life style helped to conceal their economic debility. Indeed, even at the cost of keeping Sicily poor, they naturally did what they could to twist the social relationships of feudalism still further in their favour. On the mainland, except perhaps in Calabria, the Bourbons usually managed to appropriate fiefs for failure to pay feudal dues or when a line of succession died out; but in Sicily, at least after the temporary confiscation of several 'states' early in the eighteenth century, these regalian prerogatives dwindled away.

The lawyers, moreover, elaborated a sophistical justification of this resurgent, bastard feudalism. A clever advocate, Carlo di Napoli, won a famous case in the 1740s against the village of Sortino which wanted to buy itself back from its prince into the royal demesne. The argument which prevailed was that the original Norman barons had strictly speaking not been feudatories of Count Roger, but rather his *commilitones* who, by helping him to conquer Sicily, had won for themselves a share of sovereignty in the lands. Thus fiefs were deemed to be private property. As an even more extravagant extension of this view, tenants were sometimes said to owe allegiance to their feudal lord rather than to the monarch. No wonder that a monument was erected to di Napoli at Palermo by a grateful baronage; no wonder that the personal links of vassal and client were considered to be of paramount importance; and no wonder the liberties of Sicily came to be confused with baronial privilege.

Even towns on the royal demesne were, for good or ill, frequently bossed by the local aristocracy. At Catania, for example, Prince Biscari, as the leading citizen and chief employer, was more important than any royal judge, and local government was invariably in aristocratic hands. Elsewhere royal forests, villages, castles and mines were from time to time encroached upon or even annexed outright by the rich. In the countryside the peasants could find themselves virtually bound to the soil, compelled to owe *corvées*, and to use the baron's mill and olive press. In the early nineteenth century the Prince of Palagonia was still collecting a marriage tax from his vassals in commutation of his seigneurial right to sleep with their daughters.

The Bourbons of Naples by no means always favoured the nobles, and at Naples they almost eliminated feudalism during this century; but they knew that keeping Sicily submissive would be infinitely less expensive if the baronage could be persuaded to cooperate. The barons were cheaper than royal officials in local government; with their assistance any movement for Sicilian independence could be checked; and they could be used to help inculcate respect for the established order in Church and State. The Bourbon government, in return for their political subservience, was usually ready to excuse their malpractices. 'If only other Kings would follow such a good example!', apostrophized the Marquis of Villabianca.

BANDITS AND THE LAW

Though the Austrians momentarily deluded themselves that they were eliminating crime, law enforcement remained much the same problem as in previous centuries. There was little to stop large bands of outlaws roaming the countryside; for though bandits sometimes levied a contribution on the peasants, they were protected by an environment that considered law breaking a respectable activity. One indication of this may have been the popular religious cult of the *Decollati*, in which prayers were offered up to executed criminals, and shrines erected for their dismembered relics. A more practical consequence of this extra-legal mentality was non-cooperation with the police. The Austrian authorities had been baffled to discover that 'to be a witness in any kind of criminal action brought unspeakable disgrace even on the most abject member of society'. Clearly *omertà* was not founded on fear alone.

Another fact which inevitably reduced the respect for public law was the persistence of so many different *fori*: ecclesiastics still claimed exemption from the ordinary courts as did members of the Inquisition from the bishops' courts, and so forth. Of even greater significance perhaps was the traditional lawlessness of the upper classes. Everywhere, said the early nineteenth-century historian Palmeri, there could be found nobles who protected bandits either out of fear or covetousness; and the fact that the barons could, within their own territory, often behave much as they liked added to the problem. They still had powers of life and death, and Victor Amadeus was told that in their courts injustice was the rule, for innocent people could be punished out of mere caprice.

In practice even the royal courts treated nobles differently from ordinary citizens. The Duke of San Filippo openly engaged in contraband protected by the authorities. The Prince of Villafranca, who had tortured boys with burning irons for having mocked his eight-horse carriage, successfully defended himself by saying that it was none of the royal court's business. Even murder was dealt with leniently, and when in 1771 a nobleman was executed for this offence, it was the first time for nearly a century; and even so, strong representations for a reprieve were made by his peers, one argument being that the executioner had no experience with a guillotine and would first need some practice.

The most successful governments at dealing with crime were those that suppressed their indignation and came to terms with the underworld.

Setting a thief to catch a thief often achieved a fair amount of success, and that was why notorious criminals were still employed as Captains at Arms. Like many bandits before him, the famous Testalonga was only caught when someone in his own gang betrayed him. The problem facing the government was that it was dealing not so much with isolated criminals as with a widely shared way of life. In this society, the public good was a meaningless phrase; and relations with family, patrons and clients counted for more than any idea of loyalty to the state. Sometimes there seemed to be a widespread underground conspiracy against the law; and a number of writers in the eighteenth century boasted that Sicilians had a secret sign language that had been used since the time of the Greek tyrants as a means of resistance against foreign rule. Such febrile inventiveness was later to contribute to ideas about the mafia.

Visitors from overseas were told of criminal organizations that colluded with one another and sometimes boasted aristocratic protectors. One must allow here for exaggeration and rumour: there was often a desire to impress foreigners, just as there was a desire by gullible foreigners to be impressed. The *Beati Paoli* and the Revengers may not have been serious organizations; but some delinquent groups undoubtedly did exist which levied a tax on peasants and landlords alike. They might in a sense have had their own system of justice; and it was said that members were sworn to execute their secret judgements without question. Rarely was a foreign traveller molested by these criminals; but that was mainly because they were concerned with local conflicts for power into which foreigners did not enter.

Delinquency was made much easier by the sheer variety of laws and regulations. Many foreign invasions of Sicily had left behind them a labyrinth of uncodified legislation which was extremely hard to understand or apply. This is another reason why public justice was disobeyed and even derided. In a world of overlapping and conflicting jurisdictions, of privileged exemptions from the ordinary courts, of judgeships being sold and witnesses intimidated, frequently the local boss or the local landowner was more important for law enforcement and even for law-making than the central government, and this fact was accepted, if not welcomed, by ordinary people as well as the authorities.

The law was discredited not only by its diverseness and complexity but also by its delays and costliness. Individuals were therefore inclined to seek redress by other means. Many quite poor people, according to the poet Meli, were ruined by protracted lawsuits, and this kind of fact put another premium on gangsterism; for everyone, whether peasant, landlord, priest, businessman or criminal, had an added incentive to commend himself to somebody who could show that in practice he was more effective than the regular forces of law. The courts imposed harsh deterrent penalties which included branding, public torturing and the strangling and disembowelling of criminals; but all this merely served to conceal the essential ineffectiveness of the authorities in maintaining law and order.

INTELLECTUALS AND REFORM

One important reason why the voice of reform was muffled in Sicily lay in the nature of the ties which bound the small class of intellectuals to an essentially conservative world. Anyone with genuine originality was tempted to move away from this closed, patriarchal society to find employment elsewhere: the most celebrated Sicilians of the century, the architect Filippo Juvara, the composer Alessandro Scarlatti and that talented impostor Cagliostro, lived and died abroad, as did many others of lesser fame. At home there were few jobs, and any posts which carried a good salary often went to non-Sicilians.

The main hope of preferment, apart from the Church, was through the patronage of some baron, and this is one reason why there was so little open criticism of the established order. Criticism, such as it was, tended instead to be directed against reform. It was thus fashionable to blame the Bourbons of Naples for what was wrong in society, even when the Neapolitan government was relatively enlightened. In Naples itself many lawyers supported the crown against feudal usurpations, but in Sicily the legal profession looked rather to the nobility for their living. If they ever became rich it was likely to be through lawsuits over the collateral succession to feudal estates.

When the *ancien régime* did come under attack, the impetus derived not from these people but from a new generation of reforming administrators at Naples. Their first and easiest target was the Jesuits, whose reactionary hold over education was heartily disliked. In 1767 the order was expelled and its property confiscated on the pretended grounds of worldliness and corruption. Culturally this was an act of liberation, though less than some people may have hoped. Another expressed intention, to experiment in social and economic reform by breaking down some Jesuit *latifondi* into smallholdings, was not so successful, for the peasants either were never allowed to hear about it, or else were too frightened to submit their claims as the law intended. Instead of these estates being divided into small lots, the land went to enlarge existing lay *latifondi*.

Elementary education received something of a boost when Ferdinand ordered the monasteries to open free schools for the poor. Something was also done for higher education, which till then had concentrated on law and theology, to the detriment of more liberal subjects. Symptomatic had been the treatment of Marquis Natale who once defied current traditionalism and wrote a poem on Leibnitz; but the Inquisition censored it as heretical, and its non-noble printer was imprisoned. King Ferdinand now agreed that some of the money confiscated from the Jesuits should be used to start an academy. A governing body of nobles was appointed, and some twenty chairs endowed. One or two other Jesuit houses were converted into technical schools where poor children could learn to weave and make glass and ceramics.

If the Jesuits and the Church proved the easiest target for reform, that was because the privileged classes were not united in their defence. The baronial and domanial Houses had both been protesting that ecclesiastics were evading their full share of tax, and covetous eyes were no doubt cast on Church lands. In other spheres, reform only had its individual champions; and the issues involved were either impractical or the approach to them half-hearted. Francesco Paolo di Blasi, for example, wanted a new legal code and the abolition of primogeniture; he favoured women's education and compulsory free instruction for the poor. However laudable his intentions, di Blasi's was a lone voice; furthermore, he spoke only as a theorist.

Of much greater significance than individual reformers was the fact that Sicily was now exposed more directly than before to the main currents of European thought. Suddenly it was beginning to acquire the reputation of being a highly romantic island which foreigners ought to visit. It was above all the travel volume by Patrick Brydone, published in 1773, and at once translated into German and French, which publicised Sicily's charms; and there was a spate of perhaps fifty other such volumes in the next half-century. Sicily contained something for everyone with a taste for adventure: it had earthquakes, volcanoes, bandits, all manner of discomforts and quaint local customs, as well as splendid memorials of classical antiquity and a notable hospitality towards foreigners.

These overseas visitors helped a little to shock local culture out of its complacent insularity. Brydone found many English books in family libraries, and translations were beginning to appear of Arthur Young, Pope, Hume and even Locke. Northern travellers were astonished to be served iced punch and porter, and to encounter the hands-in-the-pocket affectation which English nonchalance was thought to demand. French books were beginning to appear, and the smuggled writings of Voltaire, Diderot and Montesquieu were bringing the European Enlightenment to the fascinated attention of a select few. But the impact of these foreign influences was limited. Travellers came to Sicily, but very few Sicilians ever travelled in Europe. Books, moreover, were possessed rather than read; the new ideas were not genuinely assimilated.

CHAPTER 15

Revolution and reform, 1770–1800

THE PALERMO REVOLT OF 1773

The concentration of public life on Palermo became more pronounced than ever after the partial eclipse of Messina. Not only had Messina been overcome by military defeat in 1678, but she suffered a terrible plague in 1743 which halved the population again – two shiploads of convicts had to be sent from Palermo to clear the dead from the streets and burn all infected chattels. Then an earthquake struck the town in 1783 just when recovery was beginning, and a huge fire burned for over a week. Pamphlets went on being published with the brave message that Messina was by rights the true capital of Sicily, but physical disasters had by now taken the heart out of this controversy except with a few dedicated antiquarians.

Palermo, on the other hand, was after Naples the largest town in Italy, and it was growing faster than Rome, Milan or Turin. At a rough estimate its population doubled or almost doubled to about 200,000 in the course of the eighteenth century. In addition to the aristocracy the city boasted a large and growing slum population housed in shanty towns. The Viceroy's main concern was to provide the urban proletariat with doles and cheap bread, and to keep the nobility happy by indulging them with honours and frivolity. Festivals were an important aspect of city government. That of St Rosalia in July was one of the few occasions where a genuine collective effort overrode the individualism that blighted so many other areas of public life.

The seventy-two *maestranze* or workers' guilds played an important part in the city's ceremonial life. They also contributed to its politics. Normally their internal affairs were closely supervised by the mayor and senate, but their cohesion and habitual discipline could in an emergency give them considerable autonomy and power. The fact that their members were sometimes permitted to carry weapons was also important. They were allowed to act as auxiliary police and in times of crisis to man the city fortifications: this service was the more gratefully undertaken in that it was well paid. By being brought inside the circle of privilege, they too were given a status to defend against any insurrection of the *basso popolo*.

In 1773, when a revolt broke out in the capital, these artisan corporations suddenly found themselves to be, as they had been before in 1647 and 1708, the chief effective force in the island. The background to the revolt lay in the city aristocracy's mounting dissatisfaction with the Viceroy Marquis Fogliani, who had dared to attack some of Palermo's fiscal immunities as well as other privileges which concerned the parliamentary *donativi*. When in 1770 he also imposed new taxes on luxuries – windows, balconies, wine and the consumption of snow for cooling drinks – there was an outcry: his notices were torn down, and most people flatly refused to pay. The alliance which normally bound the aristocracy to the government was momentarily snapped.

The failure of another harvest in 1773 then triggered off a popular explosion. Many nobles escaped hurriedly to their country villas, a fact which only aggravated unemployment and class antagonism; and when the Swiss guard were provoked into opening fire, a number of people reacted by breaking into the prisons, burning police files and setting some of the convicts free. Finally the palace was attacked, to the familiar cry of 'Long live the King and out with the Viceroy'. Fogliani humanely capitulated rather than order his troops to fire, and was escorted ignominiously down to the harbour by the consuls of the guilds. Thence he sailed for Messina, judging that Messina would see this as a chance to re-establish herself against Palermo; and in fact he was given a great welcome there and showered with gifts.

As in 1697, it was the *maestranze* who saved the day. They had good reason to want law and order restored, and cannon were accordingly set up in the streets and the rioters disarmed. The guildsmen then acted as police and self-appointed magistrates, refusing to accept help from the troops and adamantly preventing the Archbishop bringing back the ordinary police as he would have liked. Food supplies were quickly reorganized, which suggests that the shortage had largely been due to illegal concealment; and the city government gradually reasserted its authority over the countryside so that supplies could be better assured. As one measure of social reform, proclamations were sent to the villages encouraging peasants to apply for land under provisions of the law which had nationalized Jesuit property.

The state of emergency lasted for a full year, but little by little the aristocratic establishment regained its lost authority. The *maestranze* were deprived of their police powers and at once, so we are told, theft and assassination became common again; whether this was because the criminal classes were now turned once more against the government, or because the official police went back to their traditional policy of partial collusion with crime, is not certain. Five thousand troops took over the fortifications, and the hundred cannon belonging to the city authorities were confiscated. There was little opposition as the city magnates supported the Neapolitan government. They had signally lost face at the hands of the *maestranze*, and there was a strong desire to destroy the guilds as a serious political force.

The revolt therefore came to an end with the town aristocracy fully restored to power. But they were now heavily in debt to the government instead of the other way round. The experience of 1773 indicated to Ferdinand and his ministers that Sicily was slightly uncivilized and even dangerous; hence the government would be compelled to intervene more directly in future to prevent any recurrence of revolt. Some kind of initiative from Naples was seen to be required in order to help reduce class tensions, improve food distribution and diminish the chances of a yet more dreadful blend of town riots and a peasants' revolt. Above all, the nobles would have to set a better example and show more sense of responsibility.

THE VICEROYALTY OF CARACCIOLO 1781–6

The Marquis Domenico Caracciolo was a Neapolitan, who had lived in Paris and London; and it was above all in the France of Turgot, Diderot and Helvetius that he had learnt to dislike all that he encountered in Sicily. So reluctant was he to take up the post of Viceroy that he delayed his arrival for a year. He was appointed as a man of the Enlightenment and as someone who had no private axe to grind. Unlike some of his predecessors, he was not so frightened of dismissal that he always waited for the King's approval before taking an initiative. Nor was he open to bribery. Being an honest man, possessed of courage, persistence and a sophisticated intelligence, he was able to initiate a more radical programme of reform than any since the thirteenth century.

His first move was to tackle the most vulnerable symbol of the old regime, the Inquisition – a relatively easy task because the Holy Office was by now just a shadow of its former self. Indeed, when it was suppressed in 1782, its prisons were found to contain only three old witches. Other measures were taken against the Church. However, they were far from drastic: the Apostolic Legateship had helped keep ecclesiastics away from political power, and as a result the Church hardly seemed to Caracciolo a major obstacle to reform. He closed some monasteries, and forbade bishops and abbots to ask papal permission before paying tax. Though he kept the ecclesiastical censorship, the jurisdiction of Church courts was further restricted, and he encouraged the police to ignore rights of asylum in churches.

A more serious objective in the hierarchy of privileges was the town of Palermo. The Viceroy had only disdain for the addiction to ceremonials of the Palermo senators, and, much to their chagrin, he tried to reduce their annual parades from over a hundred to eighteen. He also sought to curtail the multiplication of jobs in the town administration. The *maestranze*, too, came under attack: not only were their statutes reformed, but closed monopolies as well as the claim to any separate right of *foro* were abolished. This was a most substantial defeat for the Palermo guilds, and it explains why the more privileged shopkeepers and skilled workers shared with the aristocracy a fear of this Neapolitan reformer.

Caracciolo's chief target, however, was the nobility. He found that Sicily was 'inhabited only by either oppressors or the oppressed', and its troubles could almost always be traced back to 'the tyranny of the great proprietors'. His first task was to repudiate di Napoli's extreme feudal doctrines, and severe penalties were now threatened against anyone who asserted that Sicilian fiefs were not held from the King and could not revert to him. He also declared private armies and private military uniforms illegal, and servants were forbidden to use swords even for purely decorative purposes. Nobles were now arrested for protecting delinquents or for browbeating local authorities and suborning witnesses. No previous Viceroy had ever treated them so abruptly, and they began to fear that the lower orders might take advantage of this discomfiture. Every means of influence was therefore used to make the King dismiss this terrible Viceroy before it was too late.

One principal reason why Caracciolo had been selected for his post was because, as an economist, he might discover how Sicily could be made less poor and yield more revenue. As a tentative move towards progressive taxation he introduced an annual impost on carriages in order to pay for paving the streets of Palermo; and when some of the nobles refused to pay, the Viceroy sent the bailiffs into the palaces to seize the best carriages and sell them. He then turned to his favourite project which was for a land tax. A proper valuation of property, however, was an indispensable prerequisite of this, and both barons and ecclesiastics in the 1782 parliament formally objected to having one.

Caracciolo here came up against one of the chief pillars of the old regime. As a man who had seen enlightened authoritarianism in Paris and Naples, he regarded parliament as an institution which typified and protected waste, inefficiency and unfairness. The Sicilian parliament had nothing to do with liberty; on the contrary, it was arbitrary and tyrannical. Only in the domanial House did he find, alongside its aristocratic leadership, enough lawyers who might hope for preferment at his hands and could therefore be won to his views. Against the wish of the two upper Houses, these representatives of the towns were now persuaded to petition that the privileged classes should at least have their lands properly surveyed and subjected to tax.

This parliamentary petition was the crucial confrontation of Caracciolo's whole campaign. Previous viceroys had found little difficulty in packing parliament to obtain their minimal requirements of tax, and in return used to overlook its deficiencies. Caracciolo, however, scorned any craven compromise: he wanted more efficiency in mobilising the resources of the kingdom, and knew that the upper two Houses would never voluntarily agree with him. Parliament would therefore have to be reformed. However, the opposition had the advantage that the King's chief minister at Naples was still the Sicilian aristocrat, Sambuca. The Prince of Trabia, who was head of the domanial House, wrote to Sambuca to beg for 'liberation from a slavery worse than that of the people of Israel in Babylon'; and, under pressure, the King decided not to push the matter to an immediate decision.

A somewhat easier target was economic protectionism, and here Caracciolo was aided by the fact that famine conditions after the Messina earthquake made emergency remedies acceptable. In Naples and Paris he had observed that free trade might be a better prophylactic against famines than protection; he accordingly abolished the municipalised bakeries with their fixed prices for bread, because under cover of being in the consumers' interest they were open to much trickery and profiteering. He also insisted that it was against the public interest for a landowner to compel tenants to grind their corn at his mill or to crush their olives and grapes at his press; nor should they have to sell their produce to him at his own price. It was wrong for barons to impose taxes on their tenants capriciously and without appeal. Caracciolo was here laying down rules which were generally accepted in other countries, but the attempt did not ingratiate him with the Sicilian landlords.

Nor did his desire to create smaller and more profitable farms. He believed that long leases and greater security of tenure would stimulate farmers to make agriculture more intensive and more highly capitalised. Perhaps villages could also be encouraged to let out part of their communal lands in *enfiteusi*. Some villages, in order to obtain money for their tax obligations and for other minor expenses over tithes and police, had been trying to turn these commons into profitable leaseholds, but local authorities were so much under baronial influence that the leases were generally offered to existing landowners, and the *latifondi* had thereby become all the more strongly entrenched. Caracciolo here touched on a fundamental problem, but it was more complex than he knew, and for the moment he could do little more than encourage the villagers to stand up for their rights.

THE PARTIAL SUCCESS OF REFORM

Caracciolo's reforms were much less radical than some of those being carried out elsewhere in Europe, but hostility to them was immense. Up to a point his success was remarkable, especially in view of the fact that he had little force at his disposal. Nothing in Sicily was to be quite the same ever again; moreover, the opposition which he elicited was to be an important element in the country's political education. Yet his temperament was too abrasive and uncompromising. Believing in reason and progress, he was interested in the desirable rather than the possible. Perhaps he was at once too radical and insufficiently liberal to be a truly successful reformer, and he did not always stop to understand the historical roots of what he was attacking.

Caracciolo himself chose his successor, the Prince of Caramanico. This man was also a Neapolitan product of the Enlightenment who had lived in northern Europe; and another mainlander, Simonetti, who as *Consultore* had been second in charge at Palermo and an important inspiration of Caracciolo's reforms, remained in administration to show that policy had not changed. Caramanico had less imagination and energy than his predecessor, but in some ways he was a more effective Viceroy. As well as being a convinced reformer, his more accommodating temperament won friends among the barons, and they went some way to meet him just because they now realized their vulnerability.

One of Caramanico's achievements was to make parliament agree to a new distribution of tax and the very survey of property which had earlier aroused such opposition. This census was delayed by the outbreak of the French revolutionary wars, but nevertheless the decision to have it was a useful threat. Parliament thus agreed to make taxes proportional to income. It was also agreed to change the inequitable system by which baronial towns paid less than their fair share of the *donativi*. Palermitans who owned property elsewhere in Sicily were no longer to be so favoured in tax matters. By accepting these changes, the nobles were publicly admitting both the need for a new deal and the fact that their old privileges were not inviolable.

Feudalism was further weakened when, by a pragmatic sanction in 1788, the King finally supported Caracciolo's view that the thirteenth-century laws, *Volentes* and *Si aliquem*, had made no fundamental change in feudal obligations. Fiefs could not be bequeathed or alienated like allodial property. Royal confirmation and a special payment were needed before they could be inherited; and, failing a proper succession, or if a proper entitlement could not be proved, they should revert to the crown. Moreover, peasants could not, except with compensation, be dispossessed of any rights of communal usage established by law or custom, not even on a baronial fief. Of course these were only legal decisions, and considerable efforts were made to mitigate their practical application, but ordinary people now received direct encouragement to assert their rights, and this was one ingredient in the gradual changing of public opinion.

In agricultural terms, the fiefs corresponded more or less to the semi-cultivated *latifondi* that covered most of Sicily. They were owned either by the barons and higher clergy, or sometimes communally by the villages. One difficulty with them was that in many cases immemorial rights of pasture made intensive crop farming impossible even if landlords had been willing to allow it. Though helpful to many individuals, such common rights were one reason why agricultural output was not keeping pace with a rising population. The *latifondisti* understandably wanted more unfettered ownership and already, either by arbitrary enclosures or by buying out other parties, they were beginning to move in this direction. The government knew that any revocation of 'promiscuous rights' would deprive many people of a livelihood; they also believed, however, that if communal methods of extensive cultivation could only be replaced by small farms individually owned, this ought to mean increased production, and equally give landless labourers a beneficial stake in society.

An edict of 1789 therefore aimed at increasing smallholdings, by bringing new land into cultivation and old farms into more intensive use. Some of the common lands in village possession were to be divided into copyholds and given for preference to poor people in exchange for the surrender of their rights of pasture and wood collecting. In practice, however, these laws sometimes took an unexpected turn: either the peasants could not pay the ground rent, or else the plots of land were too small and too distant; or else the laws were manipulated to their own profit by the local bosses in each village, that class of 'semi-gentlemen', as Sergio ominously called them, who were taking over from absentee landlords and had gunmen to enforce their will.

Economically desirable though it was to define rights of property, and though the number of peasant owners was in fact increased, socially the result of these laws was generally to enrich people who were already rich enough and in large part parasitic on society, at the same time as a rural proletariat was created which forfeited immemorial and valuable rights in the commons without receiving due compensation. Instead of reducing revolutionary tensions as the government had hoped, there was a multiplication in the number of casual labourers who lived precariously and had little or nothing to fall back on in years of difficulty. Before long the rootlessness and desperate poverty of these largely unemployed labourers would make them a revolutionary force of real significance.

The Abbé Balsamo watched this process with some apprehension. He was one of a select body of intellectuals, mostly ecclesiastics, who had benefited from government patronage under two reforming viceroys – indeed he became a pluralist with two abbeys as a sinecure. In 1787 a chair of agricultural science was created for him at Palermo, and Balsamo used this appointment as a chance to spend three years touring northern Italy, France and England to examine the latest agricultural practices. But, unlike so many other Sicilian intellectuals in the past, he did not become a permanent expatriate, for government policies were now creating a more hopeful outlet for talent in Sicily itself. He returned with new agricultural methods and tools, and full of ideas learnt from Arthur Young and Adam Smith. He was then entrusted by Caramanico with the task of surveying the deficiencies of Sicilian agriculture.

Under Balsamo's influence, experiments now took place with irrigation, artificial leys, cattle sheds and the rotation of crops. He argued that Sicily could never become prosperous without more capital, and this could only be formed through agriculture; but it would need a wholly new attitude towards entails, mortmain, 'promiscuous rights', excises, the *tratte* and all the other restrictive practices which hindered rational development. Balsamo was remarkable chiefly because he rejected the pessimism which refused to see any possibility of improvement. Unfortunately he was much too excited about what he found in England, and too ready to believe that it could be adapted to the different physical and psychological conditions of Sicily. Yet nothing should have been so inducive to a break in the main psychological barrier as his expert conviction that there was nothing inherently wrong with the climate or the soil.

A few intellectuals, encouraged by two of the ablest viceroys in all Sicilian history, were thus beginning to question some of the fundamental principles of the *ancien régime*. The idea of progress and notions about social obligation could now occasionally make their appearance. From the writings of the poet Meli we can see that, already by the 1780s, Rousseau and Voltaire had become fashionable names to drop in the aristocratic salons of Palermo. The Prince of Aci and Prince Lanza di Trabia are examples of nobles who were interested in agricultural experiment. Especially in the much more open town of Catania there was even an infiltration of radically democratic ideas from France.

Ironically, the French Revolution of 1789 then abruptly halted this process, for the King's more reactionary advisers persuaded him that further reforms might bring a demand for political liberty and so undermine both State and Church just as in France. The danger was real, for the influence of jacobinism was not negligible in Sicily; and the threat was obviously increased by the presence of the French revolutionary army which marched down through Italy and encamped over the straits within sight of Messina. Some individual Sicilians went into exile in France because of their advanced ideas. Others made one or two minuscule attempts at revolution. Francesco di Blasi planned a republican rebellion to take place during the Good Friday processions of 1795: a number of private denunciations, some of them apparently out of mere personal rancour, revealed his intentions to the police, and he was publicly tortured and beheaded.

Di Blasi's sympathisers seem to have been mainly among the artisan classes and more in eastern than western Sicily. They were not very clear in their ideas, nor convinced enough to risk prison and death, and they had no notion how to organize a conspiracy. Almost nothing bound them to the common labourers and peasants without whom there was no propulsive force for a genuine insurrection. They themselves were not for the most part men of violence, and at the first sign of a truly popular riot most of them were quick to line up behind their patrons, the aristocracy. Such riots took place fairly often now, but in general owed less to jacobinism or politics than to the island's endemic propensity to jacqueries.

The reformers of the Enlightenment had not succeeded in prising Sicily loose from her history, and the European war that now broke out halted change, provoked a counter-revolution and temporarily restored the old balance in society. Apart from Sardinia, Sicily was the only region of Italy which Napoleon did not conquer. It thus escaped the message of the French Revolution, and this was a fact of the greatest consequence. Though di Blasi bewailed the faint-heartedness of his fellow countrymen, there is really no likelihood that any spontaneous political revolt could have succeeded. The middle class to whom he might have appealed was negligible, and even the songs of the common people were anti-jacobin. Only if Napoleon had remembered to make provision for transports at Reggio di Calabria could the work of Caracciolo and Caramanico have been taken to what might seem its logical conclusion.

CHAPTER 16

The Napoleonic Wars

BRITISH INTERVENTION

If Sicily was saved for the old regime after 1789, this was partly because the King was frightened into abandoning reform and partly because Napoleon's victories made occupation of the island an urgent strategic necessity for Britain. At the same time, the success of France made a close British alliance the one hope of survival for the Bourbons. When the French captured Malta, which was still nominally a Sicilian dependency, Neapolitan troops helped the British retake it; and though the latter at first claimed to rule in Ferdinand's name, Malta in fact found herself removed for ever from Sicilian sovereignty. Sicily, too, inevitably lost some independence as soon as it became a link in Britain's attempt to blockade Europe and keep open the Mediterranean sea routes. Though the British promised at first that they would 'not on any account interfere in the civil administration of Sicily', they did not take long to change their mind.

When Napoleon's army invaded Naples in 1798, Ferdinand fled to Palermo on Nelson's flagship. His arrival was greeted with delight, for it seemed to signify independence once again from Naples and a profitable return to court life. In all outward respects, at any rate, the country gave Ferdinand unqualified support against revolutionary France; and the ferocity of the common people in this cause was such that hundreds of sick French soldiers who landed at Augusta were murdered out of hand. The King, however, did not reciprocate the enthusiasm of his subjects, and looked on Sicily merely as a source of revenue for Naples. His Austrian Queen went further and claimed to hate Sicilians. Palermo seemed to her in every respect several generations behind Naples.

Sicily in some ways gained greatly by the arrival of these strangers. The King may have been uncouth and illiberal, but some of his entourage were, by comparison with what they encountered, sophisticated and progressive. Sicilians now learnt about new styles of architecture, new standards of personal living, and new ways of looking at politics and administration. But the debit side of the account was more in evidence, for inevitably it was very expensive to maintain the King and the hundreds of Neapolitans who came with him. Sir William and Lady Hamilton were showered with presents by the monarch; Nelson – the 'Anglo-Sicilian hero', as Meli called him – was given a huge feudal estate as Duke of Bronte, with all the perquisites of feudal jurisdiction and a large income which once had more usefully endowed the Palermo hospital.

The only regular source of revenue that might be quickly stretched was the *donativi*, though the King's failure to support some of Caracciolo's reforms meant that the privileged classes were strongly placed to fight any attempt to increase their contribution. Ferdinand was now belatedly convinced of the need to end light taxation of the aristocracy, and this threat at last brought a real constitutional opposition into being against the monarchy. Already in 1790 and 1794, the solidarity of the three Houses of parliament was visibly crumbling as the nobles became alarmed at the growth of egalitarian sentiment. Then came the demands for millions of *scudi* for yet another war from which Sicily stood to gain nothing. These were met; but in 1798 the two upper Houses asked for a prior assurance that Caracciolo's reforms would be annulled, that the King would visit Sicily, and that any new tax would not be spent just in the interests of Naples.

Here were the stirrings of resistance. Four years later, the King presided in person over parliament, in what had been intended as a purely formal occasion. But the meetings were unusually prolonged. Eventually a discreet offer of jobs and favours succeeded in neutralising some princely leaders of the opposition, and this enabled the King's friend, Prince Belmonte, to pilot an appropriate grant through the necessary stages. But Ferdinand had to promise that, if he returned to Naples, he would keep a permanent court at Palermo headed by a royal prince. Almost at once he broke this undertaking; a treaty with Napoleon allowed him to return home, and he took with him the court and a good deal of Sicilian money.

When war once again compelled the royal family to seek refuge at Palermo in 1806, they found a much chillier reception. The last four parliaments, coming on top of the challenge by Caracciolo, had given political experience and ambition to some barons; and the heavy new fiscal demands had made opposition almost an economic necessity. The nobles were now disinclined to believe that the kingdom was simply personal property given to the King by God; and they found his refusal to accept the existence of a Sicilian nation hard to bear. Indeed, so unconcerned was this philistine about the island's past glories that many twelfth-century mosaics were removed just to give him more convenient access to the palace chapel. What is more, Neapolitans were again taking over the main jobs, and this lack of employment especially for younger sons of the nobility was a serious motive of discontent.

Napoleon had every intention of capturing Sicily and so dominating the central Mediterranean. As Ferdinand had no army or navy worth the name, he was reluctantly compelled in 1806 to invite a British force to take over the main responsibility for defence. He probably did not know that the British commander had orders to occupy Sicily by force if this invitation was not forthcoming. The presence of a large foreign army brought greater prosperity than Sicily had known for centuries. Not only a direct British subsidy, but many loans, a fair amount of private investment capital from London, and large expenditure by the occupying forces all helped to create a minor boom for industry, commerce and agriculture. So considerable was Britain's commercial intervention that by 1812 she had thirty consuls or vice-consuls on the island; and the salons of Palermo even developed a snobbish affectation of speaking Sicilian with an English accent.

Continued war and inflation soon enough brought up again the question of finance and baronial tax immunities. Parliament therefore had to be summoned in 1810. Government officials explained to the three Houses that putting more taxation on the poor would be financially unproductive as well as a brake on the economy. The speech from the throne boldly appealed to the 'noble principle of equality', and the Deputation was instructed to act in accordance with this principle. The gauntlet had been thrown down. Surprisingly it was picked up. Prince Belmonte, one of the few travelled and talented aristocrats, dramatically changed sides and made a fighting speech which persuaded the barons to reduce the government's request for money by half. Even more astonishing, he persuaded the ecclesiastics to turn against the Archbishop of Palermo and join the barons in resistance.

Once the privileged classes realised that they would no longer be allowed to escape tax, there was no reason for their usual subservience. A new menace of royal interference was threatening their income and social position. To dislodge the Neapolitan ministers, and as a bid for popularity, they therefore challenged the whole structure of monarchical absolutism by agreeing to a counter-plan which accepted some of the very reforms that the nobles had strenuously rejected in the 1780s. It was proposed to abolish the eighteen different *donativi* as being much too complex and expensive to collect. They also proposed giving up their feudal dues. Instead they were ready to pay a single tax of 5 per cent on the income of all real estate – with the significance exception of property in and around Palermo.

Coming from the barons, this offer was altogether unexpected. Possibly it was meant only as a tactical move without much intention of being taken seriously. Nevertheless, it was a deliberate challenge to the royal prerogative. If the King wished to stand firm, he could fall back on British money; but this might mean some loss of independence and even acceptance of a more liberal policy, and he for one thought that too high a price to pay. Instead Ferdinand resorted to non-parliamentary taxation. The opposition was incensed, and forty barons, representing half the parliamentary votes, delivered a humble remonstrance urging that any additional taxes should come through parliament. In reply, the Deputation, that vaunted guardian of Sicilian liberties, decided with no contrary vote that the King was perfectly within his rights.

Belmonte now turned secretly to the British: he was ready to convene a rival parliament at Messina, he said, and accept any King whom Britain might impose, even if necessary a Protestant. The King, whose baronial friends gave him ample warning of this somewhat half-hearted rebellion, waited for several months; then suddenly, in a move strangely reminiscent of the Westminster episode of 1642, he arrested the five chief protesting members of parliament. Among these were Belmonte and his uncle the Prince of Castelnuovo. All five were deported to penal settlements in islands off the Sicilian shore.

This royal coup nearly succeeded, for the opposition crumbled without their leaders. But if the feudatories were unwilling to persist, it was otherwise with General William Bentinck, the British commander. He and his officers were getting concerned about the security of the 17,000 British troops in Sicily. They were also alarmed at the administrative chaos which made their task of defending the island so hard. They knew by now that they would have to control the spending of the subsidy if munitions and fortifications were to be provided. They also feared that local support might be forthcoming for a French invasion if there were not some lessening of the tension in the island. It even came to their knowledge that the court, while taking Bentinck's money, was in secret contact with the French.

What Caracciolo had failed to do by enlightened absolutism, Bentinck now tried to do by a liberal parliamentarism which was quite exotic to Sicily. By threatening to withdraw his troops and suspend the subsidy, he made the government release the five barons and withdraw the extra-parliamentary taxes. Then, at his direction, the largely Neapolitan ministry was replaced by a more representative cabinet which included three of the five ex-prisoners. In the end, he had to go further still and force the Queen into exile after using the secret service funds to pay off her enormous debts and get her jewels out of pawn. Without intending to become too closely embroiled in domestic politics, Bentinck manoeuvred himself into a position where he was the virtual governor of Sicily, and under his influence a new parliament was summoned which abolished feudalism and planned a new liberal constitution.

THE CONSTITUTION OF 1812

When parliament met in June 1812, the *ancien régime* suddenly appeared to collapse. The monarchy and the conservative feudatories accepted the most radical changes almost without a fight. The King made a desperate bid for support and offered to revoke all the reforms of Caracciolo; but this came too late to win enough acceptance. He therefore temporarily handed over authority to his son, who was strongly under Bentinck's influence. Belmonte and Castelnuovo were now ministers and could use the block vote of the domanial House to support the cause of reform. They also controlled many of the proxy votes, and this gave them a majority among the ecclesiastics. The baronial chamber was less certain; but Castelnuovo believed that the nobility, if only out of fear, could be persuaded to make some sacrifice of its prerogatives.

Balsamo and his friends had meanwhile spent several months drafting an outline constitution. During a single night session its main principles were unanimously agreed. The excitement of the moment, the general readiness to accept authority, and no doubt a little panic, all contributed to this speed and unanimity. Among its chief features was the formation of a two-chamber parliament with a House of Peers and a House of Commons. This was to meet annually, and could tax and legislate subject to royal assent; it could also hold ministers responsible. The King, however, kept executive powers, together with a veto and the right to dissolve parliament. A jury system was adopted; and torture, along with all private jurisdictions and *fori* except those of the Church and the army, were abolished. Sicily was to be quite independent; and the King was forbidden, just as he had once been in 1296, to leave the island without parliamentary consent.

Quite as revolutionary was the abolition of feudalism to which the nobles agreed in a moment of mixed generosity and shrewd calculation. Some feudatories realized the necessity of change if they were to survive economically. If entails could only be mitigated, then some land could be sold to pay off debts and the remaining property made economically sound. This would put capital and land to better use. All younger sons of the aristocracy would gain from freer inheritance laws and no primogeniture. Other nobles simply wanted an excuse to rescind the 'promiscuous rights' in their fiefs which hitherto had given the peasantry a kind of co-proprietorship in the land. Others recognized that the wartime rise in cereal prices meant vast profits if the complicated edifice of restrictions of the wheat trade could be demolished.

At the same time, partly as a result of the war and the British occupation, a middle class was appearing with enough money to buy land if only feudal law could be modified to allow the fiefs to be broken up. This middle class had come into existence either by switching from wheat to more profitable crops on land held in *enfiteusi*, or by money-lending, or by managing the *latifondi* through the contract of *gabella*. The *gabelloti* wanted land for financial profit as well as just for prestige and power, and this gave their land hunger an extra force. Under the British occupation these middlemen had many chances to make money, and money for them meant land. Therefore they too, as well as the landowners, had an interest in opening up the feudal estates and destroying communal rights of grazing on private property.

The abolition of feudalism in July 1812 was not an entirely unselfish act by the aristocracy. There were solid advantages in shedding the duties as well as the rights of feudalism. The surrender of feudal jurisdiction was certainly a loss, but the conversion of fiefs into freeholds was ample compensation. Sulphur mines, formerly considered public property, were now deemed to be in private ownership just when the industrial revolution made sulphur a product of fundamental importance in which Sicily had a near monopoly. Never again would a fief devolve to the crown for lack of an heir; and by abolishing 'promiscuous rights' on former feudal land, the nobility was making an enormous gain, without offering any compensation to the dispossessed. Equally important, and in contrast to Naples, water supplies were now more than ever to be private property; and in an arid country, this was crucial.

As a consequence, the freedoms invoked in 1812 were of little practical relevance to the peasantry. In so far as there was promise of social as opposed to private benefits, the gains turned out to be more theoretical than real; never was there any specification of precisely what was abolished, nor how the abolition should take place. All the really important decisions were left for the courts to determine, and these were rarely independent enough to decide against the landed interest. The *latifondi* went on being called 'fiefs', the landowners 'feudatories', and the peasantry 'villeins' right down to the twentieth century; and with reason.

This element of illusion was at first obscured in the general enthusiasm. Balsamo's constitution was hailed as a great victory for Sicilian liberties and was set alongside that of Britain. Subsequently, Bentinck was accused of having forced it on Sicily, but in fact he clearly warned Balsamo at the time that such an exotic transplant could hardly be expected to work very well; and other Englishmen were still more outspoken. The truth was rather that both monarch and aristocracy had a common wish to involve Britain, and it was thought that this kind of copy would compel the British to guarantee that no liberal or democratic practices would be introduced which went any further than current practice at Westminster.

Parliament met in 1813, and when sessions began, the liberal government found itself facing a reactionary House of Peers and a radical majority in the Commons. Most of the towns were effectively electing their representatives for the first time in centuries, and some of them wanted no part in the 'aristocratic' constitutional decision of 1812. These new middle class 'democrats' came more from eastern than western Sicily, and included merchants, landowners, and intellectuals, as well as lawyers. They wanted cheaper food; they had serious ideas about agrarian reform; they sought the complete abolition of entails and a further division of Church property; they wanted a new land survey and a still fairer spread of taxation. To them the constitution was a baronial sham; and until it was reformed, they refused to grant a penny of tax.

It was not only the Commons who showed that a free constitution could not work in a semi-feudal world. The nobles, said Balsamo, were quite as factious as the democrats; and they automatically rejected any bill from the other House. The opposition was many-sided. It even included a man of the Enlightenment, Natale, who was offended that his title was not grand enough for a seat in the upper House. Many barons had supported the constitution only in the hope of obtaining still more power for themselves, and they were shaken by the appearance of a democratic middle class with ideas of its own. Almost all of them, said Bentinck's secretary in July 1813, were already repentant at having given up their feudal rights. Mention of universal suffrage and land nationalisation was far more alarming than any indignity they had ever suffered from the crown in the worst days of Caracciolo.

Bentinck was the most energetic and yet the most moderate spirit behind liberal reform, and when he moved away to help liberate northern Italy, personal and sectional jealousies in Sicily became worse than ever. Belmonte gave up the cause as hopeless and retired to Paris. Castelnuovo felt similarly defeated, while the Abbé Balsamo admitted that there were simply not enough enlightened and independent people to provide 154 deputies in the Commons. 'Too much liberty,' he told Bentinck, 'is for the Sicilians, what would be a pistol, or a stiletto in the hands of a boy or a madman.' As the war drew to a close it could be seen by everyone that the constitution depended more than ever on British money and troops, but any form of government needing the permanent presence of a foreign army was an absurdity, and in any case neither the British public nor the other European powers would allow such an occupation to continue in peacetime.

– The Temple of Concord, Agrigento. Built in the mid-fifth century BC, this Greek
mple owes its preservation largely to its conversion into a church in the sixth century AD.

– The late fifth-century temple at Segesta. The building was never completed, and it
ay just have been part of a plan to lure Athens into an alliance by creating a false
npression of the city's power and wealth.

3 – The Greek theatre at Segesta. This is among the smaller of Sicily's Greek theatres, and probably dates from the late fourth or early third century BC.

4 – The Greek theatre at Taormina, looking south towards Mount Etna. It was rebuilt by the Romans, who used it for gladiatorial combats. This is one of the most breathtaking sites anywhere in the world.

5 & 6 – Pavement mosaics from the Roman villa near Piazza Armerina. They far
outstrip in scale anything else of their kind known today. *Above*: Odysseus in the cave
of the Cyclops. According to Greek legend, the Cyclops lived on Mount Etna. A cluster
of rocks in the sea off Acireale are reputedly those hurled at the fleeing Odysseus.
Below: The end of a chariot race.

7 – The Palatine Chapel, Palermo, looking west to where the Norman kings used to sit beneath the image of Christ enthroned. The wooden ceiling dates from the 1140s, and is by Arab craftsmen. Its sumptuousness, and to some extent its style, make it unique.

8 – The cathedral at Cefalù, begun by King Roger in 1131, was at one time intended as a royal mausoleum. It was almost certainly built with the help of Anglo-Noman architects.

9 – Mosaic of Christ Pantokrator from the cathedral at Cefalù. Of Greek workmanship and dating from 1148, this composition was regarded even by contemporaries as a masterpiece.

10 – The church of St John of the Hermits (San Giovanni degli Eremiti), Palermo. It was built by King Roger in the 1130s. With its five red cupolas it seems almost as much a mosque as a Christian shrine.

11 – The baronial stronghold at Caccamo. Sicily is still dotted with such castles, though few can boast such a magnificent setting as this. The site has been fortified since prehistoric times.

12 – Villa Valguarnera, Bagheria, built to designs by Tomaso Napoli in 1721. Bagheria was once the fashionable resort of the aristocracy. It is now an ugly overspill of Palermo.

13 – Figures on a garden wall in the Villa Palagonia, Bagheria. This villa was built by the eccentric Prince of Palagonia in 1715. It was a source of great curiosity to northern travellers of the Grand Tour. Goethe wrote about it with some vehemence.

14 – The 'sitting-out' room in the Palazzo Gangi, Palermo, *c.* 1750–60. This palace was the setting for the ball scenes in Luchino Visconti's *The Leopard*, a film based on the famous novel by Giuseppe Tomasi di Lampedusa.

15 – The church of San Giorgio, Ragusa. One of south-eastern Sicily's many fine baroque churches. It was built to designs by Rosario Gagliardi (after the great earthquake of 1693 which destroyed much of this area), and was completed in 1775.

16 – Auto-da-fè, 1724, in front of the Archbishop's Palace and Palermo cathedral. The inquisitors are to the right, and boxes are provided for the viceroy and the aristocracy.

17 – The Prince of Biscari's aqueduct near Catania, destroyed by a storm in 1780. A rare example of aristocratic endeavour.

18 – The town of Calatafimi where in May 1860 Garibaldi won a celebrated victory en route from Marsala to Palermo. This is a rich agricultural area, famous for its vines.

19 – Centuripe, in eastern Sicily. Many of the island's rural communities are large, hill-top clusters like this one. Bandits and malaria made it too dangerous to live in the open countryside.

– Palermo, looking north towards Monte Pellegrino, taken shortly before building ʃeculation turned the north and west of the city into a concrete jungle.

1 – The water-front at Messina, a few years after the earthquake of 1908. The arthquake and the ensuing tidal wave destroyed more than 90 per cent of the city and illed perhaps 75,000 people. The sixteenth-century statue of Neptune survived.

22 – Soil erosion below the Temple of Juno, Agrigento. Deafforestation and heavy winter rainfall have made Sicily highly susceptible to soil erosion and landslides.

23 – A typical *masseria* or farmhouse in the midst of *latifondi*. These complexes served as the administrative headquarters for the great estates. They were a favourite 'hostel' of bandits.

4 – The Quattro Canti, Palermo. The four elaborate façades at the intersection of Via
Maqueda and Corso Vittorio Emanuele mark the traditional centre of the city. They
were built in the early seventeenth century, and are decorated with statues of the
seasons, Spanish kings, and saints.

25 – The failure of industry: the Chimed plant at Termini Imerese. This massive chemical factory was built by the regional government at a cost of many millions of pounds. For reasons that are not clear, it never went into operation. It is now too rusty and overgrown to be serviceable.

CHAPTER 17

Restoration, reform
and reaction

RESTORATION AND REVOLUTION 1816–21

Before the end of 1813, royal agents were hard at work building a party among the nobles and securing popular support among the mob and the workers' guilds. Eventually, when the King resumed government, the crowds cheered him and booed the liberal constitutionalists. According to a well-placed British observer, some of those who had supported the constitution had done so merely to reduce central supervision over their management of local affairs; and the same people had by now learnt from practical experience that they had more to fear from each other than from the monarchy. Elements of Left, Right and Centre thus conspired to bring Ferdinand back. Parliament itself, even before the constitution had been approved in detail, agreed to abandon it. Subsequently Sicilians blamed Ferdinand for destroying their liberal experiment, but in fact he seems to have had a fair general consensus of local support.

He still did not act precipitately. Only in 1815, after a succession of parliaments had produced no taxation, did he dissolve the two Houses for the last time. He then left for the mainland, although this was illegal by the 1812 statute. The following year, with Austrian approval, he conceded to his very dear Sicilians an altogether new status. Hitherto he had been Ferdinand IV of Naples and Ferdinand III of Sicily; henceforward he was to be Ferdinand I of a new unitary state, the 'Kingdom of the Two Sicilies'. The Sicilian flag was abolished; so was freedom of the press; and Ferdinand had no intention of ever calling another parliament. Laws and institutions were imported from the mainland, and this meant largely the Napoleonic code and system of administration which the French had imposed on Naples. Government was to be more centralized than before, and seven new provinces were created, to be administered by Intendants and non-elected town councils.

Bentinck was naturally displeased at this outcome, but as the Austrians had borne the brunt of liberating the mainland from Napoleon, he and the British were in no position to resist. By contrast, many Sicilians seemed quite satisfied with the new arrangement. A number of the island's aristocrats voluntarily followed the King to Naples, where they were given a large share in court life. The Messinese made a special donation to indicate their pleasure at the restoration of Bourbon absolutism; while Catania, Syracuse and the other new provincial capitals felt that gains from the new system more than compensated for any loss of insular independence. Not only princes, but also liberals and democrats joined in a flood of applications for jobs, and were glad to become Intendants or sub-Intendants in the King's 'unconstitutional' administration.

Palermo, on the other hand, lost heavily, both in pride and by ceasing to be the centre of court life. The lawyers, who were concentrated there, hated having to master a new code and a new hierarchy of courts; and as parliaments no longer met, the barons in practice discovered that they had lost one ingredient in their privileged world. Moreover, enlightened despotism was now reinforced by French-trained officials who since 1806 had been applying altogether new principles of equality and centralisation at Naples; and the land tax, which the aristocracy had approved in 1810, but which they had either not paid at all or else expected to collect from their tenants, became unexpectedly heavy as land values collapsed after 1815 and rents went unpaid.

These are some reasons why many of those who at first accepted the return of monarchical authoritarianism had second thoughts later. By defeating liberalism, the nobles had unwittingly restored the monarchy of Caracciolo. It was they, surprisingly, rather than the depleted democrats and liberals who were soon trying to break out of the traditional political immobilism which had formerly been their safeguard. As the British minister wrote in 1820: 'The only chance the Barons have of retaining any of their feudal privileges is by a separation from [Naples]. The only chance the Lawyers have of reverting to the ancient system of jurisprudence, so profitable to themselves and so ruinous to all but the Barons, is by a separation.'

Opposition was aided by the fact that a grave economic slump was blamed, somewhat unfairly, on the Neapolitan government. Sicily had profited from the war, and when British expenditure of perhaps twelve million pounds a year stopped in 1815, serious unemployment followed; and as a free international market developed once again in cereals, local wheat prices fell by three-quarters. On top of this there was irritation both at the way the new government sought to push the legal termination of feudalism further than the barons themselves wanted, and at the new provincial organization which tended to cut across intricate systems of patronage and clientelage.

Naples was soon hated in a way that Spain had never been; and when a minor insurrection in the Neapolitan provinces forced Ferdinand to make concessions to the liberal constitutionalists, this was Palermo's cue to rebel. The revolution of 1820 duplicated in many of its details a number of earlier risings. Once again the peasants and peasant squads were the main forces of disorder and revolution; but once again they lacked staying power; and their political ideas were elementary and undiscriminating. The guilds were another distinct force, but they were never so revolutionary that they wanted a clean sweep of the old regime. Here and there were groups of *carbonari*, secret middle-class confraternities vowed to a variety of political reforms. But their importance should not be exaggerated. Apart from a generalised aversion to tyranny, the *carbonari* had no clear or uniform political programme; and their most active elements would almost certainly have preferred a Neapolitan constitution rather than an alliance with aristocratic separatism or a peasants' revolt.

The Two Sicilies had in 1820 been granted a joint parliament by Ferdinand, and consequently the Neapolitan liberals were extremely annoyed when rioting in Sicily upset their constitutional plans. They were determined not to recognise the island's right to secede; and when representatives were sent by the Palermo junta to Naples to discuss Sicilian autonomy, they were unceremoniously arrested by parliament. In the eyes of the Neapolitan liberals, Sicilian autonomy would at best be taking liberalism too far, and at worst would spell reactionary feudalism.

Palermo's political lead was not generally followed in Sicily. The news of the rising was sometimes taken in country districts as an excuse for social revolution, for instance in the Ragusa area where a considerable division of the land took place. At Trapani there was strong feeling for a liberal Neapolitan constitution rather than renewed submission to aristocratic rule from Palermo; but Marsala then used the opportunity to break free from the provincial capital at Trapani, and destroyed crops and woodlands belonging to this rural city. Civic quarrels were thus far more in evidence than any common feelings of Sicilian allegiance; and when Messina turned against Palermo, it was almost automatic for some of the villages near Messina to take this occasion to favour the other side.

When the Neapolitan parliament decided to subdue Sicilian separatism by force, Palermo found herself with little support elsewhere. The Palermo aristocracy had failed to impose their conservative constitution on the rest of Sicily, and now realised that the social revolution which they had partly encouraged might get out of hand; so the Prince of Villafranca, the leading figure in the Palermo junta, went with some of the guildsmen to meet the Neapolitan army at Termini Imerese and discuss surrender. But some of the anarchic forces which had helped initiate the revolution were unwilling to accept peace and the end to months of independence and impunity for crime. A mob was soon in arms for the defence of Palermo; and the city had to be bombarded before it finally surrendered to the Neapolitan army.

The Neapolitan liberals were interested only in putting down the rebellion and had few constructive ideas of how to bring reforms to Sicily. A few laws were passed, but the constitutional regime did not last long enough for such legislation to have any practical effect. In March 1821, the Austrians invaded Naples with the intention of restoring the absolutist government of King Ferdinand; and Sicilians accepted this fairly passively. Soon there were ten thousand Austrian troops in the island. Whereas the British occupation had more than paid for itself, during the next five years Sicily had to bear heavy costs to pay for this foreign army.

Once again the most common political feelings in Sicily were shown to be those connected with passive opposition – opposition to autocratic and liberal regimes alike, and almost equally to government by foreigners or Sicilians. The initial enthusiasm generated for each revolution in turn was in part illusory: it usually reflected a negative longing for change, accompanied by a desire on the part of certain individuals for anarchy and the achievement of private non-political objectives. Attempts at reform by either constitutionalists or royalist autocrats at Naples had as little permanent effect on society as those of Caracciolo and Bentinck earlier, or those of the Piedmontese and Austrians a hundred years before; and the general reaction in Sicily to each of them differed remarkably little. At root there was still a deep political pessimism which shied away from any social action or from accepting the possibility of lasting gain as a result of political commitment.

REFORM AND REACTION

Supported by Austrian bayonets, Ferdinand for the second time suspended a constitution which he had sworn to observe; and despite protests by England, even despite advice from Austria and France, he broke his own undertaking of 1816 to recall the Sicilian parliament before any increase in taxes. In fact the word 'parliament' was now expunged from official documents. Sicilian separatism had been doubly defeated by Neapolitan liberals and by Austria, yet some concessions were made to autonomist sentiment. The stamp and tobacco duties were not reimposed, and Sicily was left with one of the lowest general tax rates in Europe. Sicilians were now to have a monopoly of jobs in Sicily; and conscription was stopped, partly because deserters were taking to brigandage.

The King had learnt from the revolution that the privileged classes were still a danger. At long last, therefore, the guilds were abolished. In 1824 a law was introduced that aimed to break the hold of inefficient landlords on Sicilian agriculture. This allowed creditors to take land in settlement of debt; and since most large estates were heavily mortgaged, the hope was that a new class of efficient landowners would now emerge from among these creditors. Unfortunately, Scinà, the architect of the law, underestimated the psychological as well as the sheer practical difficulties of transforming the *latifondi*. In effect the main beneficiaries of his legislation turned out to be existing landowners and ecclesiastical corporations, or else *gabelloti* who were little if any improvement on their predecessors.

Some division of properties was gradually taking place as the pressure of population grew, and no doubt two bouts of Bourbon legislation in 1789–92 and 1818–24 contributed towards this process. But legislation could not immediately effect the tradition which encouraged younger sons not to marry; and there was still a tendency for their portion of an inheritance to return at death so that the family holdings should not be dispersed. Social conditions thus strongly favoured the retention of the large ranch as a unit of agriculture; so did physical conditions of climate, soil and communications; and there was also the fact that the ending of feudalism made enclosure easier. At Bronte, the heir of Lord Nelson more than doubled the extent of his huge domain during the century, and in the process he deprived many peasants of common rights which they had formerly enjoyed when these estates belonged to the Palermo hospital.

These common rights were another field where legislation was always defeated by vested interests. Every district had its own immemorial customs, and they had existed on both the village commons and the baronial fiefs. They varied from place to place, but usually they gave the right to obtain wood for making ploughs or charcoal, perhaps to glean in the stubble, or collect acorns and chestnuts for pigs; in one village, the residents could cut peat, in another the roots of liquorice, in another wild asparagus and berries; more rarely they could sow wheat on the common lands. Most common of all was the right to pasture animals. But naturally it was a grave restraint on agricultural development if flocks could damage standing crops and if every step in the farming cycle had to be regulated by tradition and communal considerations.

Reformers and landowners had a common interest in wanting to change this relic of the past; and the Bourbon government, on the experience of Napleonic practice in Naples, tried to transform 'promiscuous rights' wherever possible. In 1817 officials were required to work out a rate of compensation for any deprived beneficiaries. The lawyers then enjoyed decades of discussion over which precise rights were affected and the value of compensation. The peasants, even if they dared to ask, could understand little about the complicated legal proceedings involved, and so landowners were again able to round off their *latifondi* while giving little or nothing in return. Another law in 1825 tried to close some of the gaping loopholes, but the landowners had the advantage not only of occupying much of the land in question, but also of dominating the commissions set up to enforce the law.

Here was a general problem facing reformers. The administration in Naples was too remote geographically and too lacking in bureaucratic efficiency to be able to enforce legislation on the spot. If there had been greater inspiration from the top, things might have been different. But Ferdinand I, though in some ways less misguided than his opponents allowed, was neither an able ruler nor an intelligent man; and his son, Francis I (1825–30) was more inadequate still, a weakling in mind and body, narrow-minded and intolerant, whose ministers were incompetent and whose government was based essentially on the threat of force. Sicily had always suffered from rulers of insufficient tact, practice and intelligence; and the Bourbons were no exceptions.

Ferdinand II (1830–59) was at least more inspiring than his predecessors. His four visits to the island in the 1830s were something without precedent. He set up an institute to encourage industry and agriculture, and also a Central Office of Statistics. A new census was decreed in 1833 in the hope that a more accurate land tax would make it possible to reduce the *macinato* on flour. Such moderate essays in reform, however, did not reconcile Sicilians to being a Neapolitan possession. On the contrary, they can only have made the *notabili* more hostile still. Neither an increase in land tax nor reducing the *macinato*, nor championing the rights of villagers on the ex-fiefs was likely to please the aristocracy. What they would have liked was a completely separate Sicilian government which would at once satisfy their sense of honour, create jobs for their children and in general give them the power to keep reform at bay.

The King knew that there were grave administrative difficulties in the way of making policy effective. But he was by nature an idle man, and after 1835 he lost interest in remedial legislation. Clubs were shut down and foreign books excluded by a harsher censorship. 'Although the King and his ministers are fully sensible of the evils which exist in Sicily,' wrote a foreign ambassador, 'they do not possess sufficient talent or energy to meet them, and will leave things to take their chance.' As a result the impoverishment of the peasants became more acute, and other foreign observers clearly expressed their fears that social revolution could not be far away.

One cause of poverty was the high crime rate. Much talent and energy was channelled into underworld activities which crippled economic life; and the Bourbons were as powerless here as every previous regime. Smuggling continued to be widespread. Much less common, but still serious, was the illicit control of water supplies, and we know from official reports that the drying out of the water table south of Palermo had made this quite rewarding by the 1840s. The most common crime of all was animal stealing, or *abigeato*, an activity made easy by the semi-nomadic system of husbandry in the roadless interior. Protection money was extorted from landowners, and strong pressure used to make the *latifondisti* employ criminals as *guardiani* on their estates.

Early in the century, British troops had learnt of secret brotherhoods with a reputation for courage, honour, cruelty, and complete disregard for the law. Many stories were told of landowners harbouring bands of brigands; and they sometimes even led them in person. There were also groups composed, it seems, of peasants defending themselves against feudal usurpations; and we hear of one commanded by the local archpriest. Though the activities of such units may at times have been criminal, that was not always their *raison d'être*. Often they were no more than local political factions or clienteles, and this made them loose 'social' structures rather than organizations in any strict sense of the word.

The question of lawlessness in Sicily was complicated by the fact that this was a society in which honour, power and mistrust sometimes played a greater role in crime than the mere pursuit of gain. This presented a problem for the authorities, as it meant that criminals were often understood and tolerated by their communities to an unusual degree. Indeed they were frequently respected to the point where they could parade as standard bearers of a more equitable system of justice than that provided by the state. To outsiders, used to a greater harmony between public and private morality, this state of affairs was baffling. To governments, it was also frustrating, and after 1860 the convenient but improbable legend was to develop that a widespread criminal association must be secretly at work.

CHAPTER 18

The economy 1750–1850

COMMERCE

The slowness of Sicilian political development is in part explained by the slowness of the economy to expand or indeed to admit change of any kind. Until 1800, Sicily's overseas commerce was mostly carried by either the Genoese or the French, and the lack of any vigorous local competition to these foreign merchants contributed a static quality to social and economic life. The middle class, to the small extent that one existed, remained professional and bureaucratic rather than commercial or industrial, while the leaders of society lived off their rents and nourished a resolute prejudice against trade.

This genteel attitude towards commerce was a fundamental fact. Sometimes the Spanish were blamed for introducing it, though in fact many Spaniards had made fortunes out of Sicilian trade and had been despised by Palermo society for doing so. Alternatively, blame was placed on the Bourbons for either too much or too little government intervention. More plausibly, the courts were held to be at fault for not making debts easier to collect; or else the taxation of exported manufactures was said to be unfair. The system of import duties was also condemned just because it did not encourage local enterprise by taxing dyed cloth more than undyed, refined sugar more than unrefined.

Perhaps the greatest barrier to commerce was the perennial lack of trust. Mutual suspicion made it almost unknown for rich men to form a limited company except on a family basis, and this meant that one indispensable ingredient of a flourishing economy was absent. The same lack of trust, explained the economist, Francesco Ferrara, was also responsible for the absence of Sicilian insurance firms, simply because Sicilians themselves always preferred to insure abroad with companies which had the reputation for paying up at once without going to court. Any insurance firm, incidentally, would expect a high premium from a Sicilian merchant, and this was another fact which contributed to make local businesses uncompetitive.

Another hurdle was that, at a time when Naples was developing new and flourishing credit institutions, it still needed an interest rate of 12 or even 20 per cent in Sicily before money could be attracted into commerce. The government was occasionally begged to bring down interest rates by law, and to found the banks that private enterprise could not create; it was called upon to assist the formation of trading companies and to assure them by law of a monopoly; it had been asked to help industrialists by giving them cheap convict labour so as to reduce costs, and even by providing them with free factory space in the ex-Jesuit houses. But the government was not only ill-equipped to intervene in this way, it was also afraid that such action would only make the disease even worse; and meanwhile commerce and industry were left to foreigners, who incidentally managed to do quite well out of them.

The necessary spirit of association and mutual confidence could have been generated only in the towns. Part of the trouble was that communal administration had for too long been an appendage of feudalism. Long after the Spanish had gone, the most coveted privilege for an urban councillor was still to be entitled a 'grandee of Spain first class'. In the big towns the office of senator was, for prestige and financial reasons, kept as an absolute monopoly of the nobles. In these circumstances it is not altogether surprising to find that the ports were still poorly equipped for trade and empty most of the year, and the rivalry of one port with another made it difficult to agree over allocating even the small sums set aside by the government for harbour works, while the towns themselves did precious little on their own account to foster trade.

INDUSTRY

Lack of commerce and of industry went hand in hand. At the beginning of the nineteenth century, native industry hardly existed except at a household level. Basic products such as shoes, nails, pins, buttons and knives were imported, and so even were bricks. Despite this, most Sicilian economists were not enthusiastic about artificially encouraging manufacturers if this required excessive protectionism and transferring scanty capital away from agriculture where they thought it could be more usefully employed. After all, Sicily clearly lacked the main pre-requirements of an industrial revolution. She had no iron that could be mined economically, no coal except a little bad quality lignite, no navigable canals and rivers at all, and very poor internal communications of any sort.

The Neapolitan government after 1815 tried to encourage what local industries there were by protecting them against imports from Naples; but the amount of protection was either insufficient as an incentive, or else too high to be much inducement to increased efficiency; and British, French and Spanish merchants at first made things yet more difficult by insolently asserting an ancient right to be exempt from customs visitation. In 1824, some of the surviving taxes on exports were abolished and higher duties placed on imported manufactures; but the good effects of this were counteracted by the freeing of trade with Naples, and Sicily was thus exposed to imports from a country which over the previous century had outstripped the island in economic growth. Neapolitan, British and French manufactures continued to take the lion's share of the market after 1824, and certain local businesses collapsed.

Though the environment was far from propitious, the career of Vincenzo Florio shows that considerable profits could be made by people who did not accept the conventional disinclination for commerce and were prepared to take risks with their money. Florio was a Calabrian by birth, whose family had exiled itself to Sicily with the King. He began his career as commercial traveller, and, according to general belief, made his first money by smuggling. He quickly expanded his interests to include tunny fishing, sulphur, spinning and banking, and in 1841 was able to profit from government support to open the Oretea machine shop and foundry. This was the only establishment of its kind in Sicily, and by 1860 it employed two hundred people. He was a leading figure in the Marsala wine industry, and the second largest shareholder in a shipping combine organised by an English entrepreneur.

Such enterprise, however, was exceptional, and few followed Florio along this rewarding yet unfashionable path. Though two of the young Orlando brothers were making engines to mill wheat and sumac leaves after 1840, for political as well as economic reasons they eventually emigrated to the more favourable atmosphere of northern Italy, like so many other enterprising sons of Sicily. The Florio family itself married into the aristocracy and became part of the local establishment. However, they never entirely overcame the snobbish aloofness of aristocratic Palermo society.

In the absence of local initiative, it was often left to foreigners to develop the island's industrial potential. To a large extent this was true of sulphur, deposits of which stretched over several hundred square miles of central and southern Sicily. In 1794, the discovery of the Leblanc soda process revolutionized the industry, and British capitalists began to take an active interest in those areas near Sicilian ports where open-cast mining of sulphur was possible. Landowners near Girgenti and Caltanissetta suddenly discovered that they owned a near world monopoly in an essential commodity needed by the industrial revolution in Europe and America. When Ferdinand in 1808 waived his royal monopoly rights over mining in order to please the Sicilian aristocracy, a rosy future opened to many *latifondisti* and smallholders.

After the restoration of peace in 1815, there was a rush into sulphur mining, and thousands of new industrial uses for sulphuric acid were soon being developed. French firms now began to appear alongside the British. It seemed for a time as though the economy of Sicily was about to change dramatically; and despite some casualties, production was greatly expanded. By the peak year of 1834, exports of sulphur were almost three times the value of wine exports, which came next on the list. But the industry was vulnerable, as cheap labour and guaranteed exports meant there was no great incentive to improve methods of production; and this was ultimately to prove fatal.

The chief lack outside and inside the mines was wheeled transport. All the ore had to be brought to the surface on the backs of *carusi*, mostly small boys who were indentured to the trade by their families as what one can only call slave labour. Women, too, were employed as carriers, but the galleries were very low and hence boys or girls were preferred. Even on pittance wages this primitive method of transport could account for half the running expenses of a mine. As there were no proper roads, the sulphur was then taken on mules to the coast; and as there were no port establishments, stevedores waded deep into the sea to load lighters which then rowed out to ships lying beyond the dangerous inshore. All this was slow and expensive.

The Neapolitan government had some hopes that landowners would cooperate in making the industry succeed. The King set an example by renouncing his legal right to 10 per cent of the sulphur produced; but this generous gift was taken very much as a matter of course and met with no corresponding concessions from landlords. The mines as a result continued to be extraordinarily wasteful. Just as with the *latifondi*, most landowners used the *gabella* system, and the great profits of the 1830s taught them to keep leases on the mines short. But this only encouraged the manager or *gabelloto* to overproduce, and underinvest. The 'immorality and greed of producers' was given by a government inspector in 1850 as one of his main problems. Landowners, it was repeatedly said, insisted on taking between 20 per cent and 40 per cent of the sulphur as their ground rent, and this royalty must have contributed more than anything else towards making Sicilian sulphur too expensive.

AGRICULTURE

The severe slump that hit Sicilian agriculture after 1815 came as an urgent pointer to the need for radical change. Much of the area brought into production during the previous decade had to be abandoned; land values tumbled by two-thirds, and rents fell by a similar amount. How much wheat went on being produced cannot be said, because recorded figures for production according to one expert still bore little relation to reality. Export statistics were no doubt more reliable, largely because the profit had now gone out of grain smuggling. Wheat continued to be sent to Naples; and, as late as the 1830s, cereals were still exported in a good year to England, Portugal and France. Nevertheless, the pattern of trade now changed, and other crops were generally much bigger earners of foreign currency.

Sicily's wine industry was greatly boosted by the Napoleonic wars. Britain's other sources of supply were now cut off; and Nelson left for the Nile with over forty thousand gallons of Sicilian wine aboard. The man best placed to meet the new demand was John Woodhouse of Liverpool. He had originally come to the island as a dealer in vegetable potash, but in 1773 he sent an experimental consignment of wine to England. Twenty years later he profited from the vogue for sherry and port and opened a factory at Marsala for fortified wines of a similar strength and type. He brought to Sicily not only capital and enterprise but also ideas about overseas demand and marketing; and within a few years he had made a considerable fortune. Soon after 1806 another Englishman, Benjamin Ingham, set up a second establishment nearby; by 1814 there were four British firms at Marsala and several others at Mazara.

Friendly rivalry between these foreign merchants had excellent effects on quality and price. Ingham went to Spain to study the solera system, and brought back information about clarifying wine and dosing it with spirit. He used to buy rough wine from all over the island, mature it for five years, and blend it to maintain a constant standard. Nor was he too discouraged by the slump after 1815, but at once began the slow process of developing a peacetime market. Ten years later, he and the others could claim to have created an altogether new category of wine. At their own expense they built proper roads of access; at last the once famous port of Marsala was rehabilitated and reopened to shipping. Before very long, the town had tripled in size – appropriately its patron saint was the Englishman, Thomas Becket. This enterprising group of foreigners encouraged the growth of small proprietorship and intensive specialist cultivation, so that the area was eventually converted into one of the most prosperous in Sicily.

The hot coastal plains of Sicily were well-suited to fruit growing. Exports began to increase when minor uses were discovered for citric acid in industry, and when lemon and citron juice became a standard specific against scurvy in the 1790s. As demand increased, vines were even cut down to make way for lemons and oranges, and by the 1830s the value of citrus exports sometimes rivalled that of wine. But there were limitations on the potential profitability of this kind of agriculture. In the first place, enterprise was lacking to create a native citric acid industry. Secondly, arboriculture needed longer leases and cheaper credit than landowners were ready to permit. Thirdly, there was the problem of transport by mule, which caused delays, spoilage and expense. Fourthly, there was mafia activity, with its demands for protection money, and the monopolising of water supplies. When one adds to these factors the limited knowledge of farmers, who beat the trees to pick the fruit, one understands why Sicily found prosperity elusive.

Other export crops were similarly handicapped. Raw silk, for example, suffered both from poor quality and primitive techniques; and women could still be seen hatching silkworms under their clothes as they had done three centuries earlier. Foreigners would have liked to import more Sicilian cotton, and some adventurous farmers found it a rewarding crop; but again growers had the difficulty of obtaining enough capital, as well as of learning new skills and finding the most suitable varieties. Olive oil was a considerable export, and the Bourbons tried to encourage it with tax exemptions; but rough and ready methods of pressing the oil, which allowed it to ferment and become rancid, proved impossible to change.

Cattle and sheep farming, at least of a kind, was undertaken on the sparse vegetation of the inland hills. This was the typical *latifondo* country where, if water was not properly used, ten acres would barely support a single emaciated cow. Animals were therefore in continual daily movement; and there were also the long annual journeys between coast and mountains to escape the extremes of climate. The frequent journeying was bad for meat and milk production. It also meant that animal husbandry had to be largely divorced from the rest of agriculture. The ordinary farm labourer, living as he did in a village remote from the *latifondo*, was not equipped to bring sheep and cattle into his regular routine.

Balsamo said that this was one of Sicily's main problems. Evidence was available – or so he hopefully thought – that in many areas artificial leys could be created from which half a dozen crops of hay and lucerne could be taken in a single year, to say nothing of turnips and other root vegetables; but this kind of farming was in practice unknown. Balsamo travelled carefully over most of Sicily and found almost no cattle sheds and hardly any crops grown specially for stall-feeding. Everywhere the animals wandered almost wild to browse as they could, and this could be a disaster in winter time or if the rains failed and there was no grass, to say nothing of the damage done to crops and trees.

By the early nineteenth century, destruction of the forests was rapidly accelerating. In the thirty years down to 1847, according to the chief forestry inspector in western Sicily, about half the remaining woodlands had disappeared. A shortage of charcoal had been noted a century earlier, and this naturally became worse as the population grew. Apparently even oak, olive and cork trees were regularly cut for fuel, and there was soon no wood left at all near the sulphur mines. But domestic fuel requirements were perhaps the greatest cause of deafforestation, especially as the simple open stove generally employed for cooking was extremely uneconomical.

In 1819 and 1826 the Bourbons made laws which aimed to preserve what was left of the forests; but such legislation needed more community sense than could be expected from the *latifondisti* or their shepherds. The forest guards were not paid nearly enough, and they used to supplement their wages by illegally cutting trees and helping criminal gangs to deal in timber and firewood. Where 'promiscuous rights' continued to exist, villagers were often allowed to cut firewood; where they were suppressed, the new landowners or *gabelloti* found it worthwhile to sell the remaining timber. Either way the results could be serious.

Some incidental effects of this process were studied by a number of people, among them a member of the Paternò family. At Catania there were average annual rainfall figures of 785mm for 1808–12, but only 453mm for 1866–79. The river Simeto was later shown to carry twice as much sediment as the infinitely larger river Po in northern Italy, which had sixteen times as extensive a watershed. A considerable falling off was also noticed in its flow after 1824. Springs regularly dried up and did not reappear unless trees were planted again. On somewhat flimsier evidence it was said that the climate was becoming more severe, both hotter and colder and in general dryer than before.

Probably the most ominous sign of forest destruction was erosion on the hillsides, and though the Intendants had instructions to stop any ploughing on the steeper slopes, these had little effect. Cereals would grow in Sicily as high as a thousand metres or more above sea level; and since a third of the whole land surface was over five hundred metres above sea level (and, worse still, on a slope greater than one in five), land hunger, where uncontrolled, had ruinous effects. Little was known of contour ploughing. According to one forest inspector, ploughs were still used on slopes of up to 25 degrees; and on even steeper inclines peasants could be seen digging while hitched by ropes to a rock. 'All the land cultivated on slopes,' he commented, 'becomes sterile after a few years.'

CHAPTER 19

The last years of Bourbon rule

DISLIKE OF NAPLES

The last years of Bourbon Sicily were troubled by more than merely the slowness of economic growth. A brief revolt in 1837 indicated that tremendous social forces were waiting to erupt. This rising was touched off by an epidemic of cholera, a disease which struck terror because it had never been seen before in western Europe. Even university professors and the Archbishop of Palermo believed that the infection was a poison deliberately spread by the government. Many thousands died and, in the general panic, cities suddenly emptied. Villages sealed off all paths of access, channels of food supply were cut, and peasants invaded towns in search of loot.

Palermo on this occasion remained fairly quiet, but at Catania the yellow flag of Sicilian independence was raised and a revolutionary committee formed. Rich and poor were seen embracing each other in the streets, and messengers were sent to stir up a patriotic revolt in other cities, but the replies were depressingly negative. Three days after publicly swearing allegiance to the revolt, the leading members of the patrician classes realized their isolation and decided to change sides. They arrested some of their more liberal fellow-revolutionaries, and even collected money to pay for a new statue of the King. The Swiss troops were welcomed back, and a few executions then concluded this melancholy episode.

King Ferdinand II toured Sicily in 1838, and was persuaded that popular unrest was chiefly the result of existing laws not being enforced. He learnt of feudal dues and *corvées* still unlawfully being claimed, and of lawsuits deliberately being used to frustrate or delay his projects of agrarian reform. What was needed, he felt, was more property-holders and greater security of tenure. Accordingly another order was made in 1838 for further action over dividing the ecclesiastical *latifondi* in royal patronage. If properly applied, this would have affected a large area, as the King was patron of all the major benefices as well as many minor ones. Intendants were also enjoined to open up any usurped rights of way and to stop interference with rights of access to water and woodland. At the same time they were to hurry up the commutation of 'promiscuous rights'.

A remarkable law of 1841 then prescribed that landlords must compensate the villages by giving them at the very least one-fifth of any ex-feudal territories where common rights had once been enjoyed. According to the plan, the land allocated to each village would subsequently be distributed to the poor, and this should be done by lot and not by sale. Furthermore, each allotment should be free from any action by creditors for twenty years. Originally a much stronger law than this had been prepared that would have allowed prosecution of landowners who had arbitrarily enclosed common land. But the Sicilian aristocracy managed to persuade the King that actual possession of land should be taken as evidence to title. As a result, local populations had the impossible burden of producing documents to prove illegal usurpation.

The government went on trying to apply its reform policy until the revolution of 1848 brought a period of more or less enlightened despotism to a close. This maligned phase of Bourbon administration provided the last occasion for almost a century when any Sicilian government supported a serious and even-handed programme of agrarian reform. It was also the last time for decades that a comprehensive plan was drawn up for draining and irrigating the fertile plain of Catania; and the failure of this project meant that hundreds of square miles remained uninhabited. Experience now proved the impossibility of carrying out such projects given the balance of society and the existing machinery of local government. Something more drastic was needed.

Though inadequately administered and in some respects misconceived, this attempt at agrarian reform failed primarily because it was anathema to the only people who counted. Young radicals such as Filippo Cordova might support it, but they were powerless. To the local clienteles, it was clear that the Neapolitan government did not understand the traditional art of the Spanish viceroys: to leave well alone and indulge the aristocracy. The *latifondisti* and *gabelloti* therefore acted to neutralize Ferdinand's proposals. By mustering their retainers and *bravi*, by playing on local patriotism, xenophobia and the prevalent dislike of all laws and regulations, they tried to convince people that it was not they themselves but rather the hated Bourbons who prevented improvement and kept Sicily poor.

In one respect the landowners were creating future difficulties for themselves, because proletarianization made the peasants into a force more revolutionary than anything ever known before. As population grew, they became increasingly exposed to the threat of famine, and the confiscation of 'promiscuous rights' not only diminished their lives but affronted their sense of justice and made any retaliation seem fair. In every village a memory was retained of which land had been wrongly usurped; and these were the areas which in revolutionary years such as 1820, 1837 and 1848 were invaded by the peasantry. On top of all this, moreover, the *macinato* and the other food taxes condemned Sicily to a permanent state of class warfare from which everyone suffered.

The two chief potential revolutionary forces in Sicily were peasant unrest and a dislike of Naples. There was also a third force of a very different kind, which, though weak at first, was subtler and more sophisticated. This was the idea that Sicily might change her whole political alignment and join a federation of Italian states. Sicily's links with northern Italy had not hitherto been particularly close, and her commerce with England in the 1840s was ten times as great as with all the other Italian states put together. Furthermore, northern Italians did not show much awareness of any common heritage with Sicily, but rather spoke of it as somewhere remote and deserted, where brigandage made travelling unwise. Very few Italians ever travelled in Sicily and, if they did, they were liable to be taken for Englishmen.

Yet cultural contacts with Italy had never disappeared in the centuries of Spanish rule, and for political reasons they now became increasingly important. The exaltation of Rome was already a familiar theme to those with a classical education. Dante and Foscolo were eagerly read by a few intellectuals, and one English visitor in 1809 found that Alfieri's tragedies were frequently staged at Palermo. In the other direction, the poet Giovanni Meli was translated into Italian as well as into German and English; and the composer Vincenzo Bellini, like Scarlatti before him, achieved a far greater success outside than inside his own native Sicily. In the past the emigration of talented men such as Bellini had been a tremendous loss; but it was now to be in one sense a gain, as it produced a number of middle-class intellectuals of international experience and accumulated frustration who began to turn their minds to the possibility of radical change.

One person who came to believe this was a scholar and minor government official named Michele Amari. This man possessed a much wider European education than most other young Sicilians. Among his early volumes was a translation of Scott's *Marmion*, a fact which serves as a reminder that Scott as well as Byron was a strong political and literary influence on this generation. In the 1840s, Amari published a history of the Sicilian Vespers, a book which escaped censorship only because the deliverance of Sicily from the French in the thirteenth century was not immediately recognized by officialdom as an allegorical reference to winning freedom from Naples. This volume was both a catalyst to opinion and a positive act of political education.

Amari himself had to escape to Paris, and it was in exile that he and others became conscious of more sophisticated political ideas and wider loyalties. The mere fact of arriving in Paris, wrote Cordova to his father, 'is like coming to a new world'. Here were to be found men such as the lawyer Francesco Crispi, the journalist Giuseppe La Farina, and the industrialist Luigi Orlando; and these middle-class radicals now taught themselves to be political leaders of a kind Sicily had never known before. Though often out of touch with public opinion back home, they were nevertheless infected by the romanticism and patriotic idealism current in northern Europe. From a practical point of view, they could now see that Sicily needed outside help, while economists such as Busacca and Ferrara realised that freer trade with Italy would be both natural and advantageous.

These new ideas hardly took much hold in Sicily until 1848; but this was not altogether surprising. Quite apart from ideology, the social system inhibited the growth of a literate middle class which might accept revolutionary ideas of liberty and economic progress. Not only were the lawyers as a class still thoroughly obsequious, but historical accident had left Sicily with very few of the professional soldiers upon whom other countries relied for their revolution; and those few were loyal to the Bourbons almost to a man. In these circumstances it is hardly surprising that few people were prepared to take to the barricades. Though the early 1840s witnessed a growing sense of opposition, this rarely transcended the vague anarchic protest with which all governments of Sicily were familiar. It became more political only when a demand for Sicilian autonomy acted as the focus of many different animosities against Naples.

THE REVOLUTION OF 1848–9

The first days of 1848 were a time of exceptional unrest in Palermo. Rumours of a new constitution were in the air. An unsigned manifesto circulated that claimed to speak for a probably non-existent revolutionary committee. It announced that a revolt for Sicilian freedom would start under cover of the King's birthday festivities on 12 January. The ruse succeeded and, when the day arrived, a popular preacher in the Fieravecchia began an incendiary harangue which set off a riot. The streets in the richer residential districts quickly emptied, doors were barricaded, and the shutting of shops added to the general alarm by raising fears of a food shortage. By the evening, barricades were going up. Early on the 13th, squads of peasants and 'mountaineers' had already arrived in Palermo. Money had been seized from a government courier returning from the interior. The revolt was off to a flying start.

The small class of liberals suddenly discovered that political reforms might now be attainable, whether Sicilian autonomy, a liberal constitution, or possibly a federal Italy; nevertheless a parallel and far stronger social revolution was unexpectedly confusing the issue. Many of the insurgents, even those waving tricolour flags, can only have had the haziest notion, if any, of what Italy, or a constitution, was; but the inarticulate desire for social betterment, for more regular work, for land to cultivate, for the commons of which they and their forebears had been deprived, all this made the peasants by far the most revolutionary elements in an aggrieved but usually submissive society. Especially in a year of bad harvest, the need to get cheaper food and abolish the *macinato* gave them the frightening power possessed by those with little to lose from insurrection and just possibly a great deal to gain.

Revolutionaries of such a kind had no recognizable political views except the crudest; nor did they have much staying power, for life itself depended on their returning home infallibly at harvest and sowing time. Yet the news from Palermo on 12 January was a signal for all who had a grievance to rise and remedy it, and this gave the revolt an immense and unexpected force. In the villages and towns there were bread riots and attacks on the 'clubs' where the *galantuomini* used to meet. Sheep were killed, hayricks burned, and many of the surviving woodlands destroyed as land was seized and cleared for cultivation. Often the Town Hall was attacked and a bonfire made of the title deeds to property. Government ceased as officials fled for their lives. The tribal morality of a subject population was evidenced in a general assassination of policemen and suspected informers, sometimes with unbelievable cruelty.

Another element in the rising was the sudden appearance of the armed squads, often brigand bands under the leadership of a local underworld figure. Some of these men had probably been, and went on being, Bourbon employees. Others were hired by the ex-barons or even the liberals as a private police force. Still others were anarchic characters who simply used the riots as an occasion to fish in troubled waters. A breakdown of government was an ideal situation for them, especially when they could expect payment from one side or both. Men of criminal propensity, such as di Miceli in Monreale and Scordato in Bagheria, now seized effective power in their villages and marched their men into Palermo, where for several months they remained near the centre of power.

Initially, many citizens must have had mixed feelings about the dramatic events of these few days, and even some of the liberals were momentarily confused. But as soon as the Neapolitans retreated, it was as important to tame the fury of the *popolani* as it was to steer the rising into a fruitful political channel; and therefore the only group of people who had a political programme now came to the fore. Committees were hastily improvised to provide munitions, to keep order, collect money and arrange food supplies.

These committees were largely composed of the more liberal and anti-Neapolitan among the patrician classes. As the danger of counterrevolution receded, and as the revolt became more political and less social, other citizens increasingly declared their support.

On the mainland, meanwhile, the King yielded to events and granted a liberal constitution. He offered Sicilians local self-government on condition that they would accept Bourbon sovereignty. But the emergent revolutionary leaders, too excited to see the weakness of their position, bravely replied that Sicilian opinion demanded complete separation from Naples. This impelled them to revive parliament; and when it opened on 25 March, conservatives and radicals joined in a coalition government and proclaimed Ferdinand's deposition. All the deputies leapt to their feet and shouted enthusiastically for half an hour. The revolution, it was assumed, was over and Sicily independent – truly independent for the first time since the fourteenth century. The white flag of the Bourbons was replaced by the tricolour, the Bourbon lilies by the ancient three-legged emblem of Trinacria. Sicily was declared to form part of a notional federation of Italy, and a token force of a hundred Sicilians was sent north to help liberate Lombardy from the Austrians.

The revolution, however, was soon facing serious problems, as its social and political elements became increasingly uncoordinated. The armed squads were a liability now that the Bourbon troops had withdrawn: they fomented disorder, and were rather too concerned with social issues. The conservatives, therefore, decided to recruit a National Guard to protect property and, if need be, oppose the squads. It was unpaid and was intended as a class militia: manual labourers were specifically excluded; and eventually there were eighteen princes and a hundred other assorted nobles among its officers. More than once it was to intervene in politics against the radicals, and so contributed to the divisions opening up inside the coalition government.

Other signs of malaise soon helped to diminish the great initial enthusiasm aroused by this remarkable revolution. A decline in trade affected many people; the disorganization of the legal system hit the professional advocates; and conditions of public security were disastrous. In some areas the squads, displaced from Palermo, took over whole villages, pillaging, killing all the *galantuomini* or 'hats' (as distinct from 'caps') that they could find, or else forcing the peasants to abandon the fields unless they paid for protection. For some people the great patriotic year of 1848 in retrospect simply meant a moment when brigandage had gone unpunished. Many citizens must have longed for a speedy return of efficient government, even, if necessary, of Bourbon government.

Another problem facing the revolution was that the practice of parliamentary rule was not easily learnt after so many years of political authoritarianism. By early May, some of the radicals were forced out of the government coalition, and thereafter personal rancours and rivalries increasingly clouded the consideration of urgent political problems. While abduction and robbery continued unhampered in the villages, the deputies allowed themselves rhetorical displays over whether to celebrate St Rosalia's Day, or how to rename the streets of Palermo, and what kind of commemorative medal to issue. Ministries succeeded each other in rapid succession, and lack of leadership and ever-widening disagreements made it impossible to concentrate resources on winning the war.

Finance, for example, was a question which was as controversial as it was vital. People had stopped paying taxes in January, and the destruction of tax records and assessments had been a prime objective of many revolutionaries. Collection of adequate revenue was therefore impossible. An even more serious weakness was that so little was done to enlist soldiers and arm them. When some deputies asked for a debate on national defence, this was said to be inopportune and indeed unnecessary. Nor was any discussion permitted of Crispi's proposal for conscription, since the very idea of compulsory service was repudiated as intolerable to a free people.

Evidently most ordinary Sicilians were not eager to make the sacrifices implicit in the refusal by the revolutionary leaders to consider Ferdinand's offer of a separate Sicilian parliament. They had been assured by these leaders that Ferdinand was beaten and could not fight back; and when suddenly, in September 1848, a large Bourbon army landed and attacked Messina, there was consternation. The city held out for a few days, but then the victorious invaders indulged in an orgy of looting and arson. This so shocked the British and French admirals stationed at Messina that pressure was brought to bear on Ferdinand to allow a six months' armistice. He agreed, even though this was entirely to the advantage of the Sicilians.

When in February 1849 the Bourbons again offered Sicily a separate parliament and viceroy, the offer was again refused. It seems that some of the revolutionary authorities deliberately encouraged a popular hysteria which made impossible any rational discussion of the alternatives; and when some deputies cried out boldly for war, no one dared voice the obvious difficulties. Meanwhile the Bourbon army renewed its advance as soon as the armistice ended. The Sicilian levies were disorganized, untrained and mutinous; and, except at Messina and Catania, no serious resistance was offered anywhere in the island. Indeed Syracuse surrendered without a fight.

The Bourbon troops marched almost unopposed on Palermo. Hurriedly trenches were dug round the capital, and ministers, priests, titled ladies and peasants from twenty miles around all lent a hand. But the political structure of the revolution was crumbling. One by one the ministers resigned, and no one was left who would take responsibility for decisions. Many citizens fled the town. Others began to parley with the enemy. Baron Riso of the National Guard, supported by Florio and other merchants, suddenly became a convinced supporter of peace. Inflation, forced loans, social revolution, the destruction of property and the ruin of trade, all helped to separate these conservatives from La Farina, Crispi and the radical diehards. Crispi, who in time was to be revealed as the greatest Sicilian politician of the century, wrote: 'the moderates feared the victory of the people more than that of the Bourbon troops'. He may well have been right.

THE END OF THE BOURBONS

The victorious general, Filangieri, became Governor of Sicily in 1849. An amnesty was granted, from which forty-three Sicilians were excluded, and the few who now went into exile included all the potential opposition leaders. Most of the ex-deputies and peers of the revolutionary parliament begged the King's forgiveness and assured him that they had been coerced by physical threats into supporting a revolution which they truly detested. Filangieri had to govern under considerable difficulties, though on the whole he ruled with sense and humanity. Parliament was abolished, but once again some degree of local autonomy was permitted in matters of justice, finance, police and ecclesiastical affairs. The tax system remained in some ways unexpectedly favourable to Sicilians, and they were again excused compulsory service in the army.

Ferdinand II had been soured and frightened by the revolution, and he now lost his enthusiasm for reform. This was a major achievement by the revolutionaries. Like his successor, Francis, who became King in 1859, Ferdinand was inadequate as a ruler and increasingly out of touch with a new age of liberalism and nationalism. He was not interested in challenging Piedmont for political and moral leadership in the peninsula, and he failed to develop a kind of government which might have mitigated the absurdities of hereditary absolutism. This was a despotic state, based on censorship and with penal settlements. Citizens could be imprisoned on mere suspicion, and freedom of movement was greatly restricted. Police methods were sometimes cruel, and the unwillingness to allow a safety valve for public opinion added a special element of instability to public life.

Nevertheless, Naples was not the only source of the island's sufferings. Quite as harmful as foreign oppression was the fact that a growing middle class of *galantuomini* was beginning to dislodge the old aristocracy from the land, while assuming its irresponsible and reactionary attitudes. These were the *cappelli*, the men who wore hats. In any country town of about 10,000 people they might number a hundred families. They met daily in their own exclusive cafe, and their names carried the honorific prefix of 'don', a title that automatically indicated status. No one who had reached this position in society could ever completely sink back again into the undifferentiated mass, and it was the primary activity of all of them to maintain or increase the differential which was their claim to respectability.

Compared to these provincial *galantuomini*, the Bourbon administrators, even in the 1850s, were far from being the black reactionaries painted by patriotic propaganda. Bourbon prisons may have been as bad as Gladstone said, but other foreigners who saw them thought he had exaggerated the facts for political purposes, and we now know that the prisons in enlightened Piedmont were not all that much better. Bourbon justice, though it was harsh on political offences, was sometimes regretted after 1860. In the sphere of public works, good will was not lacking. Road construction, for example, was remarkably good in the 1850s when judged by previous standards; but the government was still not authoritarian enough to impose its will, and few Sicilians liked the increase in local taxes and borrowing which this essential public service made necessary.

The years after 1848 were a period of relative economic well-being. The increase in steam navigation helped trade, and the Sicilian mercantile marine in 1859 was twice what it had been in 1825. Exports of sulphur doubled in the 1850s, helped by the Crimean war and the discovery that sulphur was the only remedy against a destructive vine fungus. Nevertheless, high protective duties were a symptom and sometimes a cause of industrial stagnation. Sicily lacked the raw materials and the enterprise needed for a real industrial take-off, and what capital she possessed was ineffectively employed. An attempt to start a savings bank movement proved abortive, and the reason given was that gambling had too strong a hold; indeed when the government tried to abolish the state lottery, an outburst of popular indignation forced them to give way.

It was Bourbon taxation which was most generally resented at the time, rather than any presumed lack of reforms. The *macinato* was far more disliked than the suggestion that the Bourbons might be insufficiently 'Italian' in their outlook. Indeed the appeal of Italy, though it affected a few people such as Amari strongly, was never in any sense widespread, even among the middle classes. The *notabili* merely resented being crossed by the Intendant in local affairs; the *latifondisti* disliked the law that said they should give at least a fifth of the ex-fiefs to a new class of smallholders. The presence of so many foreign soldiers did not help either: they were deemed morally offensive as well as costly.

Estimates of 'public opinion' in Sicily are bound to be based on inference from limited information. Easier to guess are the views of the politically articulate expatriates in northern Italy, Marseilles, Malta, and even North Africa. Among these were about a dozen liberal aristocrats, but like Belmonte and Castelnuovo from whom their ideas generally derived, they were easily discouraged to the point of abjuring active politics altogether. The democratic radicals were more dynamic, although, in attempting to explain their own failure in 1848–9, La Farina and others wrote many wounding things which opened up gratuitous divisions among them. Knowing how little talent they possessed for cooperation with each other, they were the first to recognise that Sicilians were neither sufficiently agreed nor politically conscious enough to win independence on their own.

Just as the moderate liberals were hampered by their aversion to violence and social revolution, so the radicals were largely infected with a doctrinaire republicanism which prevented them looking for salvation to monarchist Piedmont. Both groups, furthermore, were moved by separatist feelings about Sicily, which made any idea of a full union with other Italian states unthinkable. Only when they began to transcend this kind of barrier would their kind of revolution become feasible. In the meantime these exiles contributed a real service of political education; not only did they keep Sicily talked about in London, Turin and Paris, but, by arguing with each other, by maintaining contact with their friends in Sicily and smuggling books into the country, they greatly contributed to the sense of frustration and the awareness of greater liberties elsewhere.

In northern Italy, meanwhile, a freelance soldier and patriot, named Garibaldi, took up what had once been Mazzini's idea of starting a Sicilian rebellion as a basis for unifying the whole peninsula. Even if Italian sentiment was not strong in the south, a special situation existed in Sicily by virtue of peasant unrest, the tradition of armed squads, and the strength of local anti-Neapolitan feeling, which could be made into a splendid temporary leveller of classes and factions. With this in mind, some of the more active exiles secretly returned home for brief visits in 1859 to propagate the programme of Garibaldi.

Among these was Francesco Crispi, the most committed of all Sicilian disciples of Garibaldi and Mazzini. Crispi was a lawyer and as such belonged to a democratic bourgeoisie much less tied than the liberal aristocracy to sentiments of regional autonomy and memories of 1812. Once back in Sicily, he established contact with some of the squad leaders and instructed his friends in how to make bombs and coordinate and synchronize a revolt.

This was an ideal country for guerrilla warfare, and intelligent leadership might make the squads into a force which not even a large army could hold in check.

The more conservative Sicilian exiles were alarmed by hairbrained schemes which seemed to threaten a repeat of the tragedy of 1849, and they directly approached the government of Piedmont to sound out the possibility of diplomatic and military intervention. Count Cavour, the liberal Prime Minister of Piedmont, had occasionally wondered about annexing Sicily from the Bourbons as one step towards creating a larger Italian state; but he decided that positive action would be premature, and he was not ready to promise any support until Sicilians had shown that they could effectively defy the Bourbons on their own. To give them some encouragement, however, he held out the expectation that Sicily would be given a large measure of self-government if ever she agreed to accept annexation by Piedmont. The fact remains, though, that Cavour, in contrast to Garibaldi and his followers, would have preferred no action at all in Sicily.

When minor disturbances by students and other radical elements in Sicily became more frequent early in 1860, the rumour began to spread that another revolution was imminent. As the government knew through its informers, clandestine groups in Palermo were beginning to discuss both the possibility of annexation by Piedmont and Garibaldi's plan to land in Sicily with a force of irregulars. Moreover, quite as important as this kind of talk was the fact that the common people were once again growing restless. Evidently a social revolution of enormous force was ready to be touched off by anyone who had enough courage and popular appeal; and a grass-roots movement was essential if the large Bourbon army in Sicily was to be defeated. This was something which Garibaldi understood but Cavour did not.

CHAPTER 20

Unification

GARIBALDI

Unrest was converted into insurrection after an armed clash with the police in a Palermo suburb on 4 April 1860. As in 1848, some kind of concerted arrangement existed between a handful of insurgents in the town and the peasantry of the surrounding villages; but the timing was imperfectly synchronized, and apparently the police had been tipped off. The rising was clearly a movement over which the patrician classes and moderate liberals had little, if any, influence; even those of them who were ready to contemplate a revolt were unwilling to rebel before they had promises of outside help. The radicals, on the other hand, had no such reservations.

Although the authorities succeeded in putting down the first outbreak of disorder, within twenty-four hours most of the military outposts around Palermo had been attacked by popular insurgents. Telegraph lines were cut, and the sudden stoppage of information caused panic among government officials who remembered the kind of ferocity which had accompanied similar outbreaks in the past. Among ordinary people the news travelled swiftly across the island. To control Palermo was not too hard for the troops, but they were not trained to fight in the countryside against 'an enemy who never shows himself'.

Any political motives among the revolutionaries were soon swamped by yet another peasants' revolt for food, land and social justice. The poorer clergy supported this movement in many villages, a fact which may have had considerable importance in helping it to succeed. More important still, the breakdown in law and order gave full play to the unruly squads which were always ready to use such a moment to extend their authority. It is not impossible that some gang leaders possessed genuinely political aims, but it is safe to assume that their main motives were much less savoury. These *mafiosi*, however, were not mere criminals. Crime was for them just one method of obtaining money and power; and political revolution was another. This strange fact now helped Sicily to contribute a decisive and partly unwitting leverage to the cause of Italian unification.

Throughout April the fortunes of the insurrection were in continual doubt. Until there was more likelihood of success, the upper classes would not commit themselves. But, as weeks went by without the Bourbons

proving that they could protect property, the unpolitically minded middle
classes began to lose confidence in them. Hostility against Naples grew
when the troops requisitioned food and fed their horses on the ripening
crops, and above all where whole villages were left unprotected and at the
mercy of the armed bands. In Palermo and Messina the shops were
frequently shut, businesses suspended, and respectable citizens reduced to
destitution.

Among the more radical exiles, some were ready for just such an
emergency. One or two landed secretly and got in touch with their former
contacts among the armed bands and the political dissidents in Palermo;
soon their story that Garibaldi was about to invade had become common
property, and this caused a dramatic release of tension and energy. When
the government circulated a photograph of Garibaldi to the port authorities,
clearly defeatism was spreading. The fact that Garibaldi had not yet decided
to come was quite irrelevant: the mere expectation was enough to keep the
revolution alive and give him time and incentive to make up his mind; in
this respect it was like the Sicilian Vespers and Peter of Aragon all over
again.

On 11 May, five weeks after the initial rising, Garibaldi arrived at the
recently reopened port of Marsala with just over a thousand ill-armed but
eager volunteers. Against him were some twenty-five battalions of infantry
as well as several artillery and cavalry regiments. Yet Garibaldi defiantly
and irresponsibly proclaimed himself a dictator, ruling on behalf of King
Victor Emanuel of Piedmont. The local inhabitants of Marsala were at first
bewildered and terrified, but Garibaldi's mesmeric personal charm and his
frank appeal to the common people quickly won support; and he was soon
being venerated as a saint, even as a reincarnation of Christ himself, come to
redeem Sicilians from centuries of ill-treatment.

Deliberately appealing to a peasants' war, Garibaldi abolished the *macinato* and promised eventual grants of land to the poor and those who took
arms. Many who had never heard the words 'Piedmont' or 'Italy' could
easily comprehend this programme, and gladly took a chance to resolve
many accumulated personal grudges and many vendettas against authority.
With savage fanaticism they swept away the last relics of Bourbon government. Farm labourers did not generally make good fighters. But they were
crucial in furnishing Garibaldi with most of the information he wanted as
well as providing lodging and food for his troops. The Bourbon soldiers by
contrast met with sullen opposition.

Garibaldi's policy was to avoid an open battle wherever possible, especially as Cavour's friends had managed to confiscate most of his firearms
before he left northern Italy. Street fighting and guerilla warfare suited his

resources much better, and these were arts at which he had no peer in Europe. His favourite stratagem was by quick marches and accurate dispersion to create the illusion of a large army; for he had at all costs to keep up a fast pace and the impression of constant success. By this means the enemy was demoralised and the squads emboldened. After a brilliant deceptive march, he eventually brought some of his advance units into Palermo. Barricades were erected in his support, and the Bourbon forces withdrew. The revolution had won against what, in purely military terms, must have seemed overwhelming odds.

Garibaldi had little time to reorganize the island, for his main preoccupation was to pursue the conquest of Naples and Rome and unite Italy. He ruled as a dictator in Sicily for five months, and his enormous moral authority allowed him to put forward an unprecedented package of reforms that included nationalisation of Church property, land distribution and freer trade. However, he clearly lacked the experience and political skill to carry them through, especially after the local *notabili* had recovered from the immediate shock of such a challenge. His political views were all in all too simple, too radical and too hastily compounded to succeed.

The revolutionary government quickly ran into the same difficulties as that of 1848. The armed bands, once their initial and essential job was over, proved a divisive force threatening social war. Garibaldi tried to replace them with a conscripted militia, but this was quite impracticable: the gangs resented the attempt to supersede them, and there was mention of possible civil war. The Sicilian irregulars had probably all been raised on a traditional basis of clientelage; they were the personal following of either a landlord or some other 'man of respect', and not even Garibaldi could enforce a different method of recruitment.

Worse still, different towns and villages were in bitter and sometimes armed conflict, while rival families and clienteles used the prevalent disorder as a chance to suppress any local opposition to themselves. When the dismissed squads returned home, the countryside became anarchic. The English wine merchants at Marsala, like other landlords, could not get rents paid; their crops and cattle were stolen, their agents attacked, and they had to pay protection money to the armed bands. Landlords had to fall back on hiring private gangs of their own, so adding to the horrors of class war.

This social question was perhaps the most serious problem of all in these months; and it had little to do with any political question. Thousands of peasants had been deprived by both big and middling landlords of any rights in the land, and when Garibaldi promised to redress this kind of wrong a spontaneous occupation occurred of parts of the old *latifondi*. 'Like wolves driven by hunger', wild men in goatskins came down from the hills, and any gentry who failed to escape ran the risk of being assassinated to the cry of 'Viva l'Italia'. One particularly savage *émeute* occurred at Bronte, which Garibaldi put down with exemplary severity. Social reformer though he was, he was no anarchist, and he needed the support of the landowners for his kind of political revolution.

The dictator, much to Cavour's annoyance, delayed handing over full sovereignty to Piedmont until he no longer needed a base for further operations on the mainland. In the meantime, he gradually introduced Piedmontese laws and institutions. The *lira*, the Piedmontese decimal system and the north-Italian flag were all officially imposed on Sicily by Garibaldi's personal fiat. Instead of reviving the centuries-old Sicilian parliament, he proclaimed the very different Piedmontese parliamentary system. Some Sicilians were surprised and offended that they were not consulted by this northern dictator and that no provision was made for local self-government: suddenly it was beginning to seem as though there was to be no Sicilian autonomy but simply an annexation of Sicily by Piedmont.

Other Sicilians, however, now realized that they wanted annexation to Piedmont even more quickly than Garibaldi was ready to go. They feared that genuine social and agrarian reforms would be introduced if he were left in sole control much longer; and it caused particular offence when he set up a 'Dictatorship of the Two Sicilies' which recalled the very same connection with the mainland against which they thought they had been rebelling. Count Cavour looked like a far safer politician; for one thing, he was further away; moreover, they already had been given reason to believe that he would allow Sicilian autonomy, and it was a fair assumption that he would reinforce the existing balance of social classes.

One of the few generalizations that can be hazarded about politically conscious opinion in Sicily by the autumn of 1860 is that nearly everyone wanted and expected some kind of regional self-government. Sicilians had been used to a degree of autonomy even under the Bourbons, and few considered that this might now completely stop. Little thought was given to what a new system of money, weights and measures would entail, let alone a completely different system of administration and justice, and what to ordinary people was an altogether new language – the Sicilian 'dialect' had only the remotest relation to Italian. Even at this late stage, most Sicilians had never heard of Cavour; and *l'Italia*, or rather *la Talia*, was for years thought by some to be the name of King Victor Emanuel's wife. Annexation to Piedmont was to prove a shock and by no means a universally welcome one.

UNION WITH ITALY

In October 1860, Garibaldi held a plebiscite in Sicily which by a 99.5 per cent majority favoured the formation of a united Italian nation under King Victor Emanuel. This plebiscite was meant as a mere demonstration to regularize something which had already happened. North Italians, however, read it rather as a test of opinion and so misunderstood what was happening. Few voters had more than a superficial awareness of what was at issue, for there was neither time nor machinery to instruct them, and opposition voices were discouraged from stating their case. Votes were accepted from anyone, even from non-Sicilians. Some peasants fled into the hills fearing a plot to press them for military service, while others were simply told that they were voting their appreciation of Garibaldi.

Some of the ambiguities concealed in this almost unanimous vote soon became explicit. Garibaldi's dictatorship was now ended and power handed over to the parliamentary leader at Turin, Count Cavour; this offended those Sicilians for whom Garibaldi was a hero and deliverer. Even more offence was caused when Cavour reneged on the vital point of regional self-government. He had suddenly realized that Garibaldi's conquests made possible a centralized state which would be far more manageable as well as more acceptable to northern public opinion. There was insufficient time, he argued, to debate a new constitution, and Piedmontese institutions were imposed on Sicily wholesale before anyone had time to object. Cavour's own snap judgement was that southern Italy was corrupt and needed a good dose of efficient and moral rule from the north.

In the prevalent conditions of emergency, Cavour had to take this fateful decision in the dark. He knew nothing of Sicilian laws and institutions, but simply assumed that they should be changed. Moreover, he relied for information either on those of the local aristocracy who wanted to use him to defeat Garibaldi and the democrats, or else on expatriate Sicilians who deceived him for not always very estimable reasons of their own. The unexpected result was to strengthen rather than weaken autonomist sentiment, and the legend was allowed to develop that Sicily had initiated a patriotic revolution only to be tricked into a false vote and then annexed as a conquered colony. Within a few weeks, therefore, the enthusiasm of the plebiscite dwindled into disillusionment; and observers remarked on a tremendous feeling against everything which smacked of Piedmontese.

The administrators who now arrived from the north were equally disillusioned. They had not been prepared to find a society so completely different from their own, and a language so unintelligible. In their most pessimistic moments some of them reported back that the southern provinces of Italy were 'a bottomless well of filth', that her people were 'bedouin', indolent and indifferent to free institutions, and that habits of clientelage made Piedmontese traditions of government unworkable. Matters were made worse by the arrogant assumption that northerners conferred great benefits on Sicily by annexation; they were surprised when the word 'annexation' aroused anger, and equally surprised when their superior knowledge and experience were not received with gratitude.

The same anti-governmental feeling which originally made possible Garibaldi's success against Naples was soon directed against Italy itself, and the first anniversary of the rebellion was celebrated with a riot. There was indignation when Garibaldi's promise of land distribution was shelved. Tax collectors and policemen were as unpopular under parliamentary government as under a despotism, all the more so when they proved more intrusive and efficient. Even though the government hesitated for a few years to restore the *macinato*, the tax burden was heavier than ever; some village authorities announced that they would not pay tax until their legitimate Bourbon sovereign returned.

Particularly hated was conscription. Some villages resorted to lynch law against the recruiting officers, and often over half the recruits simply disappeared. There was particular resentment that people with money could buy exemption, whereas poor people could be compelled to fight even though they could not vote. Conscription was a special hardship in an agricultural society where women did not work in the fields – indeed in which rigid social customs even prevented women from shopping or walking freely in the streets. It was also disliked because identified with the state, in other words with something which ancestral memory taught that it was a virtue to disobey.

Shirkers and deserters therefore went to swell the criminal underworld. Brigandage, so northerners tended to assume, should have disappeared as soon as honest, liberal, northern government had replaced Bourbon despotism and Garibaldian latitudinarianism; but instead, banditry and corruption grew out of all recognition. In part this was because liberal government proved more manipulable and less efficient at repression. Instead of one police organisation as under the Bourbons, there were to be four, without common information services, and occasionally with a strong dislike of each other. Fearful of encouraging insular patriotism, the Piedmontese stressed a division of the island into smaller provincial units, and usually allowed the Prefect of Palermo no authority over the other six provinces, so that it was as easy as ever for outlaws to escape from one jurisdiction into another.

Within a few months, gang warfare was clearly becoming worse, and it continued without respite for ten years. The sulphur miners were tyrannized into paying a tithe on their wages. On the rich agricultural land round Palermo, tolls were levied on herdsmen and the farmers; and those involved obviously had a helpful arrangement with the police. In Palermo itself a dozen people were stabbed to death in a single night; and when the British consul was kidnapped just outside the walls, a popular ballad extolling the heroism of his captor sold for a halfpenny in the streets. Arms were found even inside the prisons; contraband activities continued to involve customs officers; and ordinary Sicilians generally refused, as they always had, to give evidence for a prosecution.

In 1863 a play describing life in the main Palermo prison achieved a tremendous success: it was called *I Mafiusi della Vicaria*, and this title gave national currency to a local dialect word that until then had lacked criminal overtones. Though mafia behaviour had long existed, it flourished after 1860 on an unprecedented scale. Hard-pressed landowners resorted increasingly to strong-arm men to collect rents and intimidate labour; and the *gabelloti*, as well as coercing their workers, now looked to intimidate the owners in order to rent the *latifondi* on easy terms and even acquire their lands. The new institutions of local government helped the process by affording *mafiosi* the political means with which to strengthen their hold on communal life. The emergent rural middle class thereby became powerful as never before.

Though *mafiosi* existed, 'the mafia' almost certainly did not. The issue is complex but there is very little to suggest that there was ever a criminal organization of the kind described by the authorities. Yet in the confusion of the 1860s the idea of such an entity was undoubtedly attractive to northern bureaucrats faced with an alien culture and recalcitrant population. When Prefect Gualterio, who came from Umbria, first alluded to the mafia in a report of 1865, it is clear that political considerations as much as lawlessness were uppermost in his mind; and he even suggested that opponents of the new regime should be arrested as common criminals to avoid the embarrassment of political trials.

In local parlance, the word mafia had denoted qualities of beauty, independence and assertiveness. It now began to take root in the public imagination as a catch-all for what was least acceptable to the new dispensation in this strange society. The extra-legal world of vendettas, *omertà*, banditry, and flagrant individualism, came to be seen as emanations of a criminal conspiracy. Sicily's problems thus got reduced largely to a question of law and order. As a result, the island had to endure an unprecedented series of brutal repressive operations which did nothing to relieve that mistrust towards the state which lay at the root of so much mafia behaviour.

The idea of the mafia as a criminal organization did not however develop in isolation from changes in Sicilian society. The revolution of 1860 offered plenty of opportunities for ambitious new men to make good. Don Calogero Sedara in Tomasi di Lampedusa's novel, *The Leopard*, might be taken as representative. A long-term process whereby the old landowners were increasingly pressurized by upwardly mobile peasants, and which had been accelerated by the formal end of feudalism, was now further intensified. Men such as Sedara were undoubtedly ruthless and by no means averse to crime. But it is also true that it sometimes suited the *latifondisti* to ascribe their misfortunes to criminals rather than to their own ineptitude; and as the alliance between state and big landowner solidified, so the mafia became increasingly identified with the ambitious *gabelloto* and his acolytes.

Though in some ways adversaries, the *gabelloto* and his middle-class associates were also in important respects allies of the *latifondisti*. Not only did the *gabelloto* rent the landowner's estates and furnish him with much-needed cash, but he also helped to keep order in the countryside. What is more, with the introduction of elections he and his friends became crucial for delivering the vote. This was an enormous source of contractual power. Whereas the Bourbons had been paternalistic to the poor and suspicious of the gentry, the new parliamentarians found it advantageous to leave local affairs to the *notabili*, or local bosses, in return for electoral support. The scope for corruption was limitless.

With an electorate of little more than 1 per cent, the landlords and their friends and employees were often the only voters. If there were any doubt about the result of an election, intimidation was usually effective. As early as January 1861, when the very first parliamentary elections were held, the whole paraphernalia of mafia influence was employed, and henceforward it became habitual in many constituencies. Any prefect who honestly tried to preserve free elections could be quickly brought to heel, or else would be tactfully removed by the government after complaints had been received – in seven years after 1861 a dozen prefects quickly followed one another at Palermo. If anyone was brave enough to challenge this kind of conspiracy, it was not difficult to make life unpleasant for him.

If liberal government in many ways proved a misnomer, it was because an exciting and potentially fruitful revolution was veneered on to a traditionalist society which was quick to adapt and exploit liberal institutions. There was no parallel social revolution except in so far as the *risorgimento* brought increased power to a narrow class whose liberalism was much less genuine than that of Cavour. The jury system in their hands was a sham. It was not unknown for jurymen to protest formally if they were not bribed; but in any case conviction might invite a vendetta. The local elite was not interested in popular education, and often refused to build schools despite the law on compulsory education; and naturally this kind of society had little to say about land reform: landlords could hardly be taken to court over the enclosure of communal property since this would have meant the ruling clienteles suing themselves.

CHAPTER 21

Repression, revolt and the failure of reform

THE RISING OF 1866

Northern officials found Sicily hard to understand, and her incidence of crime as well as of radical and autonomist opposition was inexplicable as well as frightening. Desperately there was an attempt to inculpate Garibaldi and the Bourbons; for ministers in Turin could not afford to assume anything else than that these were a matter for the police. When one deputy suggested that Sicily's chief problem might be economic and social rather than one of public security, his remarks were held to be unpatriotic and indeed insulting: too many people stood to lose from a fundamental debate on such a suggestive and perilous theme. Parliament in 1863 preferred to give General Govone full powers, allowing him to hold military tribunals and shoot people on the spot.

Govone gradually restored order, but by methods which made Italian rule less popular than ever. In a world of *omertà* he had no option but to make summary arrests, and some people remained untried in prison for years; he took hostages from the more obdurate villages to coerce them into obedience; torture was sometimes used, as was the threat to cut off water supplies in the summer heat. Some Sicilians even appealed for foreign intervention against treatment so reminiscent of that from which the Piedmontese claimed to have delivered them in 1860. Govone made things worse by unguardedly telling parliament that no other methods would succeed in a country which 'has not yet completed the cycle which leads from barbarism to civilisation'.

There was a common and curious belief in northern Italy that Sicily was one of the most fertile countries in Europe. This was because Cavour and his associates only knew the island from misguided reports and from reading ancient history or modern poetry. One consequence, and it was convenient for many northerners, was the assumption that the Sicilian economy was robust enough to need no special treatment. This was patently untrue. Free trade after 1861 removed a cushion insulating the island from a fierce and competitive outside world. Far from Sicily being dragged into a new era of industrialization, standards of living diminished for many people as her handicrafts began to collapse; and over the next forty years the traditional

Sicilian industries continued to decline at the same time as those of northern Italy leapt forward.

Tax policy was equally inconsiderate. Sicily came into the union with some assets: unlike the rest of Italy she had a favourable balance of trade; she also had a smaller national deficit than other Italian states. The amalgamation of regional debts after 1860 thus appeared as a net loss. Furthermore, the servicing of this collective indebtedness required much higher taxes than Sicily was accustomed to, as did the policy of developing a big military and industrial potential. In other words, an economic pace was chosen which suited the north, and to help pay for it the island had to increase her tax contributions suddenly by about a third. This had the overall effect of taking money out of Sicilian agriculture for investment in the north; and an already dangerous regional disparity was thereby increased.

Another element of disorientation was the sudden introduction of Piedmontese anti-clerical laws. Cavour's advisers in Sicily recommended caution. They pointed out that the clergy were more popular than in Piedmont and that the charitable activities of the monasteries could hardly be replaced. Yet successive governments overruled such advice and made Sicily conform to northern practice by dissolving monasteries and confiscating ecclesiastical property. The radicals hoped this would lead to a distribution of Church lands to the poor; but they were an isolated minority. The victors in the political revolution were moderate anti-clericals, who were not enthusiasts for social reform. They vetoed the idea of distributing smallholdings by ballot, and instead the land was sold by auction.

Admittedly some attempt was made to curtail possible abuses by prescribing that no one should buy more than one unit of land; but in practice many people illegally bought a hundred units or more. The local *notabili* were able to get the peasantry excluded, auctioneers were intimidated, and a few powerful buyers formed secret rings which eliminated competition and kept prices minimal. The government thus lost in some cases nine-tenths of the value of the land, and this huge amount was simply presented to a class of rich people who were not notable for their sense of public responsibility, their humanity, or their economic enterprise. Only a small fraction went to altogether new landowners.

The dissolution of the monasteries not only entailed great hardship for the religious themselves, but also caused unemployment for an estimated 15,000 laymen in Palermo alone; and the government had no substitute for the charitable functions which had been so important to the urban poor. Politically, as prefects were quick to report, the shallowly rooted gratitude of the landlords had to be weighed against the hostile reaction of many others.

The autonomists, for example, were irritated that the land was nationalized rather than regionalized; and the peasantry were aggrieved to see existing legislation in their favour being simply abrogated by local *notabili*. Above all, there was the resentment of the Church itself.

Opposition from these quarters had not been foreseen by the politicians. Their response was to be yet more authoritarian, for they had to convince Europe that Italy was strong and indissoluble. Naturally this made the new regime seem more intolerable still. Garibaldi and his friends continued to be treated with notable ungenerosity; and Mazzini, who was several times elected to parliament at Messina, was not permitted to take his seat. At the other extreme, and even more dangerous, were nostalgic conservatives: already in 1862 some Sicilian parliamentary representatives were in secret negotiation with the Bourbon ex-King. There were also various groups, especially in Palermo, who wanted a degree of autonomy, either in the belief that centralization was illiberal, or that Sicily was being exploited economically, or because they wanted more power for themselves and their friends.

The refusal to allow adequate parliamentary expression to these various minority views not only drove them underground but also forced them into a strange alliance with each other; and the result was a major rebellion at Palermo in 1866. Basically this was another social revolt by working people whose standard of living was threatened, and who were sufficiently desperate to throw caution to the wind. As one foreign journalist put it, the cultivators of the soil were 'taxed above their means and their patriotism'. Conscription, increased unemployment, higher rents and prices and new kinds of stamp tax, all these added to the misery caused by a dry spring and a food shortage, and made trouble almost inevitable.

The squads of men such as di Miceli stood poised to profit; and when the large garrison in Sicily had to be withdrawn for a war against Austria, and above all when the national forces received several resounding defeats, the way was clear for these bands to revolt, along with all those who wanted social reform or a Bourbonist counterrevolution. Thousands of deserters reinforced the *squadre*. The British consul described a situation where 'secret societies are all-powerful. *Camorre* and *maffie*, self-elected *juntas* share the earnings of the workmen, keep up intercourse with outcasts, and take malefactors under their wing and protection'. Some of the gang leaders were the very same men who had initiated the patriotic revolts of 1848 and 1860.

Though few Palermo citizens emerged to take part in the revolt, equally few opposed it. The Marquis di Rudinì courageously remained in office as mayor; and indeed his support of the government made it difficult for him (and for others who stood with him) to go on living in the city in future years. For a week Palermo was reduced to a state of anarchy. After several days an organizing committee announced its existence, including Baron Riso and three princes of the front rank. But, unlike 1860, no Garibaldi arrived in support, and the Italian navy shelled Palermo into submission. Forty thousand troops then restored order, while the city council unanimously disclaimed responsibility for the revolt and demanded exemplary punishment for anyone who threatened social order and property.

THE 'SOUTHERN PROBLEM'

The revolt of 1866 was treated as essentially a police matter. Its deeper social causes were left undisturbed and indeed were largely unknown. But one clear inference was that Sicily could not easily be governed by the ordinary methods of liberal parliamentary government which had succeeded elsewhere. For another decade a large part of the Italian army had to be stationed there, and many Sicilians continued to feel that they were living under foreign occupation or as participants in a submerged civil war. General Medici, who combined military and civil power in his own hand, would still not travel without a large escort of soldiers when he went five miles away to dinner in Monreale.

Official reports spoke of the mafia as having widespread support from rich and poor alike. Certainly the first years of unification did little to assuage the Sicilian's traditional disregard for official channels. His first recourse if he needed help was to kinsmen; and, in dealing with the threatening wider world, he invariably needed friends whose patronage and contacts could advance his fortunes, or at least stave off disaster. These friends were people whose assistance could be claimed either in virtue of future allegiance, or else through some past service by himself or a relative. They might well be spoken of as *mafiosi*, which meant they were powerful and could command respect. Such men would probably have ties with local bandits and petty criminals as this was almost a necessary condition of power in Sicily; and in many villages they constituted the only effective authority.

In order to keep some control over the situation, officials would either have to collude with these people or else look, in traditional fashion, to criminals themselves. Giuseppe Albanese, who was General Medici's chief investigator, employed notorious delinquents as policemen. They continued in his service even when implicated in further crimes; nor were they dismissed when accused of using their office for large-scale criminal operations. This became known when the most senior member of the Palermo judiciary, Diego Tajani, issued a warrant for Albanese's arrest in 1871. As a non-Sicilian he was clearly unfamiliar with such methods. To Tajani's surprise the government ordered his warrant to be disregarded; and, almost as ominous, a number of witnesses for his case disappeared by assassination.

It was becoming clear that crime in Sicily was connected with political corruption, but it was also evident that northerners had made this worse and not better. Another sensitive point was that foreign newspapers were beginning to criticise northern Italians for displaying so little interest in their southern provinces and knowing next to nothing about them. The years 1874–6 were therefore marked by an increasing sense of guilt in the north and growing resentment among the 48,000 voters of Sicily. When an election suddenly gave 44 out of 48 Sicilian seats in parliament to opposition candidates, the alliance between governments of the Right and the local political machines had obviously collapsed.

Minghetti, the Prime Minister, reacted to this secession of the Sicilian political elite by proposing further emergency regulations. For one year his government made a genuine effort to deal both with brigandage and with what was now commonly referred to as the mafia. After defeat in the elections, Minghetti had nothing left to lose; on the contrary, crushing the existing electoral cliques was urgently needed in order to reinforce his failing majority. Not surprisingly, perhaps, Sicilian deputies and some landowners tried to make his task as difficult as possible. Minghetti, however, was no blinkered reactionary, and before resigning he appointed a special commit-tee of parliament to examine conditions in Sicily and find out what had been going wrong there.

The Bonfadini committee (Romualdo Bonfadini was the *rapporteur*) did not give themselves time for any more than a hurried and superficial study based either on official information or on evidence from the local notables who had every interest in putting up a smoke screen. They seem to have been determined to view things in the best possible light and so restore the good will of the landowning class. Political reasons ruled out any fun-damental analysis, and the conclusion was that Sicily needed no special treatment. Standards of living were deemed no worse than in some other parts of Italy, and crime was assumed to be much the same as elsewhere.

Far more thorough was a private report made by Sidney Sonnino and Leopoldo Franchetti, two of the most distinguished Italians of their gener-ation. These men were both from Tuscany; and as outsiders, and conserva-tive landowners, what they said carried particular weight. They visited many more places in Sicily and sampled a far wider range of opinion than the parliamentary committee; and their depressing conclusion was that things had changed remarkably little since Bourbon times. The old elites continued to dominate the localities, to the detriment of liberal government; the most talented and independent-minded Sicilians still preferred to leave Sicily;

local government was utterly corrupt; and, in the bitter struggle for power, the winning family group in each village took all. As far as tax money was concerned, very little was spent on roads or medical centres, and far too much went on theatres and political corruption.

This analysis enabled Franchetti to come nearer than anyone to penetrating the myths surrounding the mafia. The 'Honourable Society' was a legend, for the mafia was not an organization any more than it was a merely casual phenomenon; and though it might have some chivalrous elements, for the most part its so-called code of honour was a device to conceal self-interest. The theory that it evolved from opposition to foreign rule was implausible, because *mafiosi* generally sought the backing of whatever government was in power. The *mafia* exploited the gap left by an ineffective state, and its main function was to impose some rudimentary organization on the anarchy of Sicilian life. Crime was a means only for *mafiosi*; the main object, as always, was to win respect, power and hence money.

Both authors agreed that fundamental changes in Sicily were urgently needed; but whereas Sonnino thought that Sicilians might find their own remedy if left to fight it out among themselves, Franchetti believed that leaving power in the hands of Sicilian police and magistrates could only make things worse. This difference of opinion reflected a basic dilemma of many successive governments: if Sicilian officials were appointed, they would be exposed to intimidation, nepotism and clientelage; on the other hand outsiders could never penetrate the mysteries of this arcane world or succeed in making themselves obeyed. According to Franchetti's analysis, the government had incurred a clear responsibility by acquiescing in local corruption. Yet he also stated explicitly that the Sicilian ruling class was the chief villain. Naturally, therefore, they tried to bury his report.

This negative reaction was helped by the fact that the Left won political power in 1876. The great majority of Sicilian deputies now formed part of the government bloc; and the official attitude towards Sicily's problems, indeed towards the 'southern question' as a whole, therefore remained unchanged. Most Sicilian deputies would vote automatically for any official measure; and in return they had the assurance that Sicily would be left unreformed and the facts revealed by Tajani and Franchetti forgotten or at least forgiven. Far from the north's being able to reform and improve the south, it was rather southern methods of clientelage and political sharp practice which would soon be seeking further areas of profitable employment in the national capital itself.

SOCIETY AND THE ECONOMY

An immensely detailed report on Italian agriculture by a commission under Senator Jacini was published in 1886. The volumes on Sicily showed that union with Italy had brought some improvements but had done little for the farm labourers and share croppers who were the bulk of the population. This pessimistic view was endorsed by Sonnino, who told parliament, with possible exaggeration, that agricultural labourers in Sicily were worse off than any in Europe. He added that in twenty years the government had not introduced a single effective measure to improve the lot of poor people and make them see any material advantage in Italian rule. Instead of remedying the social malaise revealed by the revolt of 1866, the *macinato* had been reimposed in 1868, the very tax which for centuries had been the chief ingredient in Sicilian rebelliousness.

The chief problem of the Sicilian economy was the inability to keep food production in pace with a rapid rise in population; and this once again brought up the question of the *latifondi*. These large estates hardly seemed to have diminished in size, because any land transformed by intensive cultivation had been matched by more waste areas being brought under extensive cereal farming. Despite the splitting up of Church estates, the number of property owners had decreased, largely because of forfeiture for non-payment of taxes during a period of agricultural depression. The gap between rich and poor was becoming wider than ever, and the laws about dividing and sharing out the communal village lands, after decades of non-enforcement, were finally abrogated. Retrospective legal sanction was given to an enormous amount of illegal enclosure by the village oligarchies.

Some experts suggested that, with credit and secure tenure, peasant proprietors whose holdings were not too microscopic did better than most *latifondisti*, and Sonnino was optimistic enough to think that three-quarters of the *latifondi* could be profitably divided. The chief problem was to avoid pulverisation into tiny patches of land in places where improvements were not easy. In some areas even a farm of ten acres would be insufficient for subsistence, let alone able to provide a surplus for investment in increased production. Any land converted into smallholdings would therefore have to be selected with this in mind. Technical help and credit would also be needed.

The alternative was to induce the *latifondisti* to give up absenteeism and their preference for a low-yield and low-cost type of agriculture; or at least to persuade them, if they would not themselves improve their farms, to put up the capital and encourage their tenants to do so. This was an attractive possibility, just because smallholdings were in practice often too fragmented and

undercapitalized, whereas a well-planned ranch could offer genuine economies in production. Against it, however, was the simple and decisive fact
that social pressures made most existing landowners unwilling to change
their habits, and political reasons prevented them from being forced to do so.

In fairness, a few enlightened *latifondisti* did encourage their tenants to
try new methods and crops. Di Rudinì, for example, when he left the less
mobile environment of western Sicily, succeeded in converting unhealthy
marshes near Syracuse into smallholdings on long lease for the cultivation
of vines, nuts, olives, and carobs. Sicilian wine production received a fillip
after phylloxera began to devastate French vineyards in the late 1860s, and
large areas were now given over to vines. Unfortunately, in the late 1870s,
the phylloxera reached Sicily itself and, since an emergency regulation
obliging growers to destroy non-resistant vines could not be enforced, the
disease proved extremely damaging. Unfortunately it was the more enterprising farmers who had switched to vines, and it was they who suffered
most.

Other specialist crops also ran into trouble. The silk mulberries, which
were expensive in labour, continued to attract high taxation even though
competition from oriental silks now made this uneconomic. Likewise olives
were taxed at a rate fixed before mineral oils and gas supplanted olive oil as a
form of lighting. On the other hand, the orange and lemon groves still paid
relatively little in tax, and although they needed a good deal of capital, the
rewards were very large once steam navigation revolutionized transport.
For a time, Sicilian citrus developed a good market across the Atlantic, until
American competition began to be felt after 1884.

The national tariff policy continued to work against the south but now in a
very different way from before. The reduction of protective duties after
1878, and especially after 1887, aided the already industrialized parts of
Italy. If Sicilian politicians were among the architects of this discriminatory
policy, the reason no doubt is that the *latifondisti* and their dependents were
simultaneously given a duty on imported cereals. This protection of grain
was a concealed subsidy for wheat as against cattle breeding; it helped the
feudal Sicily of the interior at the expense of the more intensively cultivated
vineyards and orchards of the coast. It delayed the splitting up of the
latifondi and encouraged the already excessive cultivation of cereals on
altogether unsuitable land.

Where the central government might have compensated for this tariff
was in the provision of essential public services; but Sicily, with 10 per cent
of Italy's population, received less than 3 per cent of government expenditure on something as fundamental as irrigation and water control. Nor was
road building greatly accelerated despite all the resources of the new

government, and the main road across the centre of the island still took thirty years to complete. As a result half the villages had no access by road, and some could hardly be approached on horseback. Dried-out river beds often remained the chief means of communication. Wheeled transport was thus impossible, and the Lorenzoni report of 1910 said that many Sicilians had never seen a wheeled cart. Lack of roads was therefore still a primary fact in keeping Sicily backward and much of it uninhabited.

The sulphur industry, above all, needed better communications, for most of the mines were in the undeveloped provinces of Caltanissetta and Girgenti. Sulphur prices began to decline about 1875, but output went on increasing till the end of the century. By that time about five hundred mines were being worked, and it was said that nearly a quarter of a million people were dependent on them. Extraction was still costly and primitive, not least because the seventy-five or so families who owned most of the sulphur industry had managed to prevent the Piedmontese mining law from being extended to Sicily in 1861. As a result, landlords continued to take between 20 and 40 per cent of the profits in return for no work and no monetary investment. When a new steam process opened up the huge deposits in Louisiana at the end of the century, Sicilian sulphur quickly found itself priced out of the European market.

Inside the mines, most of the ore was still carried on the backs of children, whose daily stint might be thirty journeys to the surface and who worked anything from six to twelve hours a day. A government commission in 1875 recommended a total prohibition against using women, or children under fourteen, as carriers; but a first tentative law in 1879 merely forbade the employment of girls in general and boys under eleven. Even this could not be enforced, and any further attempt to reduce child labour encountered dozens of well-organized representations from mine owners, municipalities and Chambers of Commerce.

This shows that the failure to improve conditions in Sicily was more than just a question of official policy. Though government investment continued to be far heavier in the north than in the south, the chafing that this caused was often an excuse for avoiding self-criticism. There was an ingenuous expectation that politicians at Rome (which became Italy's capital in 1870) should unilaterally be finding an answer to Sicily's problems. The two main government enquiries, those of Jacini and Lorenzoni, both complained of a lack of local assistance: three out of seven Chambers of Commerce refused to give any evidence to Lorenzoni, while most latifondisti failed to answer his questionnaire. Northerners could hardly be expected to invest time and money in Sicily until Sicilians themselves were more disposed to change and had greater confidence in their own future.

CHAPTER 22

The failure of liberalism

CRISPI AND THE *FASCI* REBELLION

The governments of the Left at Rome after 1876 did little more for Sicily than their predecessors; and even under two Sicilians, Crispi and di Rudinì, who between them held the office of Prime Minister for almost ten years in succession, conditions worsened. Crispi was more interested in colonies than in benefiting his native island. To make Italy militarily strong he needed high taxes and a severely controlled expenditure on public works. This fell with special severity on the south. Moreover, so long as submissive deputies were returned to parliament, he too, like his predecessors, allowed corrupt local clienteles to retain the substance of power, to violate the law at their pleasure, and keep Sicily unreformed.

Though Crispi had once been, as in fact he remained, a radical reformer, he had to an extent lost touch with the realities of Sicilian life, even though his friends warned him in the 1880s that a social war was building up. Local authorities were continuing to place the main burden of taxation on people who were already too near to starvation; and agricultural prices were sharply falling, as railways and steamships brought competition from American grain. A depression was then intensified by Crispi's trade war with France, by the arrival of vine disease and a reduction in mining wages. A British consul could write in 1891: 'The price of labour has not risen in Sicily during the last 20 years, while the cost of living has doubled.'

The common people, however, were not quick to rebel against these worsening circumstances. We hear of a group of peasants electing one of themselves to be a king, but such utopian opposition was not dangerous. Only after a year of really bad harvest did they become less docile. The flagellants then processed the streets as they had done in 1647 and 1773; images of the saints again had their ornaments confiscated and were put in irons amid general derision. Just as in 1860 and 1866, religious enthusiasm could then be harnessed by popular preachers who called people to abandon the priests for a new religion of Christ. Economic distress, when over-laid with this kind of chiliastic religious excitement, easily led to acts of violence.

By 1890 there were certain changes in society which made the sense of dissatisfaction more articulate. A few farm labourers could now read and write and, as conscripts elsewhere in Italy, they had learnt of altogether new needs and possibilities. In a number of villages, minority groups among the gentry, excluded from influence and jobbery, had a casual interest in stirring up agitation; and a growing class of doctors, lawyers and other university-educated men were ready to formulate and channel a widespread feeling of frustration. There were also a few outright revolutionaries who advocated socialization of the land and the mines; and one rather idiosyncratic socialist, de Felice, formed a populist administration after winning the municipal elections at Catania in 1889.

Sicilian villlages were, on average, three times as large as those in Piedmont; and this fact, together with the concentration of workers in the mines, made it possible for agitation to spread easily, especially when groups of *fasci* began to form an embryonic trade union movement. Some of the early *fasci* were much like the old guilds, interested in sickness benefits, funeral insurance and the establishment of cooperative shops. Some were run by socialists though others were dominated by *mafiosi*, or were simply part of the faction fight which went on in each village to control municipal government. Usually, though, they were vocal champions of lower-class unrest, and this was a novel and offensive phenomenon which required a firm government response.

For the first time in history, villagers were discovering how they could organize against illegal enclosures of land, and occasionally agricultural strikes succeeded in obtaining much more generous contracts. The Prime Minister, Giovanni Giolitti, while deploring violence by either side, argued that strikes were no crime and that peasants had every right to agitate against manifest illegality. This naturally alarmed the *latifondisti*. The traditional methods of control seemed to be breaking down; and in May 1893 there was even a regional socialist congress in Sicily. Village authorities responded with greater repressiveness, and this led to an escalation of violence. Soon it was the old story of tax offices being sacked, prisons opened and land registers burned. Some demonstrators cried 'Long live the King', for they hoped that the central government was on their side; some were led by the clergy; others raised the red flag.

At this point Crispi was urgently brought back as Prime Minister, with a policy of martial law. Crispi believed, or said he believed, that the *fasci* were trying to sever Sicily from Italy with help from Russia and France: this was his remarkable excuse for sending the fleet and thirty thousand soldiers to quell the revolt. The landowners were delighted, because this was the kind of response they understood. As one Sicilian senator privately explained, Sicily was an oriental country which could be governed only by force. It was even asserted in parliament that Sicily had no particular economic hardship, no special weaknesses in local government, no discriminatory taxes which needed reform; and an unfortunately publicized meeting of Sicilian land-owners called on the government to go to the root of the trouble and abolish compulsory education.

Crispi was not at heart a reactionary. Moreover, he soon had pressing reasons for tackling the social question. The trial of two members of parliament, de Felice and Bosco, persuaded moderate opinion that Crispi's repressive policies had been miscalculated. In addition, his imperialist exploits in Africa had completely unbalanced the budget and he now thought he could disarm the reformers by tackling the land question. Suddenly, therefore, Crispi proposed a thorough reform of the *latifondi*: all uncultivated properties and private estates over 250 acres would be liable to conversion into smallholdings; so would any *latifondi* still owned by the villages. Learning from previous mistakes, the new units were to be between twelve and fifty acres in size; there were to be no auctions, and cheap credit would be provided. Most drastic of all, recalcitrant proprietors could face expropriation.

Crispi made this revolutionary proposal apparently without so much as informing his cabinet, and clearly it was a hurried and insufficiently considered move. It aroused tremendous opposition from the Sicilian deputies and had to be dropped. Crispi's successor, di Rudinì, adopted a more feasible land policy, keeping the *latifondi* intact but making them more efficient by giving tenants better credit and longer leases. In order to destroy Crispi's electoral machine he tried to ally his own conservatives with the extreme Left; he also courted the Sicilian autonomists and appointed a special regional commissioner in the island with some independence of Rome.

The idea of returning to the status of a semi-autonomous region might have been expected to attract many Sicilians, but the experiment did not prove a success. Giovanni Codronchi, the commissioner, was full of good intentions, but as a northerner he found the cards stacked against him; and since he based his administration on Palermo, there was a strong sectional opposition from Messina and elsewhere. He planned to reform local govern-ment, introduce rural banks, carry out some division of the land, and undercut the usurious rates of interest which kept the peasants in bondage. But he found Sicily a world where the ordinary rules of politics did not apply and where local cliques could easily frustrate his programme of tax reliefs and credit for the poor.

Regretfully the commissioner had to admit that nine-tenths of the Sicilian deputies were opposed to his experiment in Sicilian autonomy. Desperately, even blatantly, he tried to rig the elections using all the devices which Crispi had used before him, but with less success. De Felice, though a member of parliament, was declared under age and incapable of even voting; and in rejoinder this socialist leader accused the government of using the mafia for political purposes. Crispi was too strongly entrenched at Palermo to be ousted, and many other Sicilians deserted Codronchi when he attacked their private electoral enclaves. Clearly the local clienteles were not going to accept reform from di Rudinì any more than from Giolitti or Crispi, and they could easily play one politician off against another to ensure that things remained much as before.

THE MAFIA AND POLITICAL CORRUPTION

Some of the sinister background to this political rivalry was revealed through the unexpected publicity given to the murder in 1893 of a distinguished public servant, the Marquis Notarbartolo. This man had witnessed the corruption of municipal administration at first hand; and as a director of the Bank of Sicily he had found that a number of private fortunes had been created by the manipulation of credit and then protected through 'political contributions'. Many people must have been anxious to secure his removal before he had time to unravel the full extent of these shady goings-on; at all events he was dismissed from his job.

For years Notarbartolo for some reason remained silent, but eventually he dared to pass certain incriminating information to the government. This cost him his life: he was brutally stabbed to death on a train between Palermo and Termini Imerese. For years an inquiry to discover who paid the assassins dragged on, but one prime suspect, the deputy Palizzolo, a governor of the bank and a follower of Crispi, was not even interrogated. Only in 1899 was he indicted; but the police lied in court to secure his acquittal, and documents implicating him disappeared from the Palermo police station. At long last, in 1902, a non-Sicilian jury convicted him, but their judgement was set aside; and, ten years after the murder, another trial resulted in an open verdict after many witnesses had unaccountably changed their stories.

Many people no doubt welcomed this reversal, for mafia help and 'the Sicilian vote' were as important as ever to politicians of many different colours. A dangerously hysterical local patriotism had also been aroused among Sicilians of both Right and Left who, even while resenting Palizzolo for giving publicity to the worst side of Palermo's barbarous machine politics, resented still more the supercilious and sometimes contemptuous reaction of northerners. Some Italians were at this point writing about the south in terms of a racial inferiority which would explain Sicilian delinquency as incorrigible; and Sicilians, outraged by this attitude, lionized Palizzolo after his acquittal. A special ship was chartered to escort him home in triumph and he found himself a local hero.

The system that spawned Palizzolo was taken over by Giolitti and used on occasion to support his paramount position in Italian politics between 1900 and the outbreak of war in 1914. Giolitti had the reputation of a left-of-centre liberal, but his liberalism was more in evidence elsewhere, and he was said to think of Sicily just as a group of deputies to conciliate. In four general elections he perfected the art of winning a majority: at the lowest level, the price of votes was quoted openly in the newspapers, and private armies were allowed to intimidate voters by every means up to and including assassination. The quality of Sicilian deputies accordingly remained poor. Their job in Rome was not so much to champion Sicilian or national interests; it was rather to seek patronage for their local electors and to act as an intermediary in negotiating with government departments.

One result of this was that Sicilian parties tended to grow up around a person rather than a policy. This was the case with the best-known Sicilian politician of the early twentieth century, Nunzio Nasi. Nasi, who came from Trapani, judiciously supported Crispi and Giolitti in turn, and by so doing built up an enormously powerful clientele which included both conservatives and leftists. For forty years his careful attention to parish-pump interests enabled him to continue as Trapani's representative in parliament. But eventually he made the mistake of becoming a minister; for at Rome different standards of behaviour were required. Instinctively, and without realising the dangers, Nasi went on using the only techniques of government with which he was familiar, inflating his entertainment and travelling expenses, and occasionally misappropriating minor sums of public money to reward himself and to increase his powers of patronage.

None of this amounted to very much, and perhaps Nasi was genuinely surprised when rival politicians – some of them Sicilians – took the excuse to promote a criminal action against him. Trapani, which had done particularly well out of the minister's benefactions, then made him into a martyr: portraits of the King and Queen were burned; Victor Emanuel Street was renamed Nunzio Nasi Street; and for a short while the French flag even flew over the town hall. This sealed his fate. Nasi prudently disappeared abroad for three years, but when he returned he was impeached before the senate and found guilty of peculation. Even on the eastern seaboard of Sicily there were riots against this verdict and against the supposed slight thrown on the island by prudish, hypocritical northerners. The writer Luigi Pirandello fully shared the sense of outrage. A large subscription was raised, and Nasi was brought home to a triumphal reception as great as Palizzolo had received. Though barred from parliament, he went on being elected again and again by overwhelming majorities.

Catania on the east coast was different from Trapani, yet not unrecognizably so. With a rapidly growing population, a productive agricultural hinterland, and reputedly no mafia at all, Catania was becoming the richest industrial city in the island. On several occasions it was administered by a coalition under the socialist de Felice, who promised a general attack on corruption and inefficiency. His programme attracted many of a remarkable generation of intellectuals; but his own administration seems to have been only slightly less inefficient and corrupted than the rest. It was said that he had an arrangement with some of the most reactionary barons; and his electoral machine recruited the intimidating 'mountaineers' and goatherds at election time. By 1911 there was not a great deal to show for his reforms, and the town was heavily in debt.

The Catania of Verga, Capuana, Mario Rapisardi and de Roberto was no mean city as a cultural centre; but the impact of these men on the rest of the island was not large, and most creative artists and writers preferred to live in Rome or Milan if they could. Pirandello wrote some dialect plays, and both he and Verga had an enormous nostalgia for Sicily and a guilt about leaving it. Verga's themes were obsessively Sicilian, and it comes as a shock to find him writing from Milan for his friends to send him a collection of Sicilian phrases to make his work sound yet more authentic. Likewise Pirandello preferred to return home every few years to obtain fresh plots and local atmosphere; but he never stayed for long.

If the intellectuals failed to change Sicily, one relevant fact was the defectiveness of Sicilian education. Not only was there a general 58 per cent illiteracy in 1911, but the three local universities were still geared to producing lawyers and bureaucrats, and had a built-in prejudice against the practical agricultural and engineering studies which were much more urgently needed. Local families who could afford it preferred to send their children to universities elsewhere. The urge to leave Sicily, coupled with the strong predilection for white-collar employment, meant that educated Sicilians obtained a disproportionate number of the administrative posts at Rome, which northerners affected to despise.

As the cases of Palizzolo and Nasi suggest, the psychological as well as material gap between Sicily and the rest of Italy was great. Naturally, strong efforts were made by both sides to deal with this problem. One important source of integration was military service. Another was literature: in the spectacular short stories about his home environment, Verga tried to make his characters speak an Italian sufficiently orthodox to be generally understood. Though the process of acculturation was slow, things nevertheless were changing. Indeed by 1917 the island's most famous philosopher, Giovanni Gentile, could even hazard the opinion that there no longer existed a distinct Sicilian culture. But his was a somewhat maverick voice.

Within Sicily itself, a difference had long been noticeable between east and west; and this difference was clearly growing. Soon after 1900, for example, Palermo was overtaken by Catania as a port for overseas trade; and though the ex-feudatories of western Sicily often remained the arbiters of taste and conduct, the east of the island could boast a more open society and a more forward-looking culture. Commercial investment was here as important as landed property, and enterprise was more likely to be admired and rewarded. Even agriculture was different; over large areas of the east, tenancies were longer; there was greater diversification of crops, more intensive production, and better irrigation. In addition, socialism, just like jacobinism a century before, was stronger here and frequently acted as an idealistic and purifying force.

The east of the island also had noticeably less crime than the west. Jacini and Damiani in the 1880s found that only four villages in the province of Syracuse were subject to mafia activity, and only five in that of Catania. Why this should have been the case is far from obvious. Palermo might have contributed to the west's infection, in that it was for long a centre of government, and so the fountain-head for the patronage needed by every boss and politician. More material, though, was the fact that the east of the island offered greater opportunities for honest advancement; and with the social structure more rigid, and repression more pronounced in the west, how else, as one observer asked, could one succeed in life except by the mafia?

GIOLITTI AND THE ECONOMY

While the period of Giolitti brought prosperity to the rest of Italy, Sicily was slow off the mark. In the years 1907–10, a detailed socio-economic investigation of the island was made on behalf of parliament by Professor Lorenzoni. His report described what was still a feudal world. The old aristocracy still owned most of the large estates, and all too often they still conceived it their interest to retard economic development. Conditions of soil and climate were very difficult, but a dozen *latifondisti* gave positive evidence that some large estates could be greatly improved. The other few hundred, however, who made up less than a tenth of 1 per cent of the population but owned half of Sicily, had little intention of building farm-houses or undertaking land reclamation.

Only about 2.5 per cent of the money allocated by the government to 'bonification' between 1861 and 1920 was in fact spent in Sicily. Eucalyptus trees had been introduced from Australia via Algeria in the 1860s, and by the 1880s they were showing good results in diminishing erosion and marshland; but few private individuals had the patience or public spirit to replant trees and obey the existing forest laws. When the government tried to drain marshes or carry out irrigation works, there was sometimes opposition from landowners, who thought water supplies too valuable to be left in public ownership. Yet this traditional resistance to change was becoming more and more anachronistic, and low-production *latifondismo* was far too expensive an impediment for a fast-growing population of three and a half million.

Some changes for the better were certainly visible by 1910. For one thing, northern attitudes were changing. There was still an occasional tendency to excuse government failings by arguing that Sicily must be in some way incorrigibly inferior; but now that northern industrialization was far advanced, other Italians could afford to admit that a rise in southern standards of living was possible and would help everyone. It is doubtful if many deputies read Lorenzoni's volumes, but parliament did give more attention to the 'southern problem'; and the debates no longer took place in an almost empty Chamber. In 1911 the government went so far as to accept in principle that the *latifondi* were the chief cause of Sicilian poverty, even though tariff policy continued to discourage the transformation of these ranches towards more specialist kinds of production. The next year a widening of the suffrage dented the oligarchic monopoly of local power.

Another change was that the *fasci siciliani* had taught the peasants their strength. Agricultural strikes sometimes succeeded in securing better contracts, and although proprietors frequently asked for troops against the strikers, Giolitti usually preferred not to intervene. There was a welcome appearance of agricultural cooperatives. These cooperatives were only moderately successful at first, for strong vested interests against them did not shrink from intimidation or even murder, and in any case Sicilian peasants were too individualistic to take kindly to cooperation; but it was at least proved that altogether new types of land-ownership were feasible. Cooperatives sometimes took over and effectively administered an entire *latifondo*, completely cutting out the intermediary *gabelloto*. They did more for agricultural education than anyone had ever done before, and it was particularly under their auspices that farmers learnt about phosphates and crop rotation.

The cooperative movement in general, and the pioneer organization of Don Sturzo, Mayor of Caltagirone, in particular, recognized the need for adequate agrarian credit. The Bank of Sicily had been notoriously ineffective in this important field, preferring to lend outside Sicily and in quite other fields than agriculture. The bank also went through another bad patch when its council was dismissed again for grave irregularities. The only credit normally available to small farmers came from either the landowners or the *gabelloti*, and here Lorenzoni discovered rates of interest up to 400 per cent, even in one village 1000 per cent. On the other hand, cooperatives, where they managed to exist, could lend at 7 per cent to their members, and this was the kind of service which was indispensable if smallholdings were not to perpetuate the undercapitalization which had typified the *latifondi*.

Even more important as a cause of change was the rapidly increasing rate of emigration. Many landlords had always liked living overseas, but now the peasants, too, began desperately to leave in search of food and work; and for a people so attached to their families, this was remarkable. Already, by 1900, thousands of Sicilians had achieved in Tunisia under French rule the peasant proprietorship which was so elusive at home; and they thereby exploded a myth by showing they could create flourishing farms in conditions not unlike those of the *latifondi*. Altogether one and a half million Sicilians left the island in the years before the world war. They went chiefly to the United States, but also to Argentina and Brazil. Here was one of the most prodigious facts in all Sicilian history. Some villages lost most of their male population, and were even reduced by as much as one-fifth in a single year.

This huge exodus was a terrible exposure of Sicilian poverty and the growing imbalance which the government had encouraged between north and south Italy. Yet it had some beneficial effects. The report of large fortunes made overseas was a great stimulus to education and literacy, as was also the wish to correspond with relatives overseas. More obvious was the fact that labour shortages were created, and this in turn meant that, in 1905–11, wages went up by a third for those who stayed behind. Already by 1906 some landowners were complaining of the indignity of having to go cap in hand and beg workers to help in the fields.

Marginal land under wheat was no longer so profitable in these conditions: hence some was allowed to revert back to pasture and woodland, and cereals now took up less than 70 per cent of the agricultural surface. Many landowners discovered that they could no longer afford a type of agriculture which flourished on unemployment and led necessarily to soil impoverishment and erosion. Some proprietors who did not want to reduce their standard of life decided to reside on their estates and take over management from the *gabelloti*; in the last resort they would sell land to more practical farmers, and they were quite often ready to grant better leases. In other words, agricultural practices which many people had thought incorrigible were beginning to disappear without any of the drastic legislation which Crispi had thought necessary.

Emigration caused enormous suffering, and the loss to Sicily was in one sense irremediable; yet by 1907 the economy was gaining in return the huge sum of a hundred million *lire* a year in remittances by émigrés to their families at home – and this was only the official figure. Never before had there been such an injection of capital into Sicilian agriculture. By 1907, moreoever, many of the *americani* were also coming back home to retire, with savings to invest in buying the social position which only land could confer. They brought with them the expectation of a higher standard of life, and above all a self-respect which prevented their treating the *notabili* with the deference that custom required. All this helped to weaken the tradition of supine resignation and the refusal to look ahead which characterized the agrarian society to which they were returning.

LIBERALISM IN CRISIS

Where the politicians had failed, Sicilians were thus beginning to redress the balance themselves; but at this critical moment politics intervened to halt progress. Giolitti's conquest of Libya in 1911–12 devoured the scanty resources which might have been applied to solving problems that Lorenzoni and others had begun to define; and this colonial war was enthusiastically supported by many Sicilians, including the socialist de Felice, as well as the conservative landowner di San Giuliano, who was Giolitti's foreign minister. A close connection with North Africa had accompanied many of the island's most prosperous periods of history, and great hopes were aroused here by the prospect of a new Italian empire. But in the event, the Libyan deserts proved to be an expensive mirage.

Hard on the heels of the Libyan venture came the First World War. Sicily's markets were now largely cut off until 1919, and this was a grave blow to an economy which depended on exports. Moreover, few war industries were allocated to a region where skilled workmen and efficient transport were lacking, while job reservation as an alternative to military service applied to northern industrial workers rather than to southern peasants. The government needed cheap food and so fixed artificially low prices for flour, with the result that officially declared wheat production declined by about 30 per cent between 1914 and 1917. As if this was not enough, inflation helped displace wealth from agriculture to industry with savings being transferred to the north where they were invested in plant and stocks.

These two wars inevitably speeded up many processes of social change.

Those who went off to fight returned with new skills, new aspirations, and new grievances; those who stayed behind sometimes dramatically altered their economic circumstances. This was particularly the case with those who paid their landlords in cash. The freeze on rents, together with rising prices, allowed some sections of the rural middle class, and the *gabelloti* in particular, to make enormous profits. Their new-found wealth was then used to buy up land, and this put pressure on the *latifondisti*, who were already in straitened circumstances. By the end of the war, the process of dividing up the large estates had been greatly accelerated; and this tendency was reinforced by peasant land occupations in 1919 and 1920, particularly in the west of the island. In these circumstances, and with violence rife, there was much talk of the mafia.

Parallel with this process went a decline in the credibility of liberalism. Until the 1913 elections, Sicily had generally returned a solid majority of 'ministeriali' to Rome; but in 1913 the number of Sicilian liberals in parliament was cut from 43 to 21. Six years later, as a result of the war, direct manhood suffrage had to be introduced, and elections were held before the political machines had time to adjust to this undermining of their authority. The result was that only half a dozen liberals were returned out of 52 Sicilian deputies. The new voters were asserting themselves at the expense of the traditional agrarian bloc. The situation was one of extreme flux; and the new struggle for power was reflected, as always in Sicily, by extreme lawlessness.

Dangerous moment though this was, the political climate in Sicily was notably different from that in other parts of Italy. No fascists were elected there until after Mussolini's conquest of power in 1922. The socialists also were much weaker than on the mainland, and there was less militant labour unrest. This was largely because an industrial proletariat was still lacking, but it was partly due to the fact that, whereas the landowners of northern Italy needed Mussolini's help against trade unionism, Sicily possessed more traditional methods of intimidation. A number of union leaders and peasant agitators were assassinated, and of course the culprits ran little risk of conviction.

A renewed demand for agrarian reform was the chief threat to the existing order in this period. The soldiers had been promised land during the war in order to encourage them to fight, but they returned home to find unemployment, inflation, and a fierce resistance to their claims. Other countries now made emigration difficult, and this added to the tension. The upshot was a wave of land occupations organised either by patriotic ex-combatants, or by people who brandished the red flag and sang the *International*. Some peasants were led by their priests, since the catholic popular party of Don

Sturzo strongly favoured land reform. Hundreds of thousands of acres were transferred in this way to smallholders, and dozens of new cooperatives were formed to assist the process of cultivation.

Such a vast movement of land distribution, though it reduced the *latifondi*, could not by itself destroy the old methods of extensive agriculture. There were now other Italian regions with a greater number of large estates than Sicily, while at the other extreme Sicily possessed proportionally more smallholdings of up to two acres in extent than existed on the mainland; but these tiny plots did not necessarily mean a change for the better. Some of the new tenants were just out to draw a quick profit, and often did not possess enough land to give a balance of crops and maintain regular employment for their families. Sometimes they sold out. Sometimes, out of ignorance or miscalculated greed, they continued to overcrop with repeated plantings of wheat in a kind of 'peasant *latifondismo*' which mimicked and even aggravated previous practice.

Government action played relatively little part in this process except to sanction what could not be prevented. Three successive ministers of agriculture in 1919–20 had to legitimise retrospectively the spontaneous land occupations, and preference was given by law to cooperatives. But government decrees on the subject left much to be desired: they were not applied uniformly, and local committees for land apportionment were subject to political and other pressures. Furthermore the cooperatives often lacked the requisite technical capacity or even indeed the willingness to work together. One result, though, was that the scale of the arbitrary land occupations diminished in 1921. This was well before Mussolini's so-called 'march on Rome', which was later fatuously deemed to have saved Italy from agrarian communism.

Sicily has been called the least fascist region in Italy, and there was certainly nothing comparable to the violent conquest of power that northern Italy experienced in 1921–2. After 1922, however, many of the established interests were quick to adjust to Mussolini's regime, for they had always liked a close understanding with whoever was in power at Rome. The *latifondisti* needed Mussolini's help in stopping agrarian reform; the mine owners had to prevent nationalization, as well as overcome trade union opposition to lower wages. Local businessmen such as Vincenzo Florio found little to object to in the new regime; and among intellectuals, as one can see from the outspoken views of both Verga and Pirandello, there was plenty of contempt for a parliamentary system which was so obviously corrupt in its operation and which had signally failed to help Sicily in sixty years.

In the 1921 elections the fascists had no success at all in Sicily; but three years later, helped by the former Prime Minister Orlando and his liberals, they took 38 of the 57 seats. Here was another electoral revolution on the same scale as that of 1874. No doubt the liberals had hoped to use fascism to perpetuate their own power. But the Great War had thrown up a new category of middle-class radicals in Sicily as elsewhere in Italy; and these young 'intransigents' were eager to push the old elite aside. In the event, the threat to the established order proved only temporary. Nevertheless, the years 1924–6 caused the *latifondisti* some anxious moments.

CHAPTER 23

Fascist Sicily

THE REGIME IN SICILY

The history of Sicily under fascism is surprisingly empty. The philosopher
Giovanni Gentile was one of the few Sicilians in the party to reach the
highest ranks, where policy-making could be influenced; and he was soon
demoted. Mussolini, to judge from his writings and speeches, gave less
thought to the island than most Prime Ministers before him. Much more
money was allocated to public works than before, though a good deal of it
was inefficiently and corruptly spent; and the local oligarchies had to submit
to more central surveillance over local taxation and expenditure. But the
fascist party was never in any sense efficient, and by the 1930s lethargy and
corruption were rife. The early conflict between radical fascists and the old
elite had been resolved by 1927 in favour of the latter; and the interests of
the big landowners once again prevailed. As a result, the pace of change was
slower than almost anywhere else in Italy.

Mussolini's success as a politician was chiefly based on his skill as a
propagandist. Fine phrases were cheaper and not infrequently more effective than practical achievements. The spurious claim was made that he had
solved the southern question; and a magazine entitled *The Problems of
Sicily* therefore had to change its name. Such empty posturing condemned
the island to neglect. Surprisingly little was done for tourism. Few railway
connections existed apart from the main coastal line, and hundreds of
thousands of people accordingly still had little contact with the rest of the
nation. Furthermore, splendid roads were constructed in Africa at a time
when some Sicilian villages were linked only by the dried bed of a river.

This neglect was not altogether surprising. In the first place, Mussolini's
chief interest was to make Italy into a strong military nation, and this meant
industrialization and hence investment in northern Italy; the task of the
south was to provide cheap food and raw materials. Secondly, the alliance
between the regime and the old landowning class, cemented by the Battle for
Grain and the political liquidation of the intransigent fascists, condemned
Sicily once again to backwardness. With their income and status guaranteed, the *latifondisti* had no incentive to change; and as usual the government lacked both the inclination and the power to constrain them. Fascist
Sicily marked no fundamental break with the past.

The clash between the radical fascists and the *latifondisti* was particularly intense in western Sicily. The Palermo boss, Alfredo Cucco, represented those young middle-class elements who wanted to liberate the island from the old clienteles and seize power for themselves. Between 1922 and 1924 Cucco led a vigorous assault against his political opponents couched in terms of a fight against the mafia; and with this pretext, he managed to get many liberal administrations dissolved. The 1925 Palermo elections, however, revealed the persistent strength of the old clienteles, and this was one reason why the government now decided to launch a full-scale offensive against the mafia. Given the mystique that the word mafia had engendered, this was bound to be a good publicity stunt; but in practical terms the operation was mainly designed to consolidate Sicilian fascism.

Unfortunately for Alfredo Cucco, things went badly wrong. When the campaign was launched towards the end of 1925, the government was already looking for an accommodation with the big landowners; and the man appointed to head the operation was Cesare Mori, a middle-aged northerner who had little time for young upstarts like Cucco. He was also someone who in the course of a long career in Sicily had established close links with the *latifondisti*; and in 1923, he had categorically stated that the big landowners were always victims of the mafia, and never its accomplices. Whatever hopes Cucco had of weakening the old clienteles and reinforcing his own position were quickly dispelled; and at the beginning of 1927 he was himself accused of involvement with the mafia, and politically liquidated. Much of Sicilian fascism was now rebuilt on an aristocratic footing.

The campaign against the mafia was presented as an attack on organized crime. Mori claimed that the mafia had now degenerated into a purely criminal association, and had thereby lost the popular support it once had. He also thought that *omertà* had been undermined by the war. At the same time, he was aware that the mafia was a nebulous concept, and that the epithet *mafioso* was often bandied about indiscriminately; it could be used, for example, simply as a term of abuse for one's political opponents. Nevertheless, given the lack of witnesses, Mori had to rely heavily on 'public opinion' in deciding whom to arrest. This inevitably led to considerable arbitrariness, with the police acting on their own prejudices or more likely falling victim to the complex web of local factionalism.

Many of those arrested by Mori belonged to that stratum of rural society which had done so well out of the war. These people, of whom the *gabelloto* was the most typical figure, posed a considerable threat to the social and economic ascendancy of the big landowners. It is noticeable that many of the denunciations made to the police in the course of the campaign came from the *latifondisti*. The peasantry in general were much less willing to cooperate. In part this was because *mafiosi* such as Don Calogero Vizzini were held in some esteem by their communities and were not generally regarded as criminals by ordinary people. Their arrest can have done little to endear the mass of the peasantry to the fascist regime; after all, the material benefits went entirely to the *latifondisti* who now increased their rents by anything up to 1500 per cent.

Mori's campaign, with its sweeping round-ups, police brutality, and hasty trials, was unlikely to have done much to overcome popular misgivings about the state; and with the big landowners again solidly entrenched, many must have felt that now more than ever, the only chance of making it in this kind of society was by ruthless self-assertion and powerful protectors. Moreover, despite its initial promises, the regime did almost nothing to improve the material lot of the peasantry. Wages were cut; and the revaluation of the *lira* in 1926–9, followed by the great depression, forced many smallholders into bankruptcy. By the late 1930s reports referred to near starvation conditions in many rural areas.

The fascists had no consistent policy about the *latifondi*. In their early socialist phase they advocated introducing powers for legal expropriation; but the subsequent alliance with the big landowners worked against any reform of private ownership. More and more Mussolini realised the importance of increased wheat production, especially when foreign politics led him to isolationism and a programme of national self-sufficiency; and in 1925 he launched the Battle for Grain. Helped by heavy protective duties, marginal lands in Sicily were brought back into cultivation; and though yields did not improve to nearly the same extent as in the north of Italy, the increased use of fertilizers and mechanization did sometimes make a notable difference.

Judged as an exercise in publicity, the Battle for Grain was good politics; economically, it was less satisfactory. Government subsidies and price supports in general worked to discourage any change in the traditional methods of tenure, management and production, which were at the root of the Sicilian problem. Few agricultural experts were consulted by the government: for professional agronomists knew that Sicily needed fewer not more acres under wheat; she needed variety instead of monoculture, and intensive rather than extensive cultivation. In practice, the result of subsidies was that the same fields were repeatedly sown with wheat, and fertility decreased as the dust bowl spread; while crops were more and more easily washed away. The number of farm animals fell sharply as pasture was ploughed up; and the results of this were bad even for cereal production.

More specialized crops also suffered from clumsy attempts at state interference. Olive oil production, for example, decreased as land was cleared for wheat. Citrus fruits made up half the value of Sicily's exports and were a useful earner of foreign exchange at a time when the rest of Italy was in deficit; but they did not recover their pre-war level. Indeed fruit exports fell by half in the difficult years of 1930–4. The fascist policy of autarky, or self-sufficiency, was bound to damage these export crops just because it provoked retaliation. Yet price supports on the home market made it less urgent for fruit growers to reduce costs or find new markets, and citrus growing in Spain and Israel was thereby greatly encouraged.

The increase in government power under fascism made possible much more stringent laws on land reclamation. Some beneficial results were achieved but, despite plans and promises, few of the proposed schemes were in fact completed. In large part this was because the *latifondisti* dominated the public works' consortia; and as usual they had no compelling reason to make improvements on their land, despite extremely generous government subsidies. The greater availability of credit seems to have been used for quick-return speculative operations, rather than long-term investment, a foretaste of what was to occur on a much larger scale after World War II.

Another reason for the failure of reform was that the government lost interest in the island after the campaign against the mafia. By official reckoning it spent over three times as much money on Apulia as Sicily and fifteen times more on Emilia, where Mussolini had a much greater interest; and later figures suggest that the island now received only 1.59 per cent of the total allocated funds for drainage and irrigation, in other words a much smaller percentage even than before 1922. There was no single dramatic project in Sicily which could catch the public eye to the same extent as draining the Pontine marshes or the Volturno valley. Furthermore, the threat from unemployment was not as great as in the north of the country, where there was obviously a much stronger tradition of working-class militancy.

The absence of popular resistance to the Allies in 1943 revealed the short-sightedness of fascist policies in Sicily. Economically, the pursuit of autarky condemned the island to backwardness. It led, among other things, to a drying-up of foreign capital, and this was bound to damage a region where foreign enterprise was so involved. Sicilian manufactures remained largely at the stage of artisan industry based on the single family. The total number of industrial workers was little greater than it had been fifty years before, and the increase was mainly in the building sector. One positive achievement was that Augusta came into its own as a naval harbour, but the commercial tonnage handled in Sicilian ports fell to half of what it had been fifty years earlier, and was still apparently falling in the 1930s.

The sulphur industry at first gained from a government prepared to eliminate some of the really high-cost mines and reduce by half the royalties paid to mine owners. But like so many other good intentions in Sicily, this one too foundered on the rock of political exigency. Though a law of 1927 declared that the subsoil was public property, it was paradoxically deprived of any practical value when the mines were handed over, in perpetuity, to their former owners. As with the campaign against the mafia, all that happened was that rich *gabelloti* such as Don Calogero Vizzini were now axed; and the owner either took over the running of the mine himself or, more likely, found a new and more pliant *gabelloto*. Either way, sulphur production remained as backward as ever.

When Mussolini visited Sicily in 1937, rumour had it that he intended to set up a special kind of regional government for this depressed area. In fact he only came because the island had suddenly acquired a new importance with the Spanish war and the development of an African empire on the other side of *mare nostrum*. 'Sicily is the geographic centre of the empire', he announced, and it was therefore going to be made into an impregnable fortress. Carried away by a Sicilian audience, he unguardedly promised to make their country 'one of the most fertile in the world . . . and to inaugurate one of the happiest epochs in your 4000 years of history'; the *latifondo* would simply be 'liquidated' along with the whole practice of extensive agriculture which kept Sicilian life at such a primitive level.

Even if intended mainly as propaganda, the threat to eliminate the *latifondo* did nevertheless reflect a change of mind. Mussolini was suddenly captivated by the popular appeal of such a simple and sweeping programme. It was also the case that the growing aggressiveness of Italian foreign policy made it necessary to utilize domestic resources more efficiently. Moreover, Mussolini's own political ideas were moving into another anti-bourgeois phase as he was angered by the recalcitrance of the landowners and their failure to cooperate in making fascism a resounding success. This *volte-face*, however, came too late. A major law was passed in 1940 that was designed to break up the *latifondo*, and a group of top fascist leaders was even sent to the island to inaugurate what was announced as the greatest event in Sicilian history. But the outbreak of war prevented anything practical being done.

Fascism had failed to wrest Sicily from its past. In 1940, more than a generation after his original researches, Professor Lorenzoni reported little change in most of the areas where large estates continued to exist. Agriculture was still in great part nomadic; and short-leases were common. Most country roads could not be used even by a rough cart. The *latifondi* were still called 'fiefs' and seemed a feudal world remote from the twentieth century; for fascism had evidently not penetrated deeply into the Sicilian interior. Perhaps nearly half the peasants lived in one-roomed huts along with their animals, just as their ancestors had always done, and their economy was one of subsistence and little more.

From other official reports we can discover a further corrective to the picture of unrelieved progress put out by fascist propaganda. Unemployment was bad and was made worse by Mussolini's strong prejudice against allowing internal migration. The annual economic growth rate can hardly have been much above 1 per cent. In thirty years there had apparently been little if any rise in the standard of living. A share cropper would normally surrender at least half his produce in lieu of rent, and he still owed personal services to his master as under feudalism. Perhaps most Sicilians now ate bread, but rarely meat. Public assistance was a good deal less well organized than officials believed, and the indebtedness of Sicilian towns and villages made it impossible to supply what the state left undone.

An equally depressing record was true for other areas of the economy. In the provision of power, for instance, there is a certain irony in the fact that all Mussolini's ambition and authority could not harness the latent natural resources which after his death were to cause a minor industrial revolution. He justifiably claimed to have increased electricity supply, but by surprisingly little, and in 1939 it was only one-tenth of the average for Italy as a whole. The telephone had reached only half the Sicilian villages. It was officially admitted that there was a considerable potential for hydro-electricity which lay unexploited. Investment was rather in thermal electricity which, though cheaper, required imported coal and so made nonsense of national self-sufficiency.

WORLD WAR AND ITS AFTERMATH

The worst legacy of fascism to Italy was the world war. Because of her insular position, Sicily was bound to suffer special hardships from any conflict, and particularly one which had a major front in the Mediterranean. Export markets were largely closed, and the difficulty of importing food meant that at times Sicilians had almost nothing to eat except a glut of oranges. The extent of local frustration was reflected in the astonishing decision made by the government in August 1941, to transfer all Sicilian-born officials to the mainland because of suspected disloyalty. Though former rulers of Sicily had thought along these lines, none had ever gone so far. Like other fascist laws in Sicily, the order was disobeyed, but it tells us something about both Sicilian rebelliousness and the incompetence and essential triviality of the regime.

The island was strategically crucial during war, and the Allies chose it for their first full-scale landing in Europe against the forces of Hitler. Mussolini promised the fascist leaders that no Allied invasion could possibly succeed in Sicily, and he confirmed this a few days after his generals had given him overwhelming written evidence to the contrary. He dared not mobilize the population for defence, because arming the people would have been too dangerous; moreover, it would have indicated failure and so risked exposing the bluff upon which he depended. There were no proper coastal defences, let alone adequate air cover against an invasion, and the generals complained that most of the artillery was horse-drawn and some of it quite unusable.

Landing near Gela in July 1943, the Americans swept through the west of Sicily. In the east the British and Canadians met the brunt of German resistance. In a moment of panic, the strongly fortified port of Augusta fell to the invaders without a shot, but there followed a protracted battle on the plain of Catania. Sicilians could do little but hope for a quick decision. In the event, though, the fighting dragged on for five weeks. The Allies, despite their complete air and naval superiority, allowed the Germans to escape across the straits with most of their equipment. The Italians too, though largely abandoned by the German higher command and poorly provided with vehicles and ferry boats, were able to evacuate many of their troops. Once again the island was severed from the rest of Italy and ruled by an alien conqueror.

The war had been a disaster. In its last stages there was a great deal of physical destruction, especially at Palermo and Messina. Some villages were almost obliterated; and damage to power supplies proved highly injurious to the post-war economy. At no time was there any sign of a revolution against Mussolini; nevertheless defeat was followed by the sudden disappearance of every fascist official. The Allies brought not only food but also new drugs which at last made it possible to control malaria. Their victory also meant the restoration of free government and new possibilities of self-determination. Separatism now emerged as a strong political force; and the separatist issue was to dominate Sicilian politics for three years. There was even question of a plebiscite to decide whether the island should become an independent republic, and wild talk was heard about annexation to the United States.

The new state of political turmoil led, as after the First World War, to an outbreak of lawlessness, and once again, after more than a decade of enforced silence on the subject, there was talk of the mafia. The accusation has frequently been made that it was the Allies who deliberately reinstated it to facilitate the conquest of Sicily, and certainly Don Calogero Vizzini and Genco Russo benefited from allied support to become significant figures in the new administration. Moreover, the Sicilian-American *mafiioso* Vito

Genovese, although still wanted by the United States police in connection with many crimes including murder, strangely turned up as a liaison official in an American unit. But too much should not be made of this. The mafia has always been more widespread in fantasy than in fact. Indeed one well-placed American intelligence officer reported after the war that the Allies had owed their success in Salerno and Sardinia, as well as Sicily, to the local mafia.

An important factor in the re-emergence of men such as Vizzini and Genco Russo was that with the collapse of fascism a power vacuum opened up which they were well suited to fill. Not only were they respected local figures, but as victims of Mori's operation against the mafia, they were also in a good position to pose as anti-fascists: criminal imputations were often held to have been politically inspired in Sicily. The ordinary kind of professional politician was now unavailable as he had invariably been a fascist; and unlike other parts of Italy, no organized partisan movement had emerged in Sicily that could have furnished a new political class and upset the existing structure of society.

Another reason for the rehabilitation of old mafiosi was that, in conditions of post-war chaos and starvation, the peasants again began occupying parts of the large estates; hence the *latifondisti* turned instinctively to Vizzini and Genco Russo. The landless labourers who formed most of the population had fared much worse than landlords or peasant proprietors during the war, and land occupation was a desperate though often fruitless attempt to redress the balance. Once again, as after 1918, successive governments tried to make landowners grant more equitable leases, and sometimes had to sanction illegal actions retrospectively. Such a trend was, however, resisted strongly by many landowners and the armed gangs at their disposal. In September 1944, communist and socialist leaders dared to challenge Vizzini's prestige in his home town, Villalba. The boss was forced to outface them, and his bodyguard opened fire, injuring a number of people including the future communist deputy, Li Causi.

In the confusion that followed the demise of fascism, success depended on backing the right horse. Vizzini began by supporting the separatists. This group was strong among the landowning classes, though it also included some utopian intellectuals on the Left who naively believed that winning independence from Italy would at last mean the end of exploitation and poverty. When the Allies handed Sicily over to Italian administration in February 1944, some of the more extremist elements formed a secret army and raised the yellow and red flag with the three-legged symbol of Trinacria in a civil war against the rest of Italy. Mafiosi and bandit gangs were freely recruited for the campaign, and a Mayor of Palermo justified this fact by quoting the example of Garibaldi, who in 1860 had not hesitated to employ the dregs of society in a noble cause.

In order to defeat such a dangerous upsurge of separatist feeling, the Italian government in May 1946 granted Sicily a large measure of autonomy. Though regarded by some as excessive, this move in fact helped reconcile many Sicilians to Italian rule. It also generated quite a few fervent, though sometimes misguided hopes. A number of people claimed that the economic decline of the island dated from 1861; autonomy, they said, would lead to the industrialization of Sicily. More plausibly it was hoped that the existence of a distinct regional administration would give many more people a new political consciousness. A legislative assembly of ninety deputies was now set up at Palermo with its own cabinet of ministers. This body was endowed with almost complete control over the vital areas of agriculture, mining and industry. It was given fairly considerable power over communications, public order and many other fields of public life.

This grant of autonomy was especially pleasing to the inhabitants of Palermo, for in a sense it restored the old regional capital. Though the city continued to decline as a port, it now flourished as a metropolis of bureaucracy; and many new jobs were created. The population, which doubled between 1861 and 1921, had, by 1961, trebled. One general reason for satisfaction was that a special grant was to be paid to the region by the Italian government: this was to make up for Sicily having been inequitably treated in the past, and for the fact that her taxable income was much lower than the national average. The result was that, when the first regional parliament was elected in 1947, fewer than 10 per cent of the deputies were separatists, and by 1951 this party had been almost eliminated.

The first elections, however, caused a different kind of alarm, since communists and socialists together heavily outnumbered the Christian Democrats, while other parties had only a marginal importance. If the Left were to agree among themselves, it seemed likely that they would capture the regional government and carry out drastic reforms in society. This was the ominous possibility which caused many from both Right and Centre to rally to Christian Democracy. Vizzini and his friends quickly changed their allegiance; and the support of such people helps to explain how the Christian Democrats in 1948 doubled their representation and thereafter remained the majority party. There now followed a campaign of terror in which dozens of trade union leaders were murdered, and the point was clearly made that organized labour was unwelcome in Sicily.

The most notorious Sicilian of the post-war years, and a man who became very much involved in the campaign of violence against the Left, was the bandit Salvatore Giuliano. This popular hero and subject of laudatory ballads was at first just one of many brigand leaders roaming the country-side; but owing to his ruthlessness, his ostentatious generosity to some of the poor, his good looks and whimsical flair for publicity, he soon became a legend and a household name even outside Italy. Considerable powers of leadership and some fortunate political involvements also helped to make him someone whose support was cheap to those who could afford it; and though a notorious murderer of many policemen, he received extraordinary favours from the authorities.

Like Vizzini, Giuliano's first political allegiance was to the separatists; and in 1945 he was a colonel in the Sicilian army of independence. When separatism could no longer guarantee him subsidies and high-level spon-sorship, it was noticed that the pattern of voting in his zone of influence shifted significantly to the monarchists, and then to the Christian Demo-crats. By 1947 his considerable powers of intimidation were engaged in fighting communism; and a few days after the Left's triumph in the elections of April 1947, he and his followers turned their machine guns on a May Day rally at Portella delle Ginestre near Palermo. In the next few weeks, many Communist Party offices were systematically wrecked.

By 1947 the central government was at last strong enough to tackle brigandage seriously, but for some reason Giuliano was spared. Perhaps he was too strong to be touched; or maybe there were political revelations that people feared he might make. At all events, battalions of police were arrayed against him to no avail. Yet the curious fact remains that foreign journalists were able to visit his hiding place easily. More strange still, some senior police officers were in touch with him and deliberately – perhaps for reasons of interforce rivalry – hampered the repressive operations. As a result, it was not until 1950 that Giuliano was finally killed, and in circumstances that remain to this day mysterious.

CHAPTER 24

Autonomy

The hopes that accompanied the granting of regional autonomy served to conceal a less auspicious reality. Not only had the government been hurried into a concession in order to scotch the separatist movement, but there were also deep cracks within the fabric of the Sicilian body politic. The principal division was along class lines. The *latifondisti* had been scared by the last years of fascism. Many of them hoped to harness autonomy to the cause of reaction, and so stop the democratic drift that had given them more than a century of anxiety. At the other end of the political spectrum were a number of young radicals who saw autonomy as a way of finally breaking free from 'immobilism', and channelling peasant aspirations towards constructive goals. As so often in history, though, the Left failed to maintain a united front, and by 1948 the conservatives had gained control and dashed any hopes of fundamental change. The new dispensation thereby failed, as in 1860, to create even the illusion of good will.

Though the new regional Statute was admirably liberal and displayed a fine concern for the division of powers, it was altogether too hastily drawn up to be fully satisfying. Furthermore, it was conceived at a time when the constitutional position of mainland Italy was unclear, and there was subsequently to be a strong feeling in Rome that too much had been conceded, and unnecessarily. Attempts were accordingly made to claw back some of the initial grants, and the ensuing wrangle between region and state meant that much time was lost that should have been spent on planning and reconstruction. There was also a fresh outburst of *'sicilianismo'*, the arid local patriotism that had so often been used by the Sicilian ruling class to defuse any attempts at reform.

The bitter recriminations against Rome in the first years of autonomy injected a sterile note into Sicilian politics that has endured to this day. However, the clash between centralists and autonomists was not wholly unexpected. Insecure nationalism had been a *leitmotif* of Italian history since 1860, and remained, albeit in attenuated form, after Italy became a republic in 1946. There was strong resistance, for example, to the establishment of the Sicilian *Alta Corte*, even though the Statute ordained it as a constitutional safeguard; and in 1956 its powers were in fact abrogated and handed over to the Constitutional Court in Rome. The clause giving the

President of the Region control of the police remained a dead letter, and the government's occasional reluctance to provide sums due to Sicily under article 38 did nothing to foster good will.

Matters might have been simpler if the Sicilian bureaucracy had been either impartial or even more autonomist in spirit. Many of the new civil servants, however, came from the former Ministry for Italian Africa, with the result that a centralizing and formalistic element was introduced into the public sphere, which tended to act as a brake to the full application of autonomy. It also made for undue conservatism, and along with the growth of bureaucratic clientelism, this was to be a major factor in the region's failure to promote more reforms. Only in 1971 was a law passed that promised to improve the character of the bureaucracy; but by then much of the damage had already been done.

However polluted at source, the idealism surrounding the advent of autonomy was not without issue. In the sphere of agriculture, for example, there was intense discussion about the future of the *latifondi*, and a law was passed in 1948 to aid the formation of small farms, and another two years later which made it illegal to retain more than 500 acres of contiguous land. State agencies were instituted to oversee the distribution of new holdings, and essential services such as irrigation and roads were to be provided at public expense. Furthermore, confiscation was prescribed for any large owner who failed to improve his remaining property. Though conservative, particularly in their failure to encourage cooperatives, the laws of 1948 and 1950 did induce change, and perhaps 750,000 acres of new farms were created as a direct result. More important still, the political hold of the *latifondisti* was finally broken; and this after more than 2000 years.

But land reform was not an unqualified success. In the first place, many large estates had already been split into peasant leaseholds, and these tended to fall outside the sphere of the new laws. Wilier owners, moreover, pre-empted the legislation by dividing their property among relatives. Finally, many of the new smallholdings were composed of poor land, and their proprietors often lacked the experience, the good fortune, or sufficient capital to make them into going concerns; and subsequent competition from the north and from Common Market countries did not help either. All in all, land reform was too partial and came too late; and hundreds of thousands of Sicilian peasants were to vote with their feet and leave the countryside in search of work elsewhere.

The shortcomings of land reform cannot be attributed solely to conservatism. Equally important was the subordination of agriculture to industry and the resulting neglect of planning and investment. Progress on the land was more patchy than systematic. What modernization did occur – and it was not inconsiderable – was restricted to 'islands' such as the Plain of Catania, the Ragusano, or San Giuseppe Jato. The initiative for change, moreover, was generally 'grass roots' rather than governmental; and it is this local drive that helps account for the 1 per cent increase in Sicily's share of national agricultural production between 1949 and 1974. The onset of the industrial crisis in 1973 did induce some official reappraisal of the role of farming; but despite recent signs of dynamism, the agricultural sphere has still not developed to the point where it is a significant propulsive force in the island economy as a whole.

Italy's entry into the Common Market in 1958 was another factor in the restricted development of Sicilian agriculture. The confusion of politics with reform that had marred the post-war land settlement was now repeated on an international plane, with strong areas of the Community being favoured at the expense of peripheral ones. The island's main agricultural products were left largely unprotected; and though citrus growing improved considerably, low investment, high transport costs, and the limited growth of cooperatives, all contributed to Sicily losing ground to other Mediterranean producers. The entry of Spain and Portugal into the Community is unlikely to improve matters.

If the progress of agriculture has been disappointing, that of industry has been little short of disastrous. Failure in this field has been particularly galling given the high hopes expressed for it after the war. Autonomy, it was felt, would free Sicily from the stranglehold of national monopolies; and a new indigenous bourgeoisie would emerge, so exploding the myth of entrepreneurial ineptitude. The danger of centuries of victimization, both real and imagined, now materialized in a reinforced conviction that the island's economic ills had been the fault of others. The discovery that this was only a partial truth came as a brutal shock; and in the 1970s there was much painful soul-searching.

In the meantime, however, a number of regional agencies were created to ease the industrial birth-pangs. One of the most promising was IRFIS, a financial institution set up in 1954 to provide cheap credit for small and medium-sized firms. Unfortunately it soon revealed a preference for large, non-Sicilian industrial complexes; and it also fell victim to bureaucratic sclerosis. Other promotional agencies included ERIS and later SOFIS and ESPI. These too betrayed their initial promise by succumbing to corruption. In the case of ESE, which was established in 1947 to provide cheap electricity, the problem was one of simple non-operation. Equally disappointing was EMS, the mining organization. It failed to arrest the chronic decline of sulphur, and by 1984 output had fallen to a mere 21,000 tons.

The initial enthusiasm for industrialization was buoyed up by the discovery of oil near Ragusa in 1953. This was in large measure the outcome of a sensible law that had made Sicily attractive to foreign prospectors. When soon afterwards the Italian company ENI found another field off Gela, the island seemed set for prosperity. A large refinery was built at Augusta, and this was later linked by a pipeline to Ragusa. By 1966 it could deal with 8 million tons of crude oil a year. Another large petrochemical plant appeared at Gela, and for the first time a proper harbour was built on the south coast with a three-mile-long jetty extending out to an island terminal. There were also important discoveries of methane gas, and potash deposits.

The hopes for industrialization in Sicily were soured by experience. The chronic mistrust that had crippled trade and industry in the past was shown to be still vigorous. A law was passed in 1947 abolishing the compulsory registration of shares, but the ensuing increase in limited companies belied hope of a renaissance. The value of stock rose from 3¼ to nearly 60 billion lire in the mid-1950s, but half of this capital belonged to one holding company. Furthermore much of the investment came from outside, and the old complaint continued to be heard that Sicilians themselves were reluctant to take risks. For some people the idea of association was blighted by criminal overtones, a sign of how judicial heavy-handedness may have fostered the very individualism that underlay so much mafia behaviour.

Many of the shortcomings of Sicilian industry must be imputed to the failure of planning. A number of ambitious programmes were announced, including those of La Loggia and Alessi and the 'Piano Battelle' of 1961; but they invariably foundered. Various explanations have been suggested for this. Some people thought the plans were too often the work of experts unfamiliar with practicalities; others pointed to the unsuitability of great industrial complexes. Plants such as those at Gela and Milazzo were capital- rather than labour-intensive, and had little impact on local employment. They also failed to promote subsidiary development. All too often major national companies took advantage of generous state subsidies to set up these installations, which then remained unconnected to the Sicilian economy; and what gain there was from these 'cathedrals in the desert' went northwards.

In general the manufacturing sector has continued to be dominated by the small firm. In 1961 two-thirds of the industrial labour force was employed in small companies of ten workers or less; and twenty years later the figure was still nearly 40 per cent. The presence of so many marginal and chronically vulnerable concerns helps to explain why Sicily had the lowest growth in industrial employment anywhere in the south in the 1970s. In other parts of Italy – notably the centre and north-east – a rash of small enterprises appeared in the wake of the oil crisis. But in Sicily the only noticeable growth came in building; and by 1981 this unproductive sector absorbed more than a quarter of the industrial workforce, well above the national average.

At the heart of so many of Sicily's failings, both economic and moral, has always been the incoherence of political life. The absence of a transcendent collective ideal, despite the pretentious claims made for Sicilian nationhood, has been one factor in this. More important, perhaps, has been a fundamental mistrust of altruism. In this world of scarcity, appeals to the common good have fallen literally on barren soil. *Scaltrezza*, or shrewdness, was traditionally more esteemed than Christian virtue; and in politics, the residue of this attitude has underpinned clientelism. With resources outstripped by expectations, the belief has persisted that only with patrons, or 'saints in paradise', can there be any hope of advancement; and far from diminishing, the vertical bonds of society appear to have prospered under autonomy, at the expense of a collective ethic.

Among the casualties of clientelism have been the public agencies. By 1974 there were more than 200 of them; and together they swallowed up about 1,500 billion lire, with few visible returns. The most notorious instance of inefficiency was SOFIS. This was set up in 1958 to produce a new class of entrepreneurs, and induce a network of smaller companies which would be sustained until strong enough to stand alone. Though the failure of this agency stemmed partly from opposition by big national companies, more fundamental was the clientelistic infighting that made economic planning impossible. Furthermore, the businesses set up by SOFIS were regarded as parking lots for political placement: economic efficiency was far less of a criterion.

When SOFIS went bankrupt in 1967, it was replaced by ESPI. Though this too was supposed to encourage local initiative, it soon succumbed to the same malaise as its predecessor, and by 1976 its 45 companies were 100 billion lire in debt. Clientelism was once again largely to blame. In the early 1970s there were 369 ESPI administrators, and all but a handful of them were political appointees, mostly Christian Democrats. They in their turn exploited their positions for patronage, and payrolls as a result became grotesquely inflated. In 1976, ESPI companies were said to be costing the Sicilian taxpayer over 50 billion lire; but according to a regional commission production needed to be increased by 360 per cent if they were to become anything like competitive.

This situation was unlikely to foster a new entrepreneurial class. With industrial positions being given to political time-servers, any thought of rational economics was bound to be anathema; and with jobs guaranteed, there was no call for risk-taking, and an essential aspect of entrepreneurship was thereby suppressed. Many Sicilians, politicians among them, have been fully aware of the shortcomings of this system; but despite analysis and discussion, no viable solution has been found. The habit of favour-mongering is deeply ingrained; and even the opposition parties are alleged to send their agents scurrying around the corridors of the Palermo assessor-ates to garner whatever favours they can.

Since the war, clientelism has spread with stultifying effect to almost every corner of Sicilian life. The crucial moment in this development came in the early 1950s. Up till then the Christian Democrats in Sicily had been dominated by the old *notabili* whose leisurely approach to politics caused them to recoil before the demands of mass organization. Then in 1954 came Fanfani's triumph at the national Congress of Naples, and the 'turn to the left'. Christian Democracy set out to become a modern party, with an autonomous structure free of dependence on the Church and big business. This meant grass-roots organization. In Palermo the 'fanfaniani' were led by the young provincial secretary, Giovanni Gioia, and under his guidance party membership more than doubled between 1952 and 1959. The new political configuration heralded its advent to power as the triumph of morality over the forces of the mafia.

Sicily was crucial to Fanfani, as about a third of his faction's membership came from the island. This made Gioia, Salvatore Lima, and the other 'Young Turks' indispensable: without them the critical vote could not be delivered at the national congress. Armed with such protection, the *fanfan-iani* in Sicily proceeded to build up a vast clientele based on control of municipal, provincial and regional organizations (*enti*). Every kind of institution was exploited for political ends, including refuse disposal com-panies and even the urban police. The latter, after all, could make life miserable for an uncompliant shopkeeper, a street vendor, or a family seeking a welfare handout.

The *fanfaniani* were also able to manipulate, and with great effect, the concession of public works, contracts and building licences. The short-comings of agrarian reform, the growth of administration, and the general rise in expectations, produced an enormous drift from the countryside to the towns in the 1950s; and this in turn stimulated the market for housing and amenities. The population of Palermo grew by almost 100,000 between 1951 and 1961, and this added greatly to the accommodation shortage already occasioned by allied bombing in the war. To meet this demand, a new class of ruthless speculators appeared; and they pledged their fortunes to the *fanfaniani*.

Under the guidance of such men as Vito Ciancimino, the Palermo assessor of public works from 1959 until 1964, the face of urban Sicily was radically

remodelled. Vast tenement blocks sprang up, often in defiance of city
building plans, and such was the speculation involved that not only were all
aesthetic concerns thrown to the wind, but so too, in some cases, were
considerations of public safety. At Agrigento licences were given to build
high-rise flats on land known to be unsafe; and in July 1966 a massive
landslide occurred, which would have been catastrophic had a street cleaner
not raised the alarm in time. A subsequent enquiry revealed that many of
the construction permits had gone to relatives of the Agrigento administration, and even to the local Christian Democrat secretary.

Regional affairs were dominated by the *fanfaniani* until the mid-1970s.
With these men in charge, politics effectively ceased, and every aspect of
public life got sucked into a huge machine for the advancement of personal
and party fortunes. The common good was stifled by inefficiency; but sheer
calculation also played its part, for so long as individualism prevailed in the
public sphere, it was in everyone's interest to seek political patronage. The
enduring success of the Christian Democrats – their regional vote has
hovered around 40 per cent since 1955 – indicates that this was in one sense a
perfect system. Nor did it depend on a steady or increasing flow of
resources: despite the severe recession, the Christian Democrat vote grew in
the municipal elections of 1975 and 1980. Scarcity, it seems, makes patronage more indispensable than ever. The mere promise of help is sufficient to
kindle hope and hence to create a political bond.

Control of the bureaucracy has been a major source of power. Through it
large areas of life can be manipulated, from job allocations and commercial
licences, to regional subsidies, credits, pension benefits, tax assessments,
and the regulation of markets. To begin with, civil servants were employed
by 'direct call'. Under this system, assessors could take on whomsoever they
wanted without recourse to public competition. The result was a great influx
of ministerial friends and relatives. It was often said that a bureaucrat's date
of employment could be told from his accent: Agrigentine, for example,
would indicate 'periodo La Loggia', Catanian 'periodo Milazzo'. This
method of employment was officially stopped in 1962, but it was altogether
too valuable a political instrument to be lost. There was accordingly a great
rise in the number of part-time and clerical staff, for such people were not
subject to competition; and once inside they could easily be promoted.

In these circumstances inefficiency was widespread. People were employed who were wholly unsuitable, and in some cases – 600 according to a
survey of regional employees conducted in the early 1970s – they only
appeared on the 27th of each month to collect their pay cheques. This
resulted in rampant inertia. It took fifteen years, for example, for the
paperwork of one small public contract, begun in 1951, to reach its final

stages. In the meantime the company involved found itself confronted with far higher costs than anticipated, and this led to another two years of wrangling. Only in 1971 was the project completed, and by then the documentation relating to the case amounted to 20,000 pages.

Unfortunately the smallest aspects of public life were subject to such grotesque formalism. To repair a burst water-pipe in a school, the headmaster would have to write to the commune; the commune would then supplicate the region, which in turn would conduct a survey, the results of which would have to be approved by decree. A public competition would eventually be announced, estimates received, checked and rechecked. Finally the money would be released. According to a report in 1971, it took on average 3 years, 9 months and 23 days to complete such repairs; and the same went for roads and other public works.

The combination of this bureaucratic lethargy with political infighting and corruption has taken a heavy toll. The 'historic centre' of Palermo remains almost untouched since being bombed by the Allies in 1943; and this despite the allocation of huge sums for *risanamento* and frequent deaths from falling masonry. In the sphere of education, only one other region in 1980 had a lower ratio than Sicily of schools to population. Infant mortality was higher than anywhere else in Italy, which partly reflects the inadequacy of hospital facilities: the number of beds per thousand inhabitants was nearly a third below the average for the centre and north in 1980.

This was a dispiriting world to live in, and the more enterprising and fortunate continued, as before, to cut their losses and emigrate. Novelists such as Vitaliano Brancati and Elio Vittorini, the poet Quasimodo, the artist Renato Guttuso, and the politicians Ugo La Malfa and Riccardo Lombardi, all preferred a metropolitan existence to the cramped provincialism of Sicily. Leonardo Sciascia and Tomasi di Lampedusa were two writers who kept their base in Sicily, and they were deemed somewhat eccentric. Unfortunately the outflow of talent has not been matched by any compensating influx. Many mainland teachers still regard posts at the universities of Palermo or Messina as irksome stepping-stones, and will even commute from Rome rather than live in the island. Such absenteeism is obviously damaging, not least for the reinforcement it gives to the already low opinion that many Sicilians have of themselves.

Another form of emigration has arguably been less pernicious. Over a million people left Sicily between 1951 and 1975 and most of these were rural labourers in search of work in the north of Italy, or further afield in Germany and Switzerland. Though in one sense a severe indictment of the region, emigration did solve the problem of rural overpopulation; and the wages of those who remained behind improved accordingly. Remittances contributed to the rise in living standards, and between 1951 and 1983 *per capita* income in Sicily more than trebled, thereby narrowing the gap slightly with the centre and north. Emigration had a further advantage, in that it afforded experience of a more democratic and less individualistic environment.

But rural emigration also had its negative side. The departure of so many men produced an ageing and predominantly female population; and some Sicilian villages were almost bereft of their male inhabitants. Another problem was that emigrants were often motivated by the single-minded desire for quick enrichment and this left them with little time to acquire fresh skills, or even to absorb their new environments. Much of the blame for this must rest with the government. There was a strongly exploitative side to Italy's 'economic miracle', and many southerners were consigned to squalid ghettoes in the north, with relatively low pay and scant union protection. When the recession bit after 1973, they were usually the first to be laid off; and 60 per cent of those who returned home failed to find a job again.

In 1984, 244,000 people in Sicily – 15 per cent of the workforce – were officially registered as unemployed. Of these almost half were in search of their first job. This was a frightening statistic, and the threat posed to the already far from robust social fabric hardly bore contemplating. Equally alarming was the prospect for southerners as a whole, for in the early 1980s north and south again drifted apart after a period in which the gap between them had narrowed. Unemployment in the south represented 44 per cent of the national total in 1983; and in contrast to the north the labour force here was growing relatively fast. A further ominous sign was the suppression after twenty-five years of the Cassa per il Mezzogiorno, the national agency for southern development.

The degeneration of the south might have led to a revival of the southern question, but the issue was still muffled by the intellectual confusion that had beset it for a decade; and in the absence of social and economic discussion, the field was left open to the criminal lobby. By the early 1980s, major drives were underway against the mafia and the Neapolitan camorra. There was talk of a great association called the 'N.C.O.' (Nuova Camorra Organizzata), and mafia torture chambers were unearthed by the police, along with helicopter landing-pads and underground prisons. Imagination and zeal were fuelled by a rising tide of violence, and this reached epidemic proportions in Sicily in 1981 and 1982.

Autonomy had done little to assuage the island's violent proclivities. Relative poverty and public money acted as catalysts to unscrupulous acquisition, while the decline of the *latifondisti* and the growth of political clientelism offered the ambitious fresh opportunities. With the stakes higher than ever, the competition was ruthless. The new arena was the city rather than the countryside, for it was clear to anyone with acumen that the future now lay with the manipulation of public resources, rather than with agriculture. This was a major break with the past. For centuries peasants had dreamed of owning land, but in the 1950s new prospects appeared, and the values of urban consumerism took root. The luxury apartment, the Rolex watch and the Mercedes now became the touchstones of power.

As the emigration of the 1950s indicated, resources were ill-matched to demand. For those Sicilians who remained behind, competition was intense, with success dependent largely on the patronage of some well-placed politician. The enrolment of new clienteles after 1953 made the situation enticingly fluid. There was also a sharpening of rivalries, and by the late 1950s gang warfare had broken out in the streets of Palermo. The objects of contention were the wholesale markets, building contracts, land speculation and the growing drug traffic; and the main factions involved were those of the Grecos and the La Barbera brothers. With higher stakes went more sophisticated weapons. Machine guns replaced the traditional shotgun, or *lupara*, and in 1958 the Palermo newspaper *L'Ora* was subject to a dynamite attack after it had published a series of outspoken articles on the mafia.

The protection afforded by Rome to Gioia and his colleagues soon filtered downwards. The rising men of the 1950s were untainted by earlier political ties, and quickly found a place in the Christian Democrat fold. Like the *fanfaniani* themselves, they were often of humble origins, and this gave patron and client alike a sense of shared values. Vito Ciancimino, assessor of public works and later mayor of Palermo, was a barber's son. One of his most successful protégés was Francesco Vassallo, who began his career in the 1930s as a carter of sand and stone, but rose to become one of the richest men in Sicily. Building contracts were the key to his prosperity. Through blatant favouritism and no doubt some intimidation, Vassallo and his friends cornered the market. A report in 1964 revealed that of 4,025 construction licences issued in Palermo between 1957 and 1963, 80 per cent had been awarded to only five men.

Such selectivity had marked advantages for the political elite, for it made patronage more manageable. Vassallo passed on his political dependency to his employees, and in this way a great pyramid emerged based on reciprocal need. Such intermeshing led to easy complicity; and whenever competition or mistrust became too intense somewhere along the line, and mediation failed, violence would erupt. The level of impunity was frustrating for the authorities, and bewildering to the general public. Demands for action against the mafia grew more insistent, and, as usual, it was the opposition parties who spearheaded the attack. Though morality was undoubtedly their main concern, charges of criminality were also a very effective way of dealing with one's opponents in this society.

After much resistance from the Christian Democrats, regional and national governments finally agreed in 1962 to set up a commission of enquiry to investigate the mafia. But even now there was a degree of foot-dragging, and it was not until seven policemen had been killed in the 'massacre of Ciaculli', and the national and regional elections safely conducted, that sessions could begin. From July 1963 until January 1976, the Commission probed the mafia with varying degrees of commitment, and its findings were published in a series of large volumes from 1971. The conclusion it effectively came to was that the mafia defied remedy by its very nature. This was disappointing, but given the subjective and nebulous character of the problem, was not altogether surprising.

The Antimafia Commission accumulated a great pile of documentation. But despite evidence of high-level collusion, police activity was directed against the more vulnerable members of society. Matters were not improved by the special measures, introduced in 1965, giving the police wider powers of arrest. Soon, as in the 1920s, there was talk of arbitrariness and brutality. One difficulty facing this, as indeed any operation against the mafia, was the climate of politicized hysteria. Politicians beat their drums and demanded success; and the newspapers found a happy mixture of moral crusade and sensationalism. The situation grew particularly bad in the 1980s. An issue that should have been soberly analysed and carefully treated, was subjected to lurid simplification; and the prognosis for justice was not good.

Had *mafiosi* been easily distinguished, then repression might have been the answer. Unfortunately the activities of Francesco Vassallo, or even Luciano Liggio, Michele Greco and Tommaso Buscetta, sprang from values that were neither peculiar nor fully abhorred. A sociological report in the 1960s revealed that the mafia was seemingly invisible to those who lived in its midst; and despite official claims, many *mafiosi* still appeared to enjoy some popular support. In a cruel world, they could pose as realists. They could also turn an accusing finger to the state, and draw on the residual mistrust that many Sicilians still felt towards the authorities.

Here was a major problem for the government. Had the economic expansion of the 1960s continued, there might have been some easing of tension. But from 1973 public money grew scarce, and emigration began to dry up. The search for capital now turned more and more to illegal channels, and in particular to drugs. Though the scale of the Sicilian narcotics trade was at times inflated by paranoia, fantasy, and even political exigency, there

was no denying its importance. Between the mid 1970s and 1980, a handful
of laboratories in the Palermo area were said to have produced between four
and five tons of pure heroin. This meant an annual income of perhaps 700
billion *lire*, much of which was laundered and invested in legal enterprises
at the regional, national and international levels. '*Narcolire*', or the money
produced by narcotics, may explain why Palermo enjoyed a minor building
boom, when the construction industry elsewhere was in recession.

With drug-trafficking on the increase, the possibilities of legal mediation
declined. There was growing resort to violence, and for the first time
important state officials became targets. The assassination of Pietro Scag-
lione in 1971 marked the beginning of a long line of 'illustrious corpses'
which culminated in September 1982 with General Carlo Alberto Dalla
Chiesa, the man sent by the government to crush the mafia. Though
criminal motives were undoubtedly paramount, it was hard to ignore the
fact that these killings bore many of the hallmarks of terrorism; and their
very sophistication suggested a network of accomplices beyond the reach of
a mere criminal organization. Popular indifference and fear certainly played
a part; but so too, one must imagine, did inveterate anti-statism.

The assassination of Dalla Chiesa precipitated an all-out offensive against
the mafia. A law was hurried through parliament giving the state the right
to investigate private bank accounts; and a new penal category was introduced – 'criminal association of mafia kind' – which was of broad applicabil-
ity. Thousands of arrests followed; but despite frequent references to 'third'
and even 'fourth' mafia levels, the only major figures to fall foul of the law
were Vito Ciancimino and the tax collectors Nino and Ignazio Salvo. There
was much talk, as in the 1920s, of a new climate of opinion; but despite the
occasional pronouncement by the Church, a few student processions, and
a stream of newspaper optimism, the mood was predominantly one of
resigned indifference, with the odd outburst of indignation that the good
name of Sicily was once again being dragged through the mud.

In the summer of 1983 the Palermo magistrates proclaimed a major coup.
Tommaso Buscetta, an underworld figure of some notoriety in the 1950s
and 1960s, was caught in Brazil and induced to 'sing'; and his testimony led
to further arrests. More important, though, he furnished an account, in
unprecedented detail, of the structure and recent activities of the mafia. Its
true name, he now revealed, was 'Cosa Nostra'. It was composed of families
which were subdivided into groups of ten and regulated by provincial
'commissions' and a 'super commission'. This was the kind of information
that the authorities had been hoping for. Some people pointed out that the
evidence tallied almost too well in specifics with what the police knew
already; others stressed the fact that Buscetta was only indicting his

opponents. Whatever the truth, it was hard to avoid the feeling that the problem of the mafia was a long way from being resolved, and that Sicily still had many years to come of painful dialogue with its past.

Chronological table

44–36 Sextus Pompey in
      Sicily

31 Battle of Actium

Imperial
AD

14 Death of Augustus
306–337 Constantine

468–476 Vandal control of
       Sicily
476–535 Ostrogoth rule

BYZANTINE

527–565 Justinian

535 Belisarius captures
      Sicily

590–604 Pope Gregory the
        Great

827 Beginning of Moslem
      invasion

ARAB

831 Palermo falls to
      Moslems
878 Syracuse captured
1060–61 First Norman
        incursion into
        Sicily

NORMAN

(b.1031)–1101 Count Roger

1071 Capture of Palermo

1101–1154 King Roger II
1154–1166 King William I
        ('The Bad')
1166–1189 King William II
        ('The Good')

1189–93 Third Crusade

HOHENSTAUFEN

1194–1197 Emperor
        Henry VI
1198–1250 Emperor
        Frederick II
        (*Stupor Mundi*)
1250–1254 Conrad
1258–1266 Manfred

1266 Battle of Benevento

ANGEVIN
(1266)–1282 Charles of Anjou
        1282 Sicilian Vespers

ARAGONESE
1282–1285 Peter III
1296–1337 Frederick III

        1337–1453 Hundred Years
           War

1392–1409 Martin I
1416–1454 Alfonso
        ('The
        Magnanimous')
1479–1516 Ferdinand II

HABSBURG (Spanish)
1516–1556 Emperor Charles V
1556–1598 Philip II

        1571 Turks defeated at
           Lepanto
        1618–48 Thirty Years War

1621–1665 Philip IV
        1647 Palermo revolt
1665–1700 Charles II
        1674–78 Messina revolt

        1701–14 War of the Spanish
           Succession

PIEDMONTESE
1713–1720 Victor
        Amadeus II
        1713 Peace of Utrecht

HABSBURG (Austrian)
1720–1734 Emperor
        Charles VI

BOURBON (Spanish)
1734–1759 Charles III
1759–1825 Ferdinand III
        1773 Palermo revolt
        1781–86 Viceroyalty of
           Marquis Caracciolo
        1806–1815 British
           occupation of
           Sicily
        1806 Joseph Bonaparte
           becomes King of
           Naples
        1814–15 Congress of Vienna

1816 Ferdinand III becomes
Ferdinand I, King of
the Two Sicilies

1820 Palermo revolt

1825–1830 Francis I
1830–1859 Ferdinand II

1848–49 Sicilian
revolution

1848–49 Revolutions in
Paris, Vienna,
Berlin; Roman
Republic

1859–1860 Francis II

1860 Garibaldi captures
Sicily

ITALY

Monarchy
1861–1878 Victor
Emanuel II

1866 Palermo revolt

1878–1900 Umberto I

1892–94 Fasci

1900–1946 Victor
Emanuel III

1903 Giolitti becomes Prime
Minister

1914–18 First World War

1922–43 Mussolini,
Prime Minister

1939–45 Second World
War

Republic

1946 Sicily granted
regional autonomy

Bibliography

GENERAL

The nearest we have to a continuous history of ancient Sicily, down to the late Roman Republic, will be found in the surviving books of the *Universal History* of Diodorus (for which there is now an admirable index by R. M. Geer in the *Loeb Classical Library* edition, vol. 12, 1967). For shorter periods or episodes, there are Thucydides, books VI–VII, on the Athenian invasion of 415–413 BC; Polybius, book I, and Livy, books XXI–XXX (based largely on portions of Polybius now lost) on the Punic Wars, in which Sicily was heavily involved; Cicero's Verrine orations on the administration of Sicily in the Roman Republic; Plutarch's lives of Nicias, Alcibiades, Dion and Timoleon; Appian, *Civil Wars*, books IV–V, on Sextus Pompey; and numerous letters of Gregory the Great, pope from 590 to 604.

The fundamental work on ancient Sicily is now *La Sicilia antica* (5 vols. in 2, Naples 1980), ed. E. Gabba and G. Vallet. The pre-history of the island is best covered by S. Tusa, *La Sicilia nella preistoria* (Rome 1983), while for the archaic period (down to 480 BC), T. J. Dunbabin, *The Western Greeks* (Oxford 1948) remains essential, though his general views on the economic side and on Greek-Carthaginian relations are not accepted in this book. Archaeological publications are numerous and widely scattered, but particular mention should be made of the journal *Kokalos*, published in Palermo since 1955. There is also R. Stillwell, ed., *The Princeton Encyclopaedia of Classical Sites* (Princeton 1976).

Much interest and controversy has been generated recently by a series of remarkable Greek inscriptions from Entella, in the west of Sicily. Though their precise import has yet to be established, they will undoubtedly alter significantly our view of the island in the decades prior to the Roman conquest. Those interested will find a very full bibliographical and factual analysis in *SEG* (Supplementum Epigraphicum Graecum) Vol. 32 (1982), pp. 250ff, while the texts themselves are reproduced in Vol. 30 (1980) nos. 1117–1123. For an important discussion of the issues involved, see *Annali della Scuola Normale Superiore di Pisa*, 12(3) (1982).

For Sicilian history in general, the most ambitious recent work is the *Storia di Sicilia* (10 vols., Naples 1977–82) ed. R. Romeo. This can be supplemented for the medieval and modern periods by the relevant chapters in the projected 23-volume *Storia d'Italia* (UTET, Turin 1979–??) ed. G. Galasso. There is also the *Storia d'Italia* (15 vols., Einaudi, Turin 1972–81), though this takes a more global approach, and the material on Sicily is accordingly less accessible. Two older works can still be read with profit: G. E. di Blasi e Gambacorta, *Storia civile del Regno di Sicilia* (17 vols., Palermo 1811–1821); and R. Gregorio, *Considerazioni sopra la storia di Sicilia, dai tempi normanni sino ai presenti* (new edition, with an introduction by A. Saitta, 3 vols., Palermo 1972–3).

For social and economic history there is still nothing to replace L. Bianchini, *Storia economico-civile di Sicilia* (new edition, ed. F. Brancato, Naples 1972). F. Maggiore Perni, *La popolazione di Sicilia e di Palermo dal X al XVIII secolo* (Palermo 1892) is unreliable but remains the starting point for Sicilian demography. An excellent recent volume on economic problems is *Problemi dell'economia siciliana* (Milan 1966), ed. P. Sylos-Labini. An interesting urban history is C. De Seta and L. Di Mauro, *Le città nella storia d'Italia. Palermo* (Rome 1980). This can be supplemented in a lighter vein by the lush and enterprising guidebook published by Gruppo Editoriale Fabbri, *Sicilia* (2 vols., Milan 1985).

Byzantine rule in Sicily is still underserved, though there are indications that here, as with the Arab and Norman periods, major changes are afoot. Probably the best recent discussion is V. von Falkenhausen, *La dominazione bizantina nell'Italia meridionale* (Bari 1978). For the Arabs there is still nothing to replace the classic, if somewhat fanciful, work of M. Amari, *Storia dei Musulmani di Sicilia* (but in the edition of C. A. Nallino, 6 vols., Catania 1933–9). For the Normans the standard account remains that of F. Chalandon, *Histoire de la domination normande en Italie et en Sicilie* (Paris 1907), though the *Giornate normanno-sveve* (to which reference is given below) are emerging as a formidable modern compendium. For the long years of Spanish domination the best narrative is still that of G. E. di Blasi e Gambacorta, *Storia cronologica de' vicerè, luogotenenti e presidenti del Regno di Sicilia* (new edition in 5 vols. with an introduction by I. Peri, Palermo 1974–5). A fine though slightly stodgy history of Italian Sicily is F. Renda, *Storia della Sicilia dal 1860 al 1970* (3 vols., Palermo 1984–6).

Any consideration of Sicilian culture must begin with the works of the great ethnographer, Giuseppe Pitrè, whose *Biblioteca delle tradizioni popolari siciliane* (Palermo 1870–1913) was published in 25 volumes. The books by Danilo Dolci (three of which are given below) provide a fascinating picture of near contemporary attitudes and values. Works on the mafia are legion, and for the most part fantastical. The point of view adopted in this book is in some respects novel, but overlaps in part with H. Hess, *Mafia and Mafiosi: The Structure of Power* (tr. E. Osers, Lexington 1973), and A. Blok, *The Mafia of a Sicilian Village 1860–1960* (Oxford 1974). N. Russo (ed.), *Antologia della mafia* (Palermo 1964), provides a useful picture of changing appraisals of the phenomenon. The volumes of the *Commissione parlamentare d'inchiesta sul fenomeno della mafia in Sicilia* (Rome 1971–??) contain much source material.

There have been a number of recent Sicilian writers of international distinction. The greatest is Giovanni Verga, whose novel *Mastro-don Gesualdo* was translated by D. H. Lawrence (Penguin 1970). Of awesome power are the same writer's *Novelle*: a selection appears in *Little Novels of Sicily* (tr. D. H. Lawrence, Penguin 1973). A good starting point for Luigi Pirandello is his *Short Stories* (selected and translated by F. May, Oxford 1975). G. Tomasi di Lampedusa's *The Leopard* (tr. A. Colquhoun, London 1961) is now well established as a classic. The best contemporary Sicilian writer is Leonardo Sciascia. Two of his most acclaimed works, *The Day of the Owl* and *Equal Danger* (Il Contesto), have appeared in a single volume translated by A. Colquhoun, A. Oliver and A. Foulke (Manchester 1984).

The most satisfactory guidebooks are all in Italian. That of the Touring Club Italiano, *Sicilia* (5th ed., Milan 1968) is the best conventional one. Excellent, but less orthodox, is the already mentioned *Sicilia* (Gruppo Editoriale Fabbri, 2 vols., Milan 1985), which is lavishly illustrated. In English there is C. Kininmonth, *Sicily. Traveller's Guide* (3rd edition, London 1981). For ancient Sicily, there is a first-class archaeological guide by F. Coarelli and M. Torelli, *Sicilia* (Rome and Bari 1984); V. Tusa and E. De Miro, *Sicilia Occidentale* (Rome 1983) is less satisfactory. Of older travel books, the two most famous are J. W. Goethe, *Italian Journey* (tr. W. H. Auden and E. Mayer, Penguin 1970) and P. Brydone, *A Tour through Sicily and Malta* (2 vols., London 1773).

The following might also be useful:

ANCIENT SICILY

H. Berve, *Die Tyrannis bei den Griechen* (2 vols., Munich 1967)
– *Dion* (Akad. d. Wiss. u. der Literatur, Mainz, *Abhandlungen der geistes- u. sozial-wiss. Klasse*, 1956, no. 10)
– *König Hieron II* (Bayerische Akad. d. Wiss., phil.-hist. Klasse, *Abhandlungen*, n.F.
H. Berve, G. Gruben, M. Hirmer, *Greek Temples, Theatres and Shrines* (London 1963)
J. Boardman, *The Greek Overseas* (3rd ed., London 1980)
A. Carandini (*et al.*), *Filosofiana. The Villa at Piazza Armerina* (2 vols., Palermo 1982)
    Cf. R. J. A. Wilson, 'Roman Mosaics in Sicily: the African Connection', *American Journal of Archaeology* 86 (1982), 413–28, and his *Piazza Armerina* (London 1983)
C. M. Kraay, *Archaic and Classical Greek Coins* (London 1976), ch. 10
B. Pace, *Arte e civiltà della Sicilia antica* (4 vols., Rome & Naples 1936–49; 2nd ed. of Vol. I, 1958)
D. Roussel, *Les Siciliens entre les Romains et les Cartaginois . . . 276 à 241* (Paris 1970)
V. M. Scramuzza, 'Roman Sicily', in *An Economic Survey of Ancient Rome*, ed. T. Frank, III (Baltimore 1937)
K. F. Stroheker, *Dionysius I* (Wiesbaden 1958)
R. J. A. Talbert, *Timoleon and the Revival of Greek Sicily, 344–317 BC* (Cambridge 1974)
J. Vogt, *Ancient Slavery and the Ideal of Man*, translated by T. Wiedemann (Oxford 1974), ch. 3, with important criticisms by F. Bomer, *Untersuchungen über die Religion der sklaven in Griechenland und in Rom III* (Akad. d. Wiss. u. der Literatur, Mainz, *Abhandlungen der geistes- u. sozialwiss. Klasse*, 1961, no. 4)
B. H. Warmington, *Carthage* (Penguin 1964)
C. R. Whittaker, 'Carthaginian Imperialism', in *Imperialism in the Ancient World*, ed. C. R. Whittaker and P. Garnsey (Cambridge 1978)

MEDIEVAL AND EARLY MODERN SICILY

D. Abulafia, *The Two Italies: Economic Relations between the Norman Kingdom of Sicily and the Northern Communes* (Cambridge 1977)
V. d'Alessandro, *Politica e società nella Sicilia aragonese* (Palermo 1963)
M. Amari, *History of the War of the Sicilian Vespers* (3 vols., London 1850)
H. Bresc, *Livre et Société en Sicile (1299–1499)* (Palermo 1971)
C. Bruhl, *Diplomi e cancelleria di Ruggero II* (Palermo 1983)
O. Cancila, *Impresa, redditi, mercato nella Sicilia moderna* (Bari 1980)
– *Barone e popolo nella Sicilia del grano* (Palermo 1983)
E. Curtis, *Roger of Sicily and the Normans in Lower Italy, 1016–1154* (London 1912)
O. Demus, *The Mosaics of Norman Sicily* (London 1949)
Giornate normanno-sveve, Università di Bari, Centro di studi normanno-svevi (Rome 1975, 1977; Bari 1979–??)
F. Giunta, *Uomini e cose del medioevo mediterraneo* (Palermo 1964)
E. M. Jamison, *Admiral Eugenius of Sicily* (Oxford 1957)

E. H. Kantorowicz, *Frederick the Second, 1194–1250* (English version by E. O. Lorimer, London 1957)

E. Kitzinger, *The Mosaics of Monreale* (Palermo 1960)

H. G. Koenigsberger, *The Government of Sicily under Philip II of Spain* (London 1951)

E. G. Leonard, *Les Angevins de Naples* (Paris 1954)

J. J. C. Norwich, *The Normans in the South, 1016–1130* (London 1967)

– *The Kingdom in the Sun, 1130–1194* (London 1976)

I. Peri, *Uomini, città e campagne in Sicilia dall'xi al xii secolo* (Rome 1978)

– *La Sicilia dopo il Vespro. Uomini, città e campagna, 1282–1376* (Bari 1982)

S. Runciman, *The Sicilian Vespers. A History of the Mediterranean World in the Later Thirteenth Century* (Cambridge 1958)

A. F. C. Ryder, *The Kingdom of Naples under Alfonso the Magnanimous. The Making of a Modern State* (Oxford 1976)

C. Trasselli, *Mediterraneo e Sicilia all'inizio dell'epoca moderna, ricerche quattrocentesche* (Cosenza 1977)

T. C. Van Cleve, *The Emperor Frederick II of Hohenstaufen, Immutator Mundi* (Oxford 1972)

MODERN SICILY

P. Balsamo, *A View of the Present State of Sicily* (London 1811)

G. Barone, S. Lupo, R. Palidda, M. Saija, *Potere e società in Sicilia nella crisi dello stato liberale* (Catania 1977)

F. Brancato, *La Sicilia nel primo ventennio del Regno d'Italia* (Bologna 1956)

L. Caico, *Sicilian Ways and Days* (London 1910)

R. Campbell, *The Luciano Project. The Secret Wartime Collaboration of the Mafia and the U.S. Navy* (New York 1977)

J. Chubb, *Patronage, Power and Poverty in Southern Italy. A Tale of Two Cities* (Cambridge 1982)

C. Gower Chapman, *Milocca. A Sicilian Village* (London 1973)

F. Crispi, *The Memoirs of Francesco Crispi*, Vol. 1, 'The Thousand' (London 1912)

D. Dolci, *Waste. An Eyewitness Report on Some Aspects of Waste in Western Sicily*, translated by R. Munroe (London 1963)

– *Poverty in Sicily. A Study of the Province of Palermo*, translated by P. D. Cummins (Penguin 1966)

– *The Man Who Plays Alone*, translated by A. Cowan (London 1968)

L. Franchetti and S. Sonnino, *Inchiesta in Sicilia*, introduction by E. Cavalieri (new ed., Florence 1974)

Fulco, *The Happy Summer Days. A Sicilian Childhood* (London 1976)

M. Ganci, *Storia antologica della autonomia siciliana* (3 vols., Palermo 1981)

G. Gentile, *Il tramonto della cultura siciliana* (Florence 1963)

G. Giarrizzo, G. Torcellan, F. Venturi (eds.), *Riformatori delle antiche repubbliche, dei ducati, dello stato pontificio e delle isole* (Milan 1965)

E. J. Hobsbawm, *Primitive Rebels. Studies in Archaic Forms of Social Movement in the 19th and 20th centuries* (Manchester 1959)

– *Bandits* (Penguin 1972)

G. Lorenzoni, *Inchiesta parlamentare sulle condizioni dei contadini nelle provincie meridionali e nella Sicilia* (Vol. VI of the Faina report), (Rome 1910)

D. Mack Smith, *Cavour and Garibaldi. A Study in Political Conflict* (Cambridge 1985)

G. C. Marino, *L'ideologia sicilianista. Dall'età dei 'lumi' al Risorgimento* (Palermo 1971)

G. Maxwell, *God Protect Me from My Friends* (London 1956). This is probably the best narrative life of the bandit Salvatore Giuliano.

– *The Ten Pains of Death* (London 1959)

C. Mori, *The Last Struggle with the Mafia* (London 1933)

M. Pantaleone, *The Mafia and Politics* (London 1966)

F. Renda, *Il movimento contadino nella società siciliana* (Palermo 1956)

– *I Fasci Siciliani, 1892–94* (Turin 1977)

R. Romeo, *Il Risorgimento in Sicilia* (Bari 1982)

J. Rosselli, *Lord William Bentinck and the British Occupation of Sicily, 1811–1814* (Cambridge 1956)

E. Sereni, *La questione agraria nella rinascita nazionale italiana* (Rome 1946)

G. Servadio, *Mafioso. A History of the Mafia from its origins to the Present Day* (London 1976)

V. Titone, *Storia, Mafia e Costume in Sicilia* (Milan 1964)

G. M. Trevelyan, *Garibaldi and the Thousand* (London 1909)

– *Garibaldi and the Making of Italy* (London 1911)

R. Trevelyan, *Princes Under the Volcano* (London 1972). A portrait of a remarkable Anglo-Sicilian family.

Marchese di Villabianca, *Diario palermitano* (Biblioteca storica e litteria di Sicilia, ed. Di Marzo, Palermo 1875)

R. Villari (ed.), *Il Sud nella storia d'Italia. Antologia della questione meridionale* (Bari 1961)

Index